WEB DEVELOPER.COM® GUIDE TO BUILDING INTELLIGENT WEB SITES WITH JAVASCRIPT™

WEB DEVELOPER.COM® GUIDE TO BUILDING INTELLIGENT WEB SITES WITH JAVASCRIPT™

Nigel Ford

WILEY COMPUTER PUBLISHING

John Wiley & Sons, Inc.
New York • Chichester • Weinheim • Brisbane • Singapore • Toronto

APR 1 5 1999

Publisher: Robert Ipsen
Editor: Cary Sullivan
Assistant Editor: Kathryn A. Malm
Managing Editor: Micheline Frederick
Electronic Products, Associate Editor: Michael Sosa
Text Design & Composition: Benchmark Productions, Inc.

Designations used by companies to distinguish their products are often claimed as trademarks. In all instances where John Wiley & Sons, Inc., is aware of a claim, the product names appear in initial capital or ALL CAPITAL LETTERS. Readers, however, should contact the appropriate companies for more complete information regarding trademarks and registration.

This publication is designed to provide accurate and authoritative information in regard to the subject matter covered. It is sold with the understanding that the publisher is not engaged in rendering professional services. If professional advice or other expert assistance is required, the services of a competent professional person should be sought.

Internet World, Web Week, Web Developer, Internet Shopper, and Mecklermedia are the exclusive trademarks of Mecklermedia Corporation and are used with permission.

Library of Congress Cataloging-in-Publication Data:
Ford, Nigel.
    Web developer.com guide to building intelligent Web sites with JavaScript / Nigel Ford.
      p. cm.
    Includes index.
    ISBN 0-471-24274-8 (pbk./Online : alk. paper)
    1. Web sites--Design. 2. JavaScript (Computer program language).
    I. Title.
    TK5105.888.F68 1998
    006.3'37--dc21   97-51983
                                             CIP

Printed in the United States of America.
10 9 8 7 6 5 4 3 2 1

CONTENTS

Chapter 3   Processing the Information to Add Value   35

Chapter 4   Communicating the Results to Your Readers   65

Chapter 5   Programming Your Web Pages to "Think"   85

INTRODUCTION

Intelligent Web pages are pages that can interact with their readers to offer the same high-quality, individualized information and advice that you would provide if you were present in person. They do this by storing and retrieving aspects of *your* knowledge and expertise.

By handling tasks that would otherwise require human attention, intelligent pages can add considerable value to your website. This added value can accrue to you, the website developer, and to visitors to your site. Your Web pages can respond individually to each visitor, analyzing his or her particular requirements and giving advice accordingly.

Value can be said to have been added to your website if, by injecting "intelligence" into your pages, you can offer your visitors a level of interactive advice and support that would otherwise not be possible or that can release you from some of the intellectual activities that would otherwise require your personal attention.

The intellectual tasks that can be handled automatically by intelligent Web pages can vary from the simple to the complex—from checking and summarizing responses to an online questionnaire to offering expert individualized advice on which products best match complex individual requirements.

All this is possible using JavaScript. This exciting language enables programming commands to be integrated seamlessly into the HTML making up your Web pages. High levels of interactivity can be contained entirely within the client's browser without the need for additional requests to the server once your pages have been loaded.

However, server-side JavaScript offers powerful additional facilities, including database access, to enhance intelligent websites.

Who Should Read This Book

This book is aimed at anyone who wants to build highly interactive Web pages. Techniques are simply and clearly introduced in a manner accessible to nonprogrammers.

No previous experience of JavaScript is required. The first part of the book provides a gentle introduction to JavaScript basics. Nor is any previous programming experience assumed. Techniques are introduced with simple examples. The code is listed in full and is clearly explained.

How This Book Is Organized

There are four main sections to this book. Following Chapter One's introduction to the types of application that can be developed using intelligent JavaScript techniques, Chapters 2–4 ("JavaScript Basics") provide a gentle introduction to basic JavaScript concepts and techniques. This part is arranged, as are the other parts of the book, according to things you may want to accomplish using JavaScript, rather than according to the technical features of the language.

Chapters 5–8 build on your understanding of JavaScript basics and explore more advanced techniques for building intelligence into your Web pages. Chapters 9–11 introduce extended JavaScript capability in the form of dynamic HTML and server-side JavaScript. Appendix A provides a concise JavaScript reference designed to enable you quickly to identify appropriate JavaScript features when developing your own applications. Appendix B gives you a brief overview of the companion website, located at **www.wiley.com/ compbooks/ford**.

Overview

Chapter 1, "Adding Value To Your Web Pages Using JavaScript," introduces the concept of intelligent Web pages. It describes how simple techniques can be used to build high levels of interactivity into your Web pages. A number of example applications are illustrated.

Chapter 2, "Obtaining Information from Readers," provides a gentle introduction to basic concepts and techniques for those new to JavaScript and to programming in general. Interactivity entails three elements: obtaining information from the readers of your Web pages (for example, telling you of their requirements or responding to questions your Web pages present to them); processing this information to add value; and communicating the results to your readers. Chapter 2 deals with the first element, introducing a range of techniques for obtaining information from the readers of your Web pages.

Chapter 3, "Processing the Information to Add Value," concerns the second element of interactivity, introducing a range of basic JavaScript techniques for processing the information obtained from the readers of your Web pages. These techniques form the building blocks for the more advanced approaches to adding value introduced in Chapters 5–8.

Chapter 4, "Communicating the Results to Your Readers," covers the third element of interactivity: communicating the results to the readers of your Web pages.

A range of JavaScript techniques for displaying information in windows and frames and dynamically creating and displaying new Web pages "on the fly" are introduced.

Chapter 5, "Programming Your Web Pages to 'Think'," introduces simple expert system techniques that enable you to build high levels of interactivity into your Web pages. Your pages can engage in a dialogue with their readers, their choice of questions depending on each reader's answers to previous ones, and offer individualized advice, including explanations of their lines of reasoning. This is achieved by building into your Web pages aspects of your own decision-making knowledge and/or that of others. This chapter introduces simple ways of doing this.

Chapter 6, "Storing Knowledge in Your Web Pages," introduces further techniques for encapsulating knowledge in your Web pages. Intelligent behavior often entails deducing information without having to be told everything explicitly. This chapter examines ways in which powers of deduction can be built into your Web pages so that they can figure out answers to questions for themselves from other relevant information they possess.

Chapter 7, "Interpreting User Input," discusses the fact that allowing the readers of your Web pages to choose from lists of options is a useful—but limited—way of obtaining information from them. This chapter explores ways of analyzing information provided by readers in the form of free text. Techniques for analyzing textual information at levels deeper than simple matching are introduced. Techniques for building an intelligent front end to an Internet search engine are introduced, along with a system enabling your Web pages to engage in some primitive conversation with readers based on the classic ELIZA program.

Chapter 8, "Problem Solving and Game Playing," discusses the concept of intelligent behavior in terms of solving a problem or achieving a goal. This chapter introduces some classic problem-solving techniques in which a problem (an initial state) is transformed into a solution (an end state). These techniques are illustrated using a number of classic problem-solving puzzles and games.

Chapter 9, "Using Dynamic HTML with JavaScript," introduces more advanced dynamic HTML display techniques offered by JavaScript 1.2. Using JavaScript-based style sheets and multiple layers of HTML content on the same page, you can control features such as fonts, borders, margins, and positioning. Blocks of content can be moved, resized, made to overlap, appear, and disappear. Their content can be changed on the fly. Images on moving layers can be rapidly changed to create complex animation effects.

Chapter 10, "Server-Side JavaScript," explores using JavaScript as a server-side language. Client-side JavaScript is downloaded along with the HTML making up your Web pages and interpreted by the reader's browser. The interactivity of your Web pages is contained entirely within each reader's browser; there is no need to keep sending requests to the server. However, JavaScript can also be used to run programs on the server. Server-side JavaScript offers additional useful built-in objects and features that facilitate interactions between server and client, avoiding the need for much CGI programming. It also allows read and write access to files and databases on the server as well as interaction with Java and other languages.

Chapter 11, "Where to Go from Here", lists useful resources for continuing study of JavaScript, including books, electronic resources available over the Web, and searching tips to enable you to keep up to date with new developments.

Appendix A, "Concise JavaScript Reference," is intended as a quick reference to JavaScript features. The aim of the chapter is to enable you quickly to identify features that may be useful for a particular application and to check the version of JavaScript (and therefore the browser version) with which each is compatible. This chapter is designed to be used in conjunction with the online *JavaScript Reference* available on Netscape's website, which contains full details of all JavaScript features, along with clear examples of exactly how to use them.

Appendix B, "The Website", explains what is to be found on the companion website. It enables you to run the programs without the need for typing in code from the book, and enables you to copy parts or all of the code for use or adaptation in your own applications.

Tools You Will Need

You should have access to Netscape Navigator version 3 or above. Netscape 4 offers the fullest implementation of JavaScript (version 1.2). However, except where JavaScript 1.2 is explicitly specified, the programs in the book will also run on Navigator 3.

You do not need a connection to the Internet or to a server to use this book. Except for the server-side JavaScript section, all programs will run on a standalone computer equipped with a JavaScript-enabled browser. It is therefore possible to develop interactive Web pages and to build up your expertise without having a Web connection.

What's on the Website

The companion website can be accessed at **www.wiley.com/compbooks/ford**. All the programs introduced in the book are contained on this site. This means that all the techniques and example programs can be tested without the need for extensive typing of code.

Before You Start

Besides the more obvious benefits to be derived from developing intelligent, interactive Web pages, I hope that you manage also to experience the enormous amount of enjoyment and just plain fun that messing around with JavaScript can bring. Good luck with your explorations of JavaScript!

ADDING VALUE TO YOUR WEB PAGES
Using JavaScript

"Normal" HTML pages can present information to, and obtain information from, the readers of your Web pages. However, these processes are relatively passive. In other words, the information you present to your readers is basically the same for all your readers, and the information obtained *from* them is passed back to you verbatim (that is, intellectually unprocessed).

JavaScript can add value to your Web pages by enabling greater levels of interactivity. You can automate a number of intellectual processes that will enable your Web pages to respond individually to different readers. Your pages can themselves compose and present customized information on the basis of analyzing the particular requirements and preferences of readers. This is what we mean when we refer to *intelligent* Web pages.

This definition has important implications. Added value can accrue to you—the Web page author—and/or the readers of your pages. Your Web pages can perform intellectual processing that would otherwise require your personal presence and attention or the presence and attention of some other human being—for example, an expensive member of sales staff. Furthermore, this capability can be called into action tirelessly, 24 hours a day, always operating at peak performance. This capability may enable you to provide a level of service (for example, interactive product information or advice on a wide range of topics) that, if it relied on human staffing, would be either impossible or prohibitively expensive.

Some Real-World Examples

The readers of your Web pages, whether potential customers or, in the case of noncommercial applications, the recipients of useful information and advice, can benefit from 24-hour availability of a high-quality interactive service. The nature of the intellectual processing that can be automated in this way can range from the very simple to the highly complex—from checking and validating a reader's responses to an online questionnaire to offering expert advice in response to complex reader requirements and circumstances. Let's look at some examples of the sort of value that can be added to your Web pages in terms of product advice, interpretation of complex regulations, research, and interactive training.

Product Advice

You can automate at least some of the work that would be done by front-line sales staff in a traditional marketing environment. It is one thing to publish relatively passive product information on the Web using HTML, but you can add another dimension if your Web pages can *interactively* give product *advice* to potential customers based on their stated requirements.

Customers can "quiz" an intelligent Web page to discover which products best match their needs. They can explore a range of options and alternatives by describing different requirements. Importantly, your pages can provide interactive, customized advice that would otherwise require time-consuming and expensive staff time. If even a significant proportion of front-line queries can be handled automatically in this way, staff time can be freed to deal with more complex queries that really *do* require human interaction. Your intelligent Web page can provide you with a tireless interactive sales assistant ready to work 24 hours a day, giving quality responses to every hit on your page.

Figure 1.1 shows a simple example Web page designed to give interactive advice on mobile phones. Users can stipulate their requirements and instantly be shown a list of network providers that fulfill these requirements. Changes in the users' requirements are reflected in an instantly updated list of matching networks. All processing is done by the Web page, within each user's browser. Letters have been substituted for the names of real network providers in this example.

As shown in Figure 1.2, each reader can then fill in his or her personal requirements and compare the cost tariffs of all the networks on the list to see which offers the most economical response to his or her particular pattern of telephone usage. Readers are asked to estimate how many calls they are likely to make in the various categories (weekends, local calls, and the like).

The Web page instantly calculates and displays the costs of all the various tariffs of the different networks (Figure 1.3). Users can experiment with usage patterns and can obtain a clear picture of which network provider best suits their particular needs. Once again, all calculations are done by the Web page, within the user's browser.

Interpretation of Complex Regulations

Much information needed by people within commercial, educational, government, and research communities entails the application of complex rules and regulations.

Figure 1.1 A mobile phone advisor.

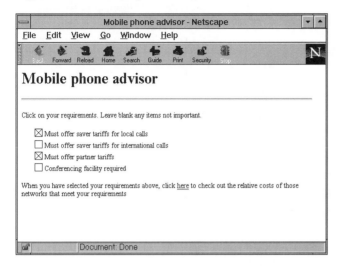

Someone may need guidance on whether they are allowed to copy a particular document according to current copyright law, for example, or they may need to know whether they are eligible for a particular benefit or to apply for a particular educational course.

Figure 1.2 Readers enter their requirements.

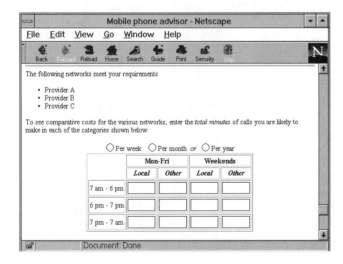

Figure 1.3 Readers can compare tariffs.

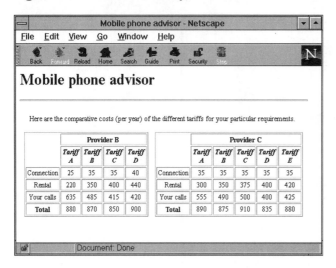

	Provider B						Provider C				
	Tariff A	*Tariff B*	*Tariff C*	*Tariff D*			*Tariff A*	*Tariff B*	*Tariff C*	*Tariff D*	*Tariff E*
Connection	25	35	35	40		Connection	35	35	35	35	35
Rental	220	350	400	440		Rental	300	350	375	400	420
Your calls	635	485	415	420		Your calls	555	490	500	400	425
Total	880	870	850	900		**Total**	890	875	910	835	880

If you are in the business of providing information to people (whether in a commercial or noncommercial context) based on the application of rules and regulations, it may be useful to provide Web pages that can filter out and deal with the more straightforward cases automatically. This can result in the releasing of staff to handle the more complex cases that really do require human intervention.

Let's take a simple example: a Web page that can give first-line advice on the U.K. Data Protection Act. Anyone wanting to set up a database in which personal information is recorded must comply with this Act.

The Web page advises the reader whether he or she is liable for prosecution under the Act. It asks a series of questions, one of which is shown in Figure 1.4. The particular questions and the order in which they are asked depend on each reader's particular circumstances. This is important; it means that only those questions relevant to each particular case are asked. The system thus filters out all the redundant questions and information that readers would normally have to plow through and filter out for themselves when accessing a more passive Web page.

Readers can ask the Web page to explain its "line of reasoning"—why a particular question is being asked and how it has reached the conclusions that form the advice given. Figure 1.4 shows the screen as it appears after a reader has asked why a particular question is being asked. If he or she wishes, the reader can inspect the detailed rules mentioned in the system's explanation by clicking the appropriate hyperlink (see Figure 1.5).

Figure 1.4 The Data Protection Act advisor explains why it is asking a particular question.

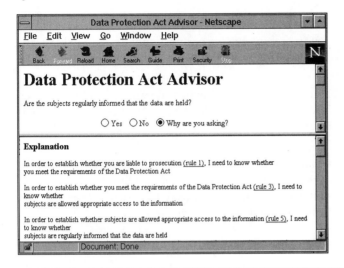

This Web page uses classic "expert system" knowledge-based techniques. Research and development into these techniques has demonstrated that it is possible

Figure 1.5 The system displays a rule in detail.

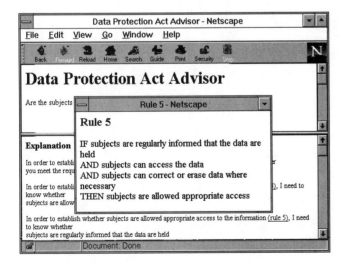

to build intelligent systems capable of emulating human decision making to high levels across a wide range of specialist activities.

Research: Web-Based Questionnaires

"Normal" HTML pages allow you to present electronic questionnaires and to have the data e-mailed to you. JavaScript can add value in that your Web pages can preprocess the data in a number of ways.

Figure 1.6 shows a Web-based questionnaire designed to evaluate an information service. As shown in Figure 1.7, when the reader clicks the button to send in his or her responses, the Web page realizes that two of the questions have not been answered and alerts the reader accordingly.

More elaborate pre-analysis can be performed—for example, to work out cumulated scores on the subscales of the questionnaire or perform more sophisticated analysis if required. Such preprocessing is all done within the Web page itself. It is all written into the HTML and JavaScript code and processed in the reader's browser.

Interactive Training

Figure 1.8 shows a page from a Web-based interactive tutorial designed to train readers in searching for information on the Internet. When the reader accesses the page, such a system can know who the reader is and which modules he or she has completed during previous sessions. It can indicate the module titles and the scores the reader

Figure 1.6 A Web-based questionnaire.

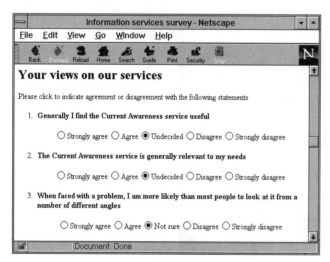

Figure 1.7 Checking questionnaire responses.

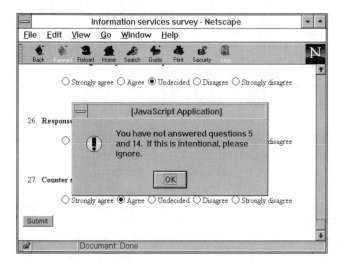

obtained on the built-in tests. It can work out which modules remain to be completed within this particular topic, and it can offer a menu of these modules as one of the options available to the user.

Figure 1.8 A Web-based interactive tutorial.

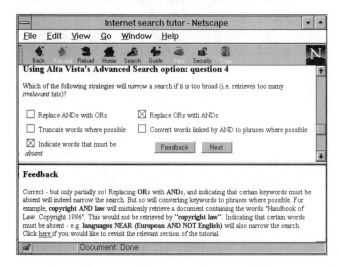

Interaction can be built into the tutorial in the form of dynamic feedback in response to users' correct and incorrect answers to questions. Figure 1.8 shows the page's response to a reader's incorrect answer to a multiple-choice question. Again, all of this is done within the reader's browser without the need for further requests to the server.

What Is JavaScript?

JavaScript is a scripting language that enables you to embed programming commands into your Web pages. This allows you to create pages capable of high levels of interaction with their readers.

JavaScript programs can be simple, consisting of a single command—for example, to display a message to the reader. They can be complex, processing information provided by the reader in sophisticated ways to add value, then displaying the results. They can be triggered by actions performed by readers as they read your page—for example, moving the mouse over areas of the screen, clicking buttons, or selecting from options you present to them.

JavaScript was developed by Sun Microsystems and Netscape Communication Corporation as a cross-platform language—that is, a language enabling the same program to run on different types of computers and operating systems. The European standards body ECMA has released a language specification, ECMA-262, derived from JavaScript. It has been submitted to the International Standards Organization for adoption as an international standard.

Client-Side and Server-Side JavaScript

JavaScript that is interpreted within the reader's browser is known as *client-side JavaScript*. Web pages written in HTML with embedded JavaScript commands are no different from normal HTML pages in that they too are downloaded from a server to the reader's browser. The browser displays the HTML and executes the JavaScript commands.

However, JavaScript can also be used for *server-side programming*. Server-side JavaScript commands are also embedded within the HTML making up your Web pages, but they are processed on the server. Server-side JavaScript can then generate and send HTML, incorporating the results of this processing for display on the reader's browser. In other words, your Web pages' responses to actions performed and information provided by their readers take place on the server as opposed to the reader's computers. Client-side and server-side JavaScript can be mixed within the same Web page.

Server-side processing allows users to respond in ways not possible using just client-side JavaScript. For example, JavaScript running on a server can read from and write to files as well as accessing databases. Your Web pages can give their readers access to information stored on such files and databases, or they can respond to readers using information stored on the server from previous visits. Information can be shared among visitors to your Web page and between different Web pages.

Server-side JavaScript requires the use of Netscape's server software.

JavaScript, Java, and "Crossware"

JavaScript is not Java. Java is a fully blown, powerful, general-purpose programming language suitable for large, complex programs. JavaScript is a scripting language designed for smaller applications. It interacts more directly with HTML than does Java. Client-side JavaScript is interpreted as it is read by the reader's browser, whereas Java must first be compiled before it is downloaded to the reader's browser. Thus, client-side JavaScript does not require a special programming environment; JavaScript commands are simply included in the text file containing HTML.

Netscape's Dynamic HTML is based on JavaScript. JavaScript style sheets allow control over the presentation of Web pages (with control of features such as margins, borders, line height, and color of particular areas of the page), content positioning (text and images can be precisely positioned, overlapped if required), dynamic change (elements can be made to appear, move, and disappear), and downloadable fonts (allowing you to specify that your Web page appear in a specific font on all platforms).

Compiled *applets* written in Java can be included within HTML documents. Netscape's LiveConnect allows JavaScript, Java, and plug-in applications to interact. For example, via JavaScript, information obtained from a reader via an HTML form can control Java applets, passing information to and from them. JavaScript can access Java variables, methods, and properties. Java can control JavaScript variables, methods, and properties. Plug-in applications can also interact with JavaScript, again allowing control from the HTML page.

JavaScript will play an increasingly central role in the development of crossware, in which software components communicate with one another, across networks and across platforms, via common interface standards. Tools such as Netscape's Visual JavaScript allow the custom building of applications using components "glued together" using JavaScript. Visual JavaScript enables complex applications to be built by "dragging and dropping" JavaScript, Java, and HTML components in a visual development environment. CORBA and JavaBean components can be imported and used as required. (JavaBeans are software components, written in Java, that adhere to JavaSoft's Bean specification and can thus be accessed by other software. CORBA objects are components that can be accessed according to the Common Object Request Broker Architecture.)

OBTAINING INFORMATION *from Readers*

Interaction is, by definition, a two-way process. So, as well as telling our readers things via our Web pages, we need our readers to tell us things. JavaScript allows us to know what our readers are saying—and doing. We can program our Web pages to respond to a wide range of actions—for example, when a reader clicks a particular button, types information into a text box, makes a selection from choices we present, or moves the mouse over a particular region of the screen.

This chapter concentrates on obtaining such information from our readers—in other words, programming our Web pages to know what our readers do and say. The way in which we *respond* to this information can vary from the simple to the highly sophisticated. However, in the interests of clarity, this chapter keeps our responses simple so that we can concentrate on ways of obtaining information. More sophisticated ways of responding are introduced in Chapter 4.

Knowing When a Button Is Clicked

Clicking buttons is central to our use of computers. Web browsers have buttons for Back, Forward, Reload, and so on. We have all seen messages appear in popup windows, which we then have to accept or cancel by clicking an OK or a Cancel button.

HTML enables us to put buttons into our Web pages to do things such as enabling readers to submit information they have provided (by typing into a text box or selecting from a range of options). Reset buttons are also often used to allow readers to erase this information and start again.

However, JavaScript allows us to create all sorts of buttons, triggering all sorts of actions. A button can perform one action or a whole range of actions.

These button actions may be obvious to the reader. For example, they may display information in another part of the screen, open a new window, or load a new page of information. An example was given in Chapter 1, where clicking the Feedback button displayed feedback on the reader's answers to a multiple-choice test. Clicking the Next button took the reader to the next question in the test.

Alternatively, the effects of clicking a button may not be seen immediately by the reader. For example, a button click may cause a calculation to be performed or some information to be stored "behind the scenes" for later use. The Feedback button referred to above, while displaying feedback to the reader, can also add the reader's score to a running total. Having done so, it can then add to its log details of which topics have caused problems for this particular reader. It can then "intelligently" suggest, either immediately or later in the learning session, a list of topics that the reader might wish to revisit.

How to Do It

In the interests of clarity, we'll take a really simple example to begin with. The disadvantage of doing so is that it may be difficult at first to appreciate just how useful a particular technique can be in "real-world," complex applications. The advantage, however, is that you can concentrate on the central procedures without being distracted by nonessential details or complexities.

For our first simple example, we will create a Web page with a button labeled "Click me". When a reader clicks the button, a little message window will pop up in the middle of the reader's screen (Figure 2.1).

Reacting in this way to something a reader does makes use of a technique called *event handling*. An *event* is simply something a reader does (in this case, clicking a button). *Handling* is what we do in response to that action (in this case, making a message window pop up). JavaScript offers a number of event handlers, listed and described fully in Appendix A. Only a selection is introduced in this chapter.

The event in this case (the popup message) is just about the simplest type of response possible and will be the main form of response to information used in the examples in this chapter. The idea is to minimize distraction from each basic information-obtaining procedure introduced. Responses can be (and usually are) more sophisticated than this example; more sophisticated examples are presented in Chapter 4, where, using a similar strategy, a simple form of *obtaining* information (the subject of the present discussion) is consistently used.

Here is our HTML code (explained below) for this example—Program 2-1 on the website:

```
<HTML>
<BODY>
```

```
<FORM>
<INPUT TYPE="button"
VALUE="Click me"
onClick="alert ('You clicked!')">
</FORM>
</BODY>
</HTML>
```

 NOTE It is good practice when publishing on the Web to give each document a title, by inserting the following before the <BODY> tag:

```
<HEAD> <TITLE> Your Title </TITLE> </HEAD>
```

In order to keep the code as uncluttered as possible, so that we can concentrate on the JavaScript techniques being introduced, titles have not been included in the examples in this book, although they have been added to the examples published on the companion website.

Figure 2.1 A popup message window.

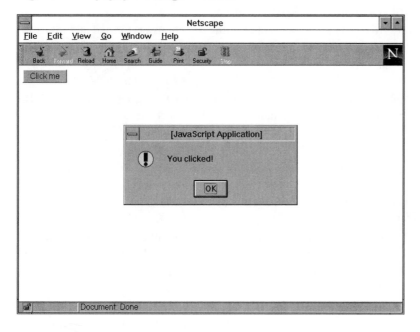

onClick and **alert** are built-in JavaScript commands. **onClick=** means "When a reader clicks on this object, do whatever comes after the **=** sign." **alert** means "Open a message box containing the words quoted in the brackets."

<table>
<tr><td>NOTE</td><td>Note the use of quotes. Whatever comes after the = sign must be enclosed within quotes. Any text you want JavaScript to display (in this case, the words "You clicked!") must also be enclosed in quotes. Whenever you have one set of quotes enclosed within another set of quotes like this, you must distinguish between them by using double (") and single (') quotes. It doesn't matter in which order you use them, so onClick="alert ('You clicked!')" and onClick='alert ("You clicked!")' are equivalent.</td></tr>
</table>

This program is not particularly useful as it stands. Generally, we will want to use our knowledge that a particular button has been clicked in order to react by triggering some appropriate action (for example, to give the reader some feedback, automatically navigate to another page, or perform some calculation using the information). To do this, we need to be able to *store* the information for later use.

Storing the Information for Later Use

Chapter 3 explores in detail various ways of reacting to actions performed and information supplied by our readers. However, what many of these actions have in common is the fact that we need to be able to *store* information for later use. This applies to *all* the ways of obtaining information that we meet in this chapter—not just to clicking buttons.

In our example so far, JavaScript will forget the fact that a reader has clicked a button as soon as the **onClick** event handler has been activated. So, although any action we specify will be executed (in this case, a simple message, "You clicked"), we cannot use the fact that the button was clicked anywhere else in our Web page.

Take, for example, an interactive training program. Early in the program, we may ask the reader to indicate whether or not he or she has used this training material before by clicking buttons marked New User or Experienced User, then clicking another button labeled Continue.

However, when the reader clicks Continue, JavaScript will have forgotten whether the reader has indicated whether he or she is a new user or has used the materials before. It will forget all about one button as soon as it begins to process information gleaned from another button!

To prevent this happening, we need to be able to store information for later retrieval. To do this, we use *variables*, or "empty containers" in which we can store information. We can create a variable using commands of the form:

```
variable name = "the information we want to store"
```

In our example, this might be translated into:

```
message = "As a new user, please go to the pre-test section"
```

which we can insert into our event handler as follows:

```
onClick="message = 'As a new user, please go to the pre-test section' "
```

Here is the new program—see Program 2-2 on the website:

```
<HTML>
<BODY>
Please indicate whether you are
<FORM>
<INPUT TYPE="button"
VALUE="New User"
onClick="message = 'As a new user, please go to the pre-test section'">
<INPUT TYPE="button"
VALUE="Experienced"
onClick="message = 'Would you like to review any sections you have already studied?'
">
<INPUT TYPE="button"
VALUE="Continue"
onClick= "alert (message)">
</FORM>
</BODY>
</HTML>
```

If the reader clicks New User, the message shown in Figure 2.2 will appear.

Clicking Experienced would result in the message "Would you like to review any sections you have already studied?"

You can give variables any name you like within the following rules:

- A variable name must be made up of valid characters. These are upper- and lowercase letters (a–z, A–Z), numbers (0–9), and the underscore character (_).

- The first character must be a letter or the underscore character.

- The variable name must not be the same as any of JavaScript's reserved words. Reserved words are listed in Appendix A.

Knowing When a Hypertext Link Is Clicked or Moved Over

We can tell when a reader clicks a hyperlink to move to another document or another place in the same document. This information can be useful if, for example, we want to interrupt the process to tell the reader more about the document he or she has selected—for example, that it has a lot of graphics that will take a long time to load—and ask the reader if he or she really wants to continue.

> **NOTE**
> If the reader clicks the Continue button before clicking either the New User or the Experienced button, a JavaScript error message will appear saying that *message* is not defined. This is because until one of these buttons is clicked, the variable *message* does not exist (remember, it is created only when the **onClick** event handler is activated). When JavaScript is asked to display the contents of *message*, it cannot do so and therefore displays an error message. This problem is easily overcome by creating the variable as soon as the Web page is loaded. One way of doing this is to include the command within the **onLoad** event handler. This is introduced more fully in the section "Knowing When a Reader Visits or Leaves Your Pages" later in this chapter. However, if you want to try it now, simply replace the <BODY> tag in the code above with the following:

```
<BODY onLoad = "message = 'Please click one of the other buttons' ">
```

Figure 2.2 Message relating to New User.

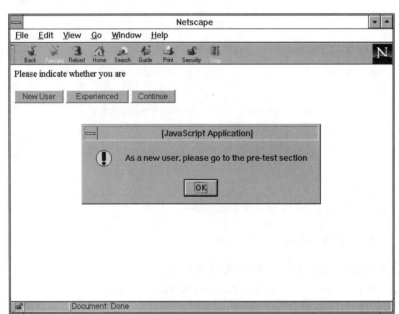

Once we have set up a variable, we can retrieve and use its contents from anywhere in our Web page. However, JavaScript will remember the contents of variables only until the reader leaves our Web page. We cannot, therefore, use information obtained from a reader next time he or she visits our page. We *can* do this, however, by using cookies, introduced in the section "Storing and Retrieving Information Over Time" in Chapter 3.

We can also tell when a reader moves the mouse over a hyperlink—and away from it again—prior to clicking it. This knowledge may be useful, for example, again to display information to the reader telling him or her more about the link. Descriptive material can be displayed in the status bar (the narrow area at the bottom of the screen), a frame, or even a popup window.

How to Do It

The first very simple example displays an alert message when the reader clicks the hyperlink—Program 2-3 on the website:

```
<HTML>
<BODY>
Click here to go to your
<A HREF="homepage.html"
onClick="alert ('So you want to go home!')">
homepage
</A>
</BODY>
</HTML>
```

In order to do something more useful—for example, to give the reader the chance to change his or her mind in the light of further information about the link—requires knowledge of JavaScript commands such as **confirm**. An example of doing precisely this is given later in this chapter in the section "Confirming Whether Something Is True."

The second example uses the **onMouseOver** and **onMouseOut** event handlers to display a message in the status bar at the bottom of the screen as the reader moves the mouse over, then away from, the hyperlink. As the mouse is moved over the link, the message "Hello" appears in the status bar. As it moves away from the link, the message "Cheerio" appears. This is Program 2-4 on the website.

```
<HTML>
<BODY>
Click here to go to your
<A HREF="homepage.html"
onMouseOver="window.status='Hello'; return true"
onMouseOut="window.status='Cheerio'">
```

```
homepage
</A>
</BODY>
</HTML>
```

 Unlike other event handlers (including **onMouseOut**), the **onMouseOver** event handler must include the command **return true** if it is to work. The semicolon before this command is the normal way to separate one JavaScript command from another. This method may be used instead of or as well as inserting a line break.

As well as triggering immediate actions, these event handlers, like any others, can be used to store information for later use. The following code stores, in a variable named *nextPage*, the name of the page whose hyperlink is clicked by the reader. The contents of this variable can then be retrieved and used elsewhere in the Web page—in this case, in the Web page's **onUnload** event handler (inside the <BODY> tag). When the reader clicks the link to move to another page, the message "You are on your way to My Homepage" will be displayed as the page is unloaded. The **onUnload** and **onLoad** event handlers are described in more detail in the next section. This is Program 2-5 on the website.

```
<HTML>
<BODY onLoad = "nextPage = '[Page not yet selected]'"
onUnload = "alert ('You are on your way to ' + nextPage)">
Click here to go to your
<A HREF="homepage.html"
onClick="nextPage='My Homepage'">
homepage
</A>
<FORM>
</BODY>
</HTML>
```

Knowing When a Reader Visits or Leaves Your Pages

There are a variety of other event handlers (described in Appendix A), two of which are **onLoad** and **onUnload**. The first allows us to specify that something should happen when a reader visits our page; the second (as we saw in the example in the previous section) when he or she leaves our page.

These event handlers can be useful. We may want, for example, to display a welcome message when the reader loads our page and another appropriate message when he or she leaves the page. However, we may want the loading or unloading of our Web page to trigger some action other than displaying a simple message. We could note the time the page was loaded, then inform the reader (or ourselves by e-mail) how long the page was read before being unloaded.

How to Do It

The following command:

```
onLoad = "alert ('Welcome to my Web page')"
```

displays a message as soon as the reader visits our Web page. The following code:

```
onUnload = "alert ('Cheerio -- come again')"
```

displays a message when a reader leaves our Web page.

These particular event handlers should be placed within the <BODY> tag of our Web page. (They can also be used within the <FRAMESET> tag. The **onLoad** event handler can also be used in the <IMG> tag.)

The following code—Program 2-6 on the website—uses both the **onLoad** and the **onUnload** event handlers:

```
<HTML>
<BODY onLoad="alert ('hello')"
onUnload="alert ('cheerio')">
Welcome to my Web page
</BODY>
</HTML>
```

As in the case of storing information about a button being clicked, we can create a variable to store this information as follows—Program 2-7 on the website:

```
<HTML>
<BODY onLoad="timeLoaded = new Date ();
alert (timeLoaded)">
</BODY>
</HTML>
```

The command:

```
new Date ()
```

is a built-in JavaScript command that establishes the current day and time. We can now calculate, for example, the length of time a reader has spent looking at our page. This information can be useful in the context of an online interactive training program. We can allow readers a particular amount of time to take a test or we can obtain feedback on those parts of the training program that take learners a particularly long time to get through (which may be an indicator of difficulty).

Here is the code—Program 2-8 on the website:

```
<HTML>
<BODY onLoad="timeLoaded = new Date ()"
onUnload = "timeUnloaded = new Date ();
secondsSpent = (timeUnloaded - timeLoaded)/1000;
alert ('You spent ' + secondsSpent + ' seconds reading this page')">

When you leave this page I will tell you how long you stayed!

</BODY>
</HTML>
```

When readers leave our page, they are told how long they have spent reading it (Figure 2.3).

This example uses a number of operators that are discussed in more detail in Chapter 3. They include the following:

* multiply

/ divide

– subtract

+ add (including concatenating text)

The fourth line of the program above calculates the number of seconds that have elapsed between loading and unloading the page by subtracting the time of unloading from the time of loading. This figure is then divided by 1,000 to convert it into seconds, because the command **Date** returns the time in milliseconds.

Prompting the Reader for Information

We examine ways of offering readers lists of options they can click to choose (checkboxes, radio buttons, etc.) shortly. However, there are many occasions on which we want readers to type in text (or numbers) freely—not just choose from a ready-made list of options. This is necessary if, for example, we want the reader to tell us his or her name and address or to send us comments on our Web pages.

The quickest and easiest way of doing this is to use the **prompt** command. This command causes a popup window to appear asking the reader to type in some information. An OK button and a Cancel button also appear in the window.

The advantage of using **prompt** is that it is very quick and easy. Only the one command is needed to do what otherwise would require a more complex set of commands to open a window, display buttons, and so on. The disadvantages include the fact that the **prompt** window is arguably a rather clumsy and ungainly way of interacting with readers. If you want more subtlety and control, you are well advised to use a *text box* or *text area*, which are introduced in the following sections.

Figure 2.3 onLoad and onUnload in action.

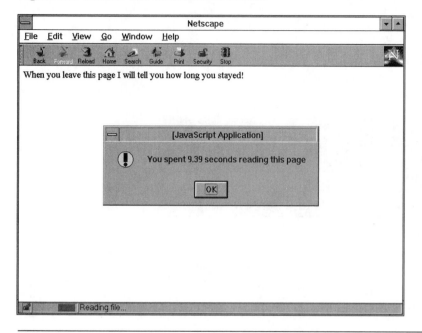

How to Do It

Let's prompt our reader for some information, then use it to generate a simple message. The following command:

```
prompt ("Please type in your name ", "Type here")
```

displays the **prompt** box shown in Figure 2.4.

If we want a blank box, without the default text "Type here," we should put empty quotes ("") in the place of the "Type here" text, as follows:

```
prompt ("Please type in your name ", " ")
```

We can put this code into our **onClick** event handler so that the **prompt** box appears when the reader clicks the Click me button. Here is the code—Program 2-9 on the website:

```
<HTML>
<BODY>
<FORM>
<INPUT
TYPE="button"
VALUE="Click me"
```

Figure 2.4 A prompt box.

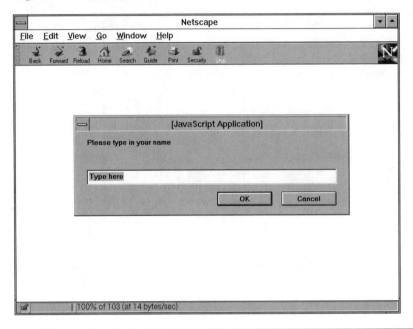

```
onClick="answer = prompt ('Please type in your name ', 'Type here'); alert ('Hello
there ' + answer) " >
</FORM>
</BODY>
</HTML>
```

The variable *answer* will be filled with the result of executing the **prompt** command (that is, what the reader types into the prompt box). This answer is then added to the words "Hello there" and displayed in an alert message box.

A shortcut way of achieving this is to use the following code:

```
onClick="alert ('Hello there ' + prompt ('Please type in your name
', 'Type here'))"
```

This first displays a prompt box asking the reader for his or her name, then adds the result to the words "Hello there," and finally displays the result in an alert box.

Confirming Whether Something Is True

There are many occasions on which we may want to display information or perform actions in response to information given by a reader. We may on occasion, for instance,

Figure 2.5 Interrupting a hyperlink with a message.

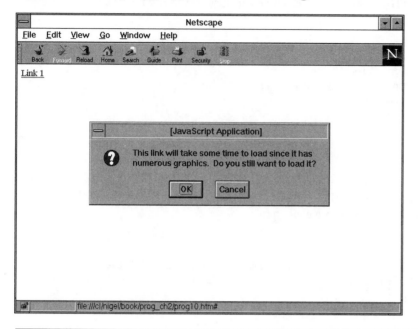

want to check whether the reader really means to do what he or she has just done. Figure 2.5 shows a message warning the reader that the link he or she has just clicked will entail loading a lot of graphics; the message asks whether he or she still wants to continue.

The point of doing this is that if the reader decides not to go ahead, we can tell JavaScript to cancel the action and continue to display the current page instead of going to the new one.

How to Do It
Using rules of the form:

> IF *some condition(s)*
> THEN *some action(s)*
> ELSE *some other action(s)*

can be useful in allowing us to respond differently to various answers given by our readers. The following example (Program 2-10 on the website) displays a message that differs according to the reader's response to the question "Are you happy?" If the reader replies that he or she *is* happy (by clicking OK), the message "Glad to hear it!" is displayed. If the reader is *not* happy, the message "Oh dear!" is displayed. Note the required syntax:

parentheses surrounding the condition of the rule (the IF part) and braces around the conclusion (the THEN part) and alternative conclusion (the ELSE part).

```
<HTML>
<BODY>
<FORM>
<INPUT TYPE="button" VALUE="Click me"
onClick = "if (confirm ('Are you happy?'))
{alert ('Glad to hear it!')}
else {alert ('Oh dear!')}">
</FORM>
</BODY>
</HTML>
```

Here is a more realistically useful example (Program 2-11 on the website). This example interrupts a hyperlink, asking the reader whether he or she really wants to continue. If not, the click is canceled.

```
<HTML>
<BODY>
<A HREF = "homepage.html" onClick = "if (confirm ('This link will take some time to
load since it has numerous graphics. Do you still want to load it?')) {return true}
else {return false}">
Link 1
</A>
</BODY>
</HTML>
```

If the reader confirms that he or she wishes to carry on and load the new page, the rule returns *true*, which has the effect of allowing the hyperlink to be executed as normal. However, if the reader replies in the negative by clicking the confirm box's Cancel button, *false* is returned. This has the effect of canceling the hyperlink even though it has been clicked. The idea of "returning" values is discussed in more detail in Chapter 3.

 A slightly shorter way of doing the same thing would be to replace the hyperlink with the following code:

```
<A HREF = "homepage.html" onClick = "return confirm ('This link will
take some time to load since it has numerous graphics. Do you still
want to load it?')">
```

Using a Text Box

The **prompt** and **confirm** commands are quick and easy. However, using a text box gives you more control. Like the prompt box, a text box enables readers to type information freely, as opposed to having to choose ready-made options. But it differs in a number of ways.

When a prompt box appears, readers are not allowed to do anything else except enter text in the box, then click either OK or Cancel. Only one prompt box can appear at a time, and each must be dealt with by the reader before the next one can appear. If readers attempt to do anything else (follow a hypertext link or use their browser's Back or Reload buttons, for example), they will find these functions and all other functions disabled.

The problem with this is that you may want to have a number of boxes on the screen at the same time, asking readers for several items of information. You may also want your readers to have full control—for example, to follow a help link if they require assistance or an explanation before they answer.

A text box can overcome these limitations. *You* decide how the text box is presented. You can place it anywhere in your normal Web page, and you can control all the text surrounding and introducing it. You can place a number of text boxes on the screen at the same time, and you can allow readers full control, as opposed to forcing them to deal with the text box before they can go on to do anything else. You can decide what will "trigger" the submission of the information. For example, you may place a button on the screen or program a text box to submit its information as soon as the reader finishes typing and clicks outside the box (by using the **onBlur** event handler).

How to Do It

Here is a simple example of a text box—Program 2-12 on the website:

```
<HTML>
<BODY>  Please type your name
<FORM NAME="myForm" >
<INPUT NAME="myTextBox"
TYPE="text">
<INPUT
TYPE="button"
VALUE="Click me"
onClick="alert ('Hello there ' + document.myForm.myTextBox.value)" >
</FORM>
</BODY>
</HTML>
```

Note that we can give objects *names*. As you can see from the code above, we have used the NAME attribute to give the name **myForm** to the form and the name **myTextBox** to the text box. We need to do this in order to retrieve and use the information the reader types into the text box. We use these names to build a unique address for this information. We can then put this unique address in the button's **onClick** command as follows:

```
onClick="alert ('Hello there ' + document.myForm.myTextBox.value)"
```

Whenever JavaScript comes across this "address." it will retrieve the information contained in it. Here is a breakdown of how the address is made up:

value	*that is, the information contained in...*
myTextBox	*the text box that is contained in...*
myForm	*the form that is contained in...*
document	*the document making up the Web page*

At present, the reader has to click within the text box before he or she can begin typing. Also, the reader will have to delete any default text appearing in the box. However, we can make things more convenient for the reader if we automatically set the cursor in the text box (so that the reader can begin typing immediately) and by highlighting the default text (so that whatever the reader types will automatically replace the default text). To do this, we need to put the *focus* on the text box, and to *select* the text box.

We can do this by using the built-in commands **focus** and **select**. We can tell JavaScript to process these commands as soon as the page has loaded in our reader's browser, by including them in the page's **onLoad** event handler. We tag the commands onto the "address" of the object that we want to receive the focus and to be selected. Here is the code—Program 2-13 on the website:

```
<HTML>
<BODY onLoad="document.myForm.myTextBox.focus ();
document.myForm.myTextBox.select ()">
Please type your name
<FORM NAME="myForm" >
<INPUT NAME="myTextBox"
TYPE="text" VALUE="Your name">
<INPUT
TYPE="button"
VALUE="Click me"
onClick="alert ('Hello there ' + document.myForm.myTextBox.value)" >
</FORM>
</BODY>
</HTML>
```

> **NOTE** The address of the text box appears (in the **onLoad** event handler) *before* the text box has actually been created. You may wonder why we don't get an error message saying that the address is not valid. The reason is that the **onLoad** event handler carries out its instructions *after* the rest of the page has loaded, so the address will in fact have been created before the **onLoad** event handler refers to it.

Figure 2.6 A text area.

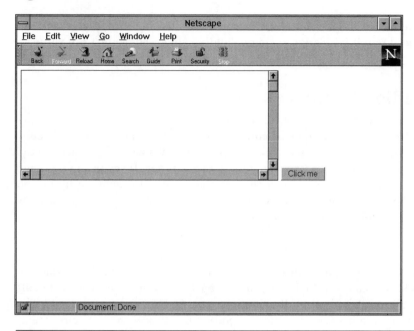

Using Text Areas

Text areas are similar to text boxes, but they can extend more than one row down the screen. They can be useful if we want our readers to enter a relatively large volume of text. A text area will automatically scroll vertically and horizontally as required to accommodate the text as it is typed in. Text can be made to wrap automatically at the end of lines (instead of scrolling horizontally) if required. Figure 2.6 shows a text area 10 rows deep and 50 columns wide.

How to Do It

Here is the code for the text area shown in Figure 2.6. This is Program 2-14 on the website.

```
<HTML>
<BODY>
<FORM NAME="myForm">
<TEXTAREA NAME="myTextArea" COLS=50 ROWS=10> </TEXTAREA>
<INPUT TYPE="button" VALUE="Click me"
onClick="alert ('You wrote ' + document.myForm.myTextArea.value)">
</FORM>
```

```
<BODY>
</HTML>
```

Just as with text boxes, in order to retrieve and use what the reader types into the text area, we need to tell JavaScript its unique address, followed by the word **value**:

```
document.myForm.myTextArea.value
```

Using Radio Buttons

Radio buttons are another useful way of obtaining input from our readers, allowing them to select from a list of options. If required, radio buttons can be made mutually exclusive—that is, the reader can select only one option, each new choice canceling the previous one. An example of this type of option is an age range. If you present a range of age categories and ask people to tick the one that applies to them, naturally you want them to choose only one. We can then make our Web pages react appropriately according to which choice the reader has made.

How to Do It

Here is the code for a set of radio buttons—Program 2-15 on the website. Note that the first radio button is already selected by default. If you do not want to preselect a default button in this way, you should simply leave out the word "CHECKED" in the code. The buttons are also mutually exclusive; clicking on one will cancel the previous choice. This is achieved by giving all the buttons the same name (in this example, "myRB"). The **reset** command resets the choices to the default each time the page is reloaded.

```
<HTML>
<BODY onLoad="selection = 'good'; document.myForm.reset ()">
I think your Web page is
<FORM NAME="myForm">
<INPUT NAME="myRB" TYPE="radio" CHECKED onClick="selection ='good'"> good
<INPUT NAME="myRB" TYPE="radio" onClick=" selection ='bad'"> bad
<INPUT NAME="myRB" TYPE="radio" onClick=" selection ='indifferent'"> indifferent
<INPUT TYPE="button" VALUE="Click me" onClick="alert ('You have chosen ' + selec-
tion)">
</FORM>
</BODY>
</HTML>
```

When the reader clicks one of the buttons, the button's **onClick** event handler creates a variable named *selection* and fills it with a value ("good," "bad," or "indifferent").

Another way of retrieving the reader's choice is to use the address of the radio buttons. As each is created, it is given a unique number (starting at 0), so

```
document.myForm.myRB[0]
```

is the address of the first radio button. The addresses of the others are:

```
document.myForm.myRB[1]
document.myForm.myRB[2]
```

If the first radio button has been selected, the following command

```
document.myForm.myRB[0].checked
```

will return the value *true*. We can therefore include the following code (Program 2-16 on the website) in our event handler to act on this information:

```
<HTML>
<BODY>
I think your Web page is
<FORM NAME="myForm">
<INPUT NAME="myRB" TYPE="radio" CHECKED> good
<INPUT NAME="myRB" TYPE="radio" > bad
<INPUT NAME="myRB" TYPE="radio" > indifferent
<INPUT TYPE="button" VALUE="Click me" onClick="if (document.myForm.myRB[0].checked)
{alert ('You have chosen Good -- an excellent choice!')} else {alert ('Oh dear --
please tell me what is wrong')}">
</FORM>
</BODY>
</HTML>
```

Alternatively, we could use the VALUE of the radio button. The address:

```
document.myForm.myRB[0].value
```

will return the contents of the VALUE property of the first radio button. The following code (Program 2-17 on the website) will display the value of the radio button selected. Note that this can be done more economically using loops rather than having a separate IF...THEN rule for each radio button. Loops, and an example of finding the value of selected radio buttons using them, are introduced in Chapter 3.

```
<HTML>
<BODY>
I think your Web page is
<FORM NAME="myForm">
<INPUT NAME="myRB" TYPE="radio" VALUE = "Good" CHECKED> good
<INPUT NAME="myRB" TYPE="radio" VALUE = "Bad"> bad
<INPUT NAME="myRB" TYPE="radio" VALUE = "Indifferent"> indifferent
<INPUT TYPE="button" VALUE="Click me" onClick="if (document.myForm.myRB[0].checked)
{answer = 0}; if (document.myForm.myRB[1].checked) {answer = 1}; if
(document.myForm.myRB[2].checked) {answer = 2}; alert ('You have chosen ' + docu-
ment.myForm.myRB[answer].value)}">
</FORM>
</BODY>
</HTML>
```

Figure 2.7 Retrieving the value of a radio button.

Figure 2.7 shows this program in action.

Choosing Options in List Boxes

List boxes are another way of presenting the reader with a list of options. If required, only one option may be displayed, along with an arrow that, when clicked, will reveal all the other choices in a dropdown list (see Figure 2.8). Alternatively, we can specify the number of rows to be displayed.

How to Do It

Here is the code for a simple list box—Program 2-18 on the website:

```
<HTML>
<BODY>
<FORM NAME="myForm">
<SELECT NAME="myListBox">
<OPTION VALUE="First">First choice</OPTION>
<OPTION VALUE="Second">Second choice</OPTION>
<OPTION VALUE="Third">Third choice</OPTION>
</SELECT>
```

```
<INPUT TYPE="button"
VALUE="Click me"
onClick="alert ('This is the text of your choice: ' +
document.myForm.myListBox.options[document.myForm.myListBox.selectedIndex].text);
alert ('This is the VALUE of your choice: ' + document.myForm.myListBox.options[docu-
ment.myForm.myListBox.selectedIndex].value)">
</FORM>
</BODY>
</HTML>
```

As with radio buttons, finding out which choice a reader has made so that we can act upon it is a little more tricky than is the case with text boxes and text areas. Each OPTION in the SELECT set has its own unique number that is automatically assigned to it when our document loads.

Here is the full address (including this unique number) of each of the three options:

```
document.myForm.myListBox.options[0]
document.myForm.myListBox.options[1]
document.myForm.myListBox.options[2]
```

Figure 2.8 Dropdown lists.

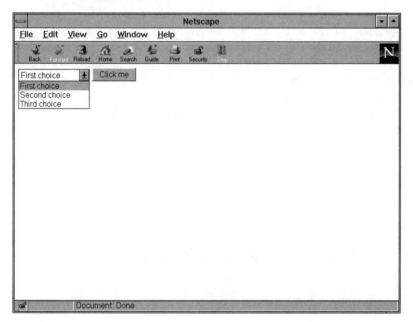

Note that the numbering starts at 0, so the first button is numbered 0, the second is numbered 1, and the third is numbered 2. Now we simply add the word "text" to the unique number of a radio button in order to retrieve its contents. Therefore:

```
document.myForm.myListBox.options[0].text
```

retrieves the text associated with the first option (in this case, "First choice"), and

```
document.myForm.myListBox.options[1].text
```

retrieves the text associated with the second radio button (in this case, "Second choice"), and so on.

The **value** of the option (that is, whatever follows VALUE = in the OPTION tag) can be retrieved by adding **value** in place of **text**. Thus:

```
document.myForm.myListBox.options[0].value
document.myForm.myListBox.options[1].value
document.myForm.myListBox.options[2].value
```

retrieves "First," "Second," and "Third."

We now know how to retrieve the contents of a given option. But how do we know which option has been selected by our reader? We can find this out by using the JavaScript command **selectedIndex** as follows:

```
document.myForm.myListBox.selectedIndex
```

This rather long-winded statement is in fact simply the address of the *number* of the radio button that has been selected by our reader. Assuming that our reader has selected the first radio button, the content of this address will simply be the number 0. Had he or she selected the second button, it would have been 1, and so on.

We use this second address (that is, the address of the number of the selected option) inside our first address (that is, the address of the set of all three options) as follows:

```
document.myForm.myListBox.options[document.myForm.myListBox.selectedIndex].text
```

Assuming that our reader has selected the first option (that is, option number 0), this is equivalent to:

```
document.myForm.myListBox.options[0].text
```

The content of this address will be "First choice."

Selecting Options by Checking Boxes

Checkboxes are another way of allowing the reader to choose one or more of a range of options. They are generally used when you want to offer people choices that are not mutually exclusive. In other words, choosing one option does not automatically exclude all the other options presented. Mutually exclusive options are best handled by radio buttons. Checkboxes offer a quick way for the reader to make "yes" and "no" choices.

How to Do It

The following code (Program 2-19 on the website) displays a checkbox followed by the words "Click this box." When the box is clicked, it will appear checked. Click it again and it will become unchecked. When the Your selection button is clicked, an alert message will tell you whether the box is checked or not. If we ask readers to check a box if they want, for example, a catalog of products to be sent to them, we need to know whether or not they have done so in order that the appropriate action can be triggered.

```
<HTML>
<BODY>
<FORM NAME="myForm">
<INPUT TYPE="checkbox" NAME="catalogWanted">
Click this box
<INPUT TYPE="button" VALUE="Your selection" onClick="alert ('It is '
+ document.myForm.catalogWanted.checked
+ ' that you want a catalogue')"
</FORM>
</BODY>
</HTML>
```

Figure 2.9 Displaying the state of a checkbox.

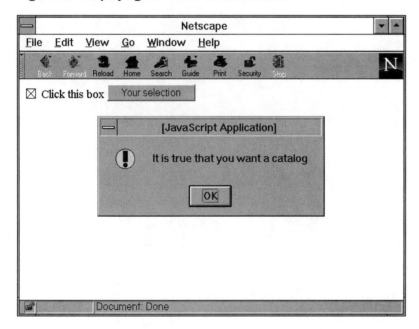

We can tell whether a particular checkbox is or is not checked because if it is, then

`document.myForm.catalogWanted.checked`

will return *true*. If it is not, it will return *false*. In the example above, assuming that the box is checked when the Your selection button is clicked, the message "It is true that you want a catalogue" will be displayed (Figure 2.9).

The example here serves simply to illustrate how to capture knowledge that a checkbox is or is not checked. Normally the action triggered by this knowledge would be to act upon the information—in this case, to e-mail you so that you could send the reader the catalog.

PROCESSING THE INFORMATION

to Add Value

3

S
o far, we have examined ways of obtaining information from the readers of our Web pages and of storing this information for later use. This chapter explores this "later use," which in fact consists of a powerful range of techniques to enable us to add value to the information provided by our readers. Communicating this added value to them is explored in Chapter 4.

Proactivity: JavaScript Outside Event Handlers

So far, all our JavaScript commands have appeared within event handlers, so nothing happens until the readers of our Web pages *do* something, such as clicking a button or hypertext link (**onClick**), loading or leaving a page (**onLoad** and **onUnload**), and so on.

In fact, we need not wait until our readers do something before we execute JavaScript commands. We can put them almost anywhere in the HTML code making up our Web pages. Arguably, this is not much different from putting JavaScript commands in the **onLoad** event handler of a page, because nothing will happen anyway until our page is loaded. However, it is less constraining if we are not restricted to placing all our JavaScript code in event handlers.

First, trying to fit complex code into event handlers and coping with further embedded quotation marks within the quotation marks signifying event handler commands can be clumsy and difficult. Second, we may want to have some control over when JavaScript commands are executed relative to the appearance of "normal" HTML text. (This is explained with practical examples in the following section.) Third, we may want to load into a Web page JavaScript commands that are not executed immediately; we might want them to be executed only when they are explicitly "called." (This technique is explained in the "Storing and Retrieving Information Over Time: Functions" section later in this chapter.)

How to Do It

If we want to place JavaScript commands outside event handlers, we can place the commands between the tags:

```
<SCRIPT LANGUAGE="JavaScript"> </SCRIPT>
```

or simply:

```
<SCRIPT> </SCRIPT>
```

 NOTE Netscape Navigator will try to interpret any code included within the <SCRIPT> or <SCRIPT LANGUAGE = "JavaScript"> tags. However, we can specify which version of JavaScript we are using in the whole—or any part—of our programs by including the following attributes. Netscape will ignore code written in a version of JavaScript that it cannot handle, if the version is specified as follows:

```
<SCRIPT LANGUAGE = "JavaScript1.1"> will be ignored by Navigator 2.0
<SCRIPT LANGUAGE = "JavaScript1.2"> will be ignored by Navigator 2.0
and Navigator 3.
```

We can, for example, display two alert message boxes (one after the other) as follows (Program 3-1 on the website):

```
<HTML>
<BODY>
<SCRIPT LANGUAGE="JavaScript">
alert ("Hello there");
alert ("Hope you are feeling OK today!")
</SCRIPT>
</BODY>
</HTML>
```

These two alert boxes will be displayed as soon as this Web page loads into the reader's browser. Note that each command must be separated from others by a semicolon and/or placing each new command on a new line.

We can place these commands in the BODY of our Web page (as in the example above) or in the HEAD, as shown below (Program 3-2 on the website):

```
<HTML>
<HEAD>
<SCRIPT LANGUAGE="JavaScript">
alert ("Hello there");
alert ("Hope you are feeling OK today!")
```

```
</SCRIPT>
</HEAD>
</HTML>
```

or indeed, if we want, using a combination of both (Program 3-3 on the website):

```
<HTML>
<HEAD>
<SCRIPT LANGUAGE="JavaScript">
alert ("Hello there")
</SCRIPT>
</HEAD>
<BODY>
<SCRIPT>
alert ("Hope you are feeling OK today!")
</SCRIPT>
</BODY>
</HTML>
```

It is important to note that the order in which information is displayed can be controlled. The following code (Program 3-4 on the website):

```
<HTML>
<BODY>
This is written first
<SCRIPT>
alert ("This is written second")
</SCRIPT>
</BODY>
</HTML>
```

results in the alert message "This is written second" being displayed *before* the text, "This is written first." However, by adding a command such as <BR>, <P>, or <HR> after the text:

```
This is written first <BR>
```

"This is written second" will in fact be displayed *after* "This is written first." If JavaScript finds no command that results in some break in the normal HTML text, it executes any JavaScript commands *before* any HTML commands.

As well as displaying messages, we can set up variables in our HTML code whenever we want. We do this as follows:

```
<HTML>
<BODY>
<SCRIPT LANGUAGE="JavaScript">
var readerName = prompt ("What is your name?","")
</SCRIPT>
```

```
</BODY>
</HTML>
```

The word **var** may be omitted when creating a variable.

When the reader types his or her name in response to the prompt box, whatever he or she types will be stored in the variable *readerName*. (Variables are explained in detail in the next section of this chapter.)

Now whenever you use the word *readerName* in your program, JavaScript will retrieve whatever the reader typed. Let's use this procedure to ask our reader for name, gender, and age, then display an appropriate message using all three pieces of information. This is Program 3-5 on the website.

```
<HTML>
<BODY>
<SCRIPT LANGUAGE="JavaScript">
readerName=prompt ("What is your name?","");
age=prompt ("How old are you?","");
gender=prompt ("Are you a man or a woman?","");
alert ("Hello there " + readerName + " you are not looking bad for a " + gender + "
of " + age + " years")
</SCRIPT>
</BODY>
</HTML>
```

Had we wanted to, we could have interspersed a message *between* the **prompt** commands—for example:

```
var readerName=prompt ("What is your name?","");
alert ("Thanks " + readerName + " -- two more questions coming up...");
var age=prompt ("How old are you?","");
alert ("One more question to go...");
var gender=prompt ("Are you a man or a woman?","");
```

Storing and Retrieving Information Over Time

We can store information more permanently in a variety of ways. First (as we have already seen in Chapter 2 and the previous section of this chapter), we can set up *variables*. Variables allow information to be remembered—and therefore used as required—at any point in a program. However, the information stored in variables will be forgotten as soon as the Web page in which they were created is unloaded.

Second, information and procedures can be stored in *functions*. Functions contain code that will be used only when the function is "called," as required, in a program. This code will also be forgotten as soon as the Web page is unloaded.

We can retain information for longer periods in a number of ways. First, we can create variables in the parent of several frames. Different pages can then be loaded in and out of the frames without the information being lost. Indeed, new pages can be created "on the fly" which take advantage of information in the variables. This process is described in Chapter 4.

Third, server-side JavaScript enables us to store information permanently on our server. This is explained in Chapter 10.

Fourth, information can be stored in *cookies* on each reader's computer. It can remain after the reader has left our pages and even after his or her computer has been switched off. We can specify how long the cookie should remain. Cookies are useful if we want to do the following:

- Store time-related information to remind the reader of something on a particular date
- Remember where a user left off, such as on a tour or training package
- Remember reader choices from a previous session or across multiple pages (for instance, in a shopping cart)
- Know which pages have been accessed previously by each reader
- Know which pages have been updated since each reader's last visit
- Tell if it is the reader's first visit (and give an appropriate welcome)

It may be useful to store information in this way on the reader's computer (as opposed to your server) if information relating to a large number of readers needs to be stored. However, the volume of information we can store is limited. Details are given in the section "Cookies" later in this chapter. Also, the reader may elect not to have cookies stored on his or her computer and can at any time delete the cookie file.

How to Do It

Let's explore each of these techniques in turn. We'll start with variables, then move on to functions and cookies. Storing information on the server requires the use of server-side JavaScript, which is introduced in Chapter 10.

Variables

Variables may be simple or complex. A simple variable acts as a container for a single value—for example:

```
answer = prompt ("What is your name?", " ")
```

More complex variables known as *objects* can act as containers for more complex information—in particular, for *arrays*. For example, a *staffMembers* array could contain the following information:

```
staffMembers[1]["name"]="Fred J. Smith"
staffMembers[1]["job"]="Technician"
staffMembers[1]["department"]="Technical Support"
```

```
staffMembers[2]["name"]="Mary G. Cheney"
staffMembers[2]["job"]="Programmer"
staffMembers[2]["department"]="Information Technology Centre"
```

and so on.

 Recall the rules for naming variables introduced in Chapter 2.
Variable names must be made up of valid characters, which consist
of upper- and lowercase letters (a–z, A–Z), numbers (0–9), and the
underscore character (_). The first character must be a letter or the
underscore character. The variable name must not be the same as
any of JavaScript's reserved words, listed in Appendix A.

Simple Variables

Variables can be created inside event handlers or indeed anywhere in our program if
they appear within SCRIPT tags. We can set up a variable inside an event handler as
follows (Program 3-6 on the website):

```
<HTML>
<BODY onLoad = "pricePerDisk = 50">
How many disks do you require?
<FORM NAME = "myForm">
<INPUT TYPE = "text" NAME = "myBox" VALUE = 0>
<INPUT TYPE = "button"
VALUE = "Total"
onClick = "total = pricePerDisk * myForm.myBox.value; alert ('It will cost you ' +
total + ' cents')">
</FORM>
</HTML>
```

As soon as the page is loaded, the variable *pricePerDisk* is set to 50 cents. This variable is not used until the reader has typed in the number of disks required (in the text box) and has clicked the Total button. A new variable *total* is set up inside the **onClick** event handler, and its value is calculated by multiplying the price per disk by the number of disks required.

These variables, once established, can be referred to and used elsewhere in the program. For example (Program 3-7 on the website):

```
<HTML>
<BODY onLoad = "pricePerDisk = 50">
How many disks do you require?
<FORM NAME = "myForm">
<INPUT TYPE = "text" NAME = "myBox" VALUE = 0>
```

```
<INPUT TYPE = "button"
VALUE = "Order"
onClick = "total = pricePerDisk * myForm.myBox.value; alert ('It will cost you ' +
total + ' cents')">
<INPUT TYPE = "button"
VALUE = "Total including delivery"
onClick = "total = total + 45; alert ('Total is ' + total + ' cents')">
</FORM>
</BODY>
</HTML>
```

Load this page. Click the first button, Order, and the variable *total* will be created. When you click the Total including delivery button, you will be shown the cost of the number of disks you entered in the text box—plus a delivery charge of 45 cents. The variable *total*, although created within the event handler of the Order button, is accessible by another button—in this case the Total including delivery button.

 If we are creating a variable inside an event handler like this, it does matter whether we include the word **var**.

> onClick = "**var** total = pricePerDisk * myForm.myBox.value"

would make the variable *total* "local" to the button—in other words, it will be forgotten as soon as the event handler has been processed! So by the time the Total including delivery button is clicked, JavaScript will have forgotten all about *total*, and will display an error message saying the variable was undefined! *Omitting* **var** makes the variable a "global" variable—that is, a variable that does not exist solely within the object in which it was created. We will find that the same distinction between local and global variables applies also to *functions*, introduced later in this chapter.

However, if you click the Total including delivery button without having first clicked the Click me button, an error message will appear saying that the variable *total* is undefined.

This message appears because a variable cannot be used until it has been created. One way to avoid this problem is to create the variable as soon as your Web page loads. We can create the variable with a default value—for example:

```
total = 0
```

In order to avoid the potential error message, we can set up the variable as we did with the variable *pricePerDisk* in the **onLoad** event handler as shown below (Program

3-8 on the website). We could equally well create these variables up within a SCRIPT tag in the HEAD or BODY of the document.

```
<HTML>
<BODY onLoad = "pricePerDisk = 50; total = 0">
How many disks do you require?
<FORM NAME = "myForm">
<INPUT TYPE = "text" NAME = "myBox" VALUE = 0>
<INPUT TYPE = "button"
VALUE = "Order"
onClick = "total = pricePerDisk * myForm.myBox.value; alert ('It will cost you ' +
total + ' cents')">
<INPUT TYPE = "button"
VALUE = "Total including delivery"
onClick = "total = total + 45; alert ('Total is ' + total + ' cents')">
</FORM>
</BODY>
</HTML>
```

Complex Variables: Objects and Arrays

Objects are variables that allow us to store information in more complex ways. We can use them to create an *array* as follows:

```
roses = new Array ()
```

This command will create an array into which we can then put information:

```
roses[0] = "Floribunda"
roses[1] = "English Rose"
roses[2] = "Dog Rose"
```

and so on. We can achieve the same effect with the following command:

```
roses = new Array ("Floribunda", "English Rose", "Dog Rose")
```

We can retrieve the values in the array as follows. The command

```
alert (roses[1])
```

will display "English Rose." Similarly,

```
alert (roses)
```

will display "Floribunda,English Rose,Dog Rose."

We can also create properties of the array *roses* by name rather than number, as follows:

```
roses["Latin name"] = "rosa"
roses["Stockist"] = "Newlands Garden Centre"
```

and so on, which we must then retrieve by name. The following code:

```
alert (roses["Latin name"])
```

will display "rosa."

The properties of an array can themselves be arrays. The following *plant* array contains both plain text ("Azalea" and "Begonia") and the *roses* array we have already created. The *roses* array must have already been created before being used in another array in this way.

```
plants = new Array ("Azalea", "Begonia", roses)
```

Now the command:

```
alert (plants[1])
```

will display "Begonia." However, the following command:

```
alert (plants[2]["Latin name"])
```

will display "rosa."

It may be instructive to examine the results of the program below (Program 3-9 on the website):

```
1.  <HTML>
2.  <BODY>
3.  <SCRIPT>
4.  roses = new Array ("Floribunda", "English Rose", "Dog Rose")
5.  roses["Latin name"] = "rosa"
6.  roses["Stockist"] = "Newlands Garden Centre"

7.  plants = new Array ("Azalea", "Begonia", roses)

8.  alert (plants)
9.  alert (plants[1])
10. alert (plants[2]["Latin name"])
11. alert (plants[2][1])

12. </SCRIPT>
13. </BODY>
14. </HTML>
```

Line 8 will display "Azalea,Begonia,Floribunda,English Rose,Dog Rose," and line 9 will display "Begonia." Line 10 will display "rosa," and line 11 will display "English Rose."

We can retrieve the values of all members of an array using loops. Loops are discussed in more detail later in this chapter.

Functions

Functions allow us to store information and procedures in such a way that they will not be acted upon immediately. Rather, they will be acted upon only when we *call* the function from anywhere in our Web pages. Functions take the form:

```
functionName (values passed to the function) {
statements
}
```

Functions can have zero—or several—values passed to them. Here is an example of a function accepting zero values. It is hardly the most useful program we will write, but it does illustrate how to create and call a function. It is Program 3-10 on the website.

Note that to call the function (in this case in the event handlers of the buttons, lines 14 and 16), the function's name must be followed by parentheses—empty if no parameters are to be passed, as in this example, and containing values if parameters are expected (as in the case of the **showMessage** function in the example following this one).

```
1. <HTML>
2. <HEAD>
3. <SCRIPT>

4. var numberOfClicks = 0

5. function countClicks () {
6. numberOfClicks ++
7. alert ("The number of times you have clicked is " + numberOfClicks)
8. }

9. </SCRIPT>
10. </HEAD>
11. <BODY>
12. <FORM>
13. <INPUT TYPE = "button" VALUE = "Click me"
14. onClick = " countClicks ()">
15. <INPUT TYPE = "button" VALUE = "And me!"
16. onClick = " countClicks ()">
17. </FORM>
18. </BODY>
19. </HTML>
```

The example illustrates how a single function can be called by different objects—in this case, two different buttons. Whichever button is clicked (lines 14 and 16) will call the function **countClicks**, which increments the variable *numberOfClicks* by one each time (the instruction *numberOfClicks* ++ in line 6 is a short way of saying *numberOfClicks* = *numberOfClicks* + 1).

This is one of the advantages of creating functions. They can reduce the need to repeat sets of commands if they are required repeatedly at different points in a program. Without them, all instructions would have to be written in full each time they were needed—in this case, in the event handlers of each button.

Using parameters (that is, passing values to the function) can enable a single function to handle a range of situations. The following **showMessage** function can be used to display any number of messages. A different message can be passed to the function each time it is called. This code (Program 3-11 on the website) displays four text boxes and a button. The reader is invited to type into any of the first three text boxes. A message is then displayed in the fourth box as appropriate—for example, "You typed Hello in text box 1," "You typed How are you? in text box 3," and so on.

```
1.  <HTML>
2.  <HEAD>
3.  <SCRIPT>

4.  function showMessage (textBox) {
5.  document.myForm.messageBox.value = "You typed "
6.  + textBox.value
7.  + " in "
8.  + textBox.name
9.  }

10. </SCRIPT>
11. </HEAD>
12. <BODY>
13. <FORM NAME = "myForm">
14. Please type into one of the top three boxes then click Continue <BR>
15. <INPUT TYPE = "text" NAME = "text box 1" onBlur = "showMessage (this)">
16. <INPUT TYPE = "text" NAME = "text box 2" onBlur = "showMessage (this)">
17. <INPUT TYPE = "text" NAME = "text box 3" onBlur = "showMessage (this)">
18. <INPUT TYPE = "text" NAME = "messageBox" SIZE = 30>
19. <INPUT TYPE = "button" VALUE = "Continue">
20. </FORM>
21. </BODY>
22. </HTML>
```

When the reader enters text in, say *text box 1*, and clicks outside the box (thus invoking the **onBlur** event handler, which is activated when the text box loses the focus), the **showMessage** function is called and passed the value *this*. In JavaScript, the word *this* can be used to refer to the *current object*—in this case, *text box 1*. The only function of the Continue button (line 19) is to make the reader click outside the text box into which he or she has just typed. It is the **onBlur** event handler of each box (lines 15, 16, and 17) that calls the function **showMessage**. **onBlur** is an event handler that operates whenever the reader, having first clicked the mouse or typed within the text box, then clicks anywhere outside the text box. A full list of event handlers, and the objects in which each can be used, is given in Appendix A.

If the reader types into the first text box, the value *text box 1* is passed to the function **showMessage** (from line 15 to line 4) as the parameter in brackets following the function's name. As it is passed this value, the function copies it as *textBox* (the name in brackets—line 4). When *text box 2*'s event handler calls the function, *textBox* will contain the value *text box 2*. When *text box 3*'s event handler calls the function, *textBox* will contain the value *text box 3*.

The function contains code that takes the value of the text box and the name of the text box and builds them into a message that is then displayed in *messageBox*.

Functions are generally located within the HEAD section of a document. One reason for placing them there is to ensure that they are fully loaded into memory before text appears. This method avoids the possibility that, for example, a button may appear before a function that the button calls in its event handler is fully loaded. However, functions can also appear in the BODY section of our documents if required.

Variables may be declared within functions. These variables may be global or local. *Global variables* may be used anywhere in the Web page. *Local* variables may be used only within the function in which they are created. To declare a local variable within a function, you precede it with **var** (line 6 below). If it is not preceded by **var** (as in line 5), the variable will be made global. The following program (Program 3-12 on the website) illustrates the difference.

```
1.  <HTML>
2.  <HEAD>
3.  <SCRIPT>

4.  function showMessage () {
5.  message1 = "Hello"
6.  var message2 = "How are you?"
7.  alert ("Message 1 is " + message1 + " and Message 2 is " + message2)
8.  }

9.  </SCRIPT>
10. </HEAD>
11. <BODY>
12. <FORM NAME = "myForm">
13. <INPUT TYPE = "button" VALUE = "Show message function"
14. onClick = "showMessage ()">
15. <INPUT TYPE = "button" VALUE = "Message 1"
16. onClick = "alert (message1)">
17. <INPUT TYPE = "button" VALUE = "Message 2"
18. onClick = "alert (message2)">
```

```
19. </FORM>
20. </BODY>
21. </HTML>
```

If the reader clicks the Show message function button, the function **showMessage** will be called and the variables *message1* and *message2* are created (lines 5 and 6). An alert message is then displayed (line 7), showing the values of message1 (that is, "Hello") and message2 (that is, "How are you?").

If the reader then clicks the Message 1 button, "Hello" will be displayed. If the reader then clicks the Message 2 button, JavaScript will display an error message saying that *message2* is not defined. This is because *message2* is a local variable and does not exist outside the function **showMessage**.

Functions can *return* values. Consider the following program (Program 3-13 on the website):

```
1.  <HTML>
2.  <HEAD>
3.  <SCRIPT>

4.  function calculateTotal (A, B) {
5.  return A * B
6   }

7.  total = calculateTotal (3,4)
8.  alert (total)

9.  </SCRIPT>
10. </HEAD>
11. </HTML>
```

Line 7 sets the value of the variable *total* as the value returned by the **calculateTotal** function after it has been passed the numbers 3 and 4. Line 5 of the function returns the result of multiplying the two numbers. This returned result becomes the value of *total*, which is then displayed in an alert box (line 8).

A shorter way of achieving lines 7 and 8 would be to replace them with:

```
alert (calculateTotal (3,4))
```

The following version of the program enables the reader to enter different figures to submit to the **calculateTotal** function. This is Program 3-14 on the website.

```
<HTML>
<HEAD>
<SCRIPT>

function calculateTotal (A, B) {
return A * B
```

```
}

</SCRIPT>
</HEAD>
<BODY>
<FORM NAME = "myForm">
Enter first number <BR>
<INPUT TYPE = "text" NAME = "textBox1"> <P>
Enter second number <BR>
<INPUT TYPE = "text" NAME = "textBox2">
<INPUT TYPE = "button" VALUE = "Submit" onClick = "alert (calculateTotal
(document.myForm.textBox1.value, document.myForm.textBox2.value))">
</FORM>
</BODY>
</HTML>
```

Once a function has returned a value, it cannot return any other value. Take the following example (Program 3-15 on the website). The function **eligible** checks whether the reader is eligible for a local children's event. If the reader is more than 16 years old or lives more than 10 miles away, he or she is not eligible. If he or she is over 16, the function returns *false*. Having done so, it does not go on to ask whether the reader lives more than 10 miles away. The function returns *true* only if neither question is confirmed.

```
<HTML>
<HEAD>
<SCRIPT>

function eligible () {
if (confirm ("Are you over 16?")) {return false}
if (confirm ("Do you live more than 10 miles from here?")) {return false}
return true
}

alert ("The eligible function has returned " + eligible ())

</SCRIPT>
<HEAD>
</HTML>
```

JavaScript 1.2 implemented in Netscape 4 allows functions to be nested within other functions.

Cookies

In client-side JavaScript, the most permanent form of storage of information for later use is the *cookie*. Cookies allow us to store information on our reader's computer. We can specify how long (in seconds, weeks, months, even years) the information should remain stored. However, the volume of information is limited, and beyond this limit new information being stored will overwrite old information.

A cookie is information stored in a text file called *cookie.txt*, located in the Netscape directory on the reader's computer. The cookie file can contain a total of 300 cookies, each of a maximum of 4K (including the cookie name). Twenty cookies are permitted per server or domain.

The following code (Program 3-16 on the website) sets up a cookie, in which the reader's name is stored. If the reader clicks the Show cookie button (line 7), assuming that he or she has not previously clicked the Create cookie button, a blank alert message will be displayed (line 8) because there is as yet no cookie. Clicking the Create cookie button will cause a prompt box to appear (line 5), asking the reader for his or her name. This name will be stored in the variable *readerName*, which is then stored in a cookie. If the reader has typed "Jane," the cookie will contain "name=Jane."

The reader may now unload the page and visit other Web sites. Whenever the reader returns to this page, he or she may click the Show cookie button (without needing to click the Create cookie button) and be shown his or her name. The variable *readerName*, in which the name was originally stored, is forgotten as soon as the page is unloaded. The information stored in the cookie is, however, retained. The default length of time it is retained is until the reader finishes the current Web session—that is, until he or she exits the browser. However, the expiration time of cookies can be set to hours, days, weeks, months—even years.

```
1.  <HTML>
2.  <BODY>
3.  <FORM>
4.  <INPUT TYPE = "button" VALUE = "Create cookie"
5.  onClick = "readerName = prompt ('What is your name?', '');
6.  document.cookie = 'name=' + readerName">
7.  <INPUT TYPE = "button" VALUE = "Show cookie"
8.  onClick = "alert (document.cookie)">
9.  </FORM>
10. </BODY>
11. </HTML>
```

The following code (Program 3-17 on the website) sets the expiration date of the cookie to a specific date. Lines 6 through 8 set up the cookie. Line 8 specifies the expiration date. The date must be correctly formatted as shown below.

```
1.  <HTML>
2.  <HEAD>
3.  <SCRIPT>
```

```
4. function createCookie () {
5. readerName = prompt ("What is your name?", "Enter your name")
6. document.cookie = "name="
7. + readerName
8. + "; expires=Mon, 01-Jul-99 12:00:00 GMT"
9. }

10. </SCRIPT>
11. </HEAD>
12. <BODY>
13. <FORM>
14. <INPUT TYPE = "button" VALUE = "Show me the cookie"
15. onClick = "if (document.cookie == '')
16. {alert ('There is no cookie')}
17. else {alert (document.cookie)}">
18. <INPUT TYPE = "button" VALUE = "Create the cookie"
19. onClick = "createCookie ()">
20. </FORM>
21. </BODY>
22. </HTML>
```

Alternatively, as in the example below (Program 3-18 on the website), we can set a *relative* expiration date—for example, 24 hours after the cookie is created. Line 6 below puts the current date and time into a variable *expiration* using the built-in JavaScript object **Date**. Line 7 uses the built-in command **setTime** to set *expiration* to 24 hours after its original value—that is, 24 hours from now. The **Date** object stores the date and time in milliseconds. To add 24 hours, we therefore have to calculate 24 (hours) * 60 (minutes) * 60 (seconds) * 1,000 (milliseconds). We then create the cookie to contain the reader's name and the expiration time.

```
1. <HTML>
2. <HEAD>
3. <SCRIPT>

4. function createCookie () {
5. readerName = prompt ("What is your name?", "Enter your name")
6. expiry = new Date ()
7. expiry.setTime (expiry.getTime () + 24 * 60 * 60 * 1000)
8. document.cookie = "name="
9. + readerName
10. + "; expires="
11. + expiry
12. }

13. </SCRIPT>
14. </HEAD>
```

```
15. <BODY>
16. <FORM>
17. <INPUT TYPE = "button" VALUE = "Show me the cookie"
18. onClick = "if (document.cookie == '')
19. {alert ('There is no cookie')}
20. else {alert (document.cookie)}">
21. <INPUT TYPE = "button" VALUE = "Create the cookie"
22. onClick = "createCookie ()">
23. </FORM>
24. </BODY>
25. </HTML>
```

This cookie will be retained for 24 hours. Try switching off your computer, then reloading the page anytime within the expiration limit. The Show me the cookie button will show that the information is retained on your computer.

If information to be stored in a cookie contains spaces, semicolons, or commas, it must be converted using the **escape** function. For example:

```
document.cookie = escape (readerName)
```

If *readerName* contained "Mary Cheney," the cookie value would be

```
name=Mary%20Cheney
```

The information can then be converted into its original form using the **unescape** function. The command

```
alert (unescape (document.cookie))
```

will display "name=Mary Cheney."

Cookies can be set with a number of other parameters:

path specifies the URL path for which the cookie is valid (the default is the path of the current document).

domain specifies the domain for which the cookie is valid (the default is the domain of the current document).

secure specifies that the cookie is sent over a secure link.

Bill Dortch has produced an excellent set of functions that enable you to create, update, get the value of, delete, and set the parameters of cookies. These are available free at the following address:

    www.hidaho.com/cookies/cookie.txt

Using Conditional Actions

Many intelligent applications, including those introduced later in this book, use *conditional reasoning*. This type of reasoning entails using rules of the form:

```
IF some condition(s)
THEN some conclusion(s) or action(s)
ELSE some other conclusion(s) or action(s)
```

To take a very simple example:

```
IF car will not start
    AND gas is OK
    AND battery is OK
THEN check the starter-motor
ELSE consult a mechanic
```

Other permutations are possible. For simplicity in the following examples, the conditions and conclusions have been replaced by the letters A, B, C, D, and E.

```
IF (A AND B)
    OR C
THEN D
ELSE E

IF A
    AND (B OR C)
THEN D
ELSE E

IF A
    IF B
        THEN C
        ELSE D
    ELSE E
```

The JavaScript format for the same rules is as follows. Note that the ELSE part of the rules is optional.

```
if ((A && B) || C)
    {D}
    else {E}

if (A && (B || C))
    {D}
    else {E}

if (A)
    if (B)
        {C}
        else {D}
    else {E}
```

Here is a simple example (Program 3-19 on the website):

```
<HTML>
<BODY>
<SCRIPT>

if (confirm ("Is it raining?"))
{alert ("Then take an umbrella")}
else {alert ("Thank goodness for that")}

</SCRIPT>
</BODY>
</HTML>
```

Here is a more complex set of rules (Program 3-20 on the website):

```
<HTML>
<BODY>
<SCRIPT>

if (confirm ("Is gas OK?"))
     {if (confirm ("Is battery OK"))
          {advice = "Gas and battery are OK -- check the starter motor"}
          else {advice = "Get a new battery and try again"} }
     else {advice = "Get some gas then try again"}

alert (advice)

</SCRIPT>
</BODY>
</HTML>
```

Variables can be tested in the IF part of rules. For example (Program 3-21 on the website):

```
<HTML>
<BODY>
<SCRIPT>

gas = "OK"
battery = "OK"

if (gas == "OK")
     {if (battery == "OK")
          {advice = "Gas and battery are OK -- check the starter motor"}
       else {advice = "Get a new battery and try again"} }
else {advice = "Get some gas then try again"}
```

```
alert (advice)

</SCRIPT>
</BODY>
</HTML>
```

as can values returned by functions (Program 3-22 on the website):

```
<HTML>
<HEAD>
<SCRIPT>

function gas () {
if (confirm ("Do you have enough gas?"))
{return "OK"}
else {return "Not OK"}
}

function battery () {
if (confirm ("Is the battery OK?"))
{return "OK"}
else {return "Not OK"}
}

</SCRIPT>
</HEAD>
<BODY>
<SCRIPT>
if (gas () == "OK")
    {if (battery () == "OK")
          {advice = "Gas and battery are OK -- check the starter motor"}
       else {advice = "Get a new battery and try again"} }
else {advice = "Get some gas then try again"}

alert (advice)

</SCRIPT>
</BODY>
</HTML>
```

A number of comparison operators can be used in the IF part of rules. These are as follows:

== [equals (numeric and text)]

!= [not equal to (numeric and text)]

> [greater than (numeric and text—"b" is greater than "a")]

$>=$ [greater than or equal to (numeric and text)]

$<$ [smaller than (numeric and text—"a" is smaller than "b")]

$<=$ [smaller than or equal to (numeric and text)]

Conditions can be linked using the following:

&& [AND]

|| [OR]

Using Loops

Loops allow us to apply repeatedly one or more instructions until some condition is met. This ability can be useful if, for example, we want the reader to enter information that meets certain criteria—perhaps a correct answer in the case of a training package or quiz.

Loops allow us to do this as well as setting a limit on the number of times an action (such as asking the reader a question) takes place. Loops also allow us to retrieve the values of all the members of an array easily.

How to Do It

There are three basic types of loop: **while** loops, **for** loops, and **for ... in** loops.

While Loops

The following code (Program 3-23 on the website) will repeatedly show an alert message box displaying the value of *counter*, then increment the counter by 1. It will keep on doing this so long as *counter* is smaller than or equal to 5.

```
<HTML>
<BODY>
<SCRIPT>

counter = 1

while (counter <= 5) {
alert ("Counter is now " + counter)
counter ++
}

</SCRIPT>
</BODY>
</HTML>
```

In the code below (Program 3-24 on the website), the reader is presented with a prompt box asking, "What is 10 multiplied by 10?" So long as he or she does *not* answer

"100," the question will be continually presented. Note, however, that if the reader types a character that is not a number, JavaScript will display an error message. Ways of overcoming this problem—for example, interrupting the error message and display a more user-friendly message instead—are introduced in the section "Validating Reader Input" in Chapter 7.

```
<HTML>
<BODY>
<SCRIPT>

correctAnswer = 100
readerAnswer = ""

while (readerAnswer != correctAnswer) {
readerAnswer = prompt ("What is 10 multiplied by 10?", "")
}

</SCRIPT>
</BODY>
</HTML>
```

Generally, it is a good idea to set some limit on the number of times a loop can execute, as in the first example. Loops can contain multiple conditions, so we can combine the two examples as follows (Program 3-25 on the website):

```
<HTML>
<BODY>
<SCRIPT>

correctAnswer = 100
readerAnswer = ""
counter = 1

while (readerAnswer != correctAnswer && counter <= 5) {
readerAnswer = prompt ("What is 10 multiplied by 10?", "")
counter ++
}

</SCRIPT>
</BODY>
</HTML>
```

This version of the program will allow the reader five attempts only.

For Loops

The example below (Program 3-26 on the website) performs the same function as our previous **while** loop. However, it does not require a *counter* variable. Line 4 does a variety of things. It sets up a local variable *i* (often used in programming to denote a number) and sets it to 1. It then specifies that the commands in the loop should be executed repeatedly so long as *i* is less than or equal to 5. It then specifies that each time through the loop, *i* should be increased by 1.

The result of this code is that a message displaying the value of *i* will be displayed each time through the cycle. It will increase by 1 each time until it is 5.

```
1. <HTML>
2. <BODY>
3. <SCRIPT>

4. for (var i=1; i<=5; i++) {
5. alert ("Counter is now " + i)
6. }

7. </SCRIPT>
8. </BODY>
9. </HTML>
```

For ... in Loops

Another type of loop represents a very easy way to retrieve the values of *arrays*. Recall from the section "Storing and Retrieving Information Over Time" earlier in this chapter that arrays allow us to store a number of values in the same object.

The example introduced there included the following command:

```
roses = new Array ("Floribunda", "English Rose", "Dog Rose")
```

resulting in the creation of the array:

```
roses[0] = "Floribunda"
roses[1] = "English Rose"
roses[2] = "Dog Rose"
```

The **for ... in** loop allows us to retrieve the values of each member of an array as follows (Program 3-27 on the website):

```
<HTML>
<BODY>
<SCRIPT>

roses = new Array ("Floribunda", "English Rose", "Dog Rose")

for (i in roses) {
alert (roses[i])
}

</SCRIPT>
```

```
</BODY>
</HTML>
```

This code will display an alert message showing each value stored in the array. It will do so for all members of the array.

Here is a slightly more complex version (Program 3-28 on the website). This code will show five alert messages, one after the other. These messages will contain, in order, "Floribunda," "English Rose," "Dog Rose," "rosa," and "Newlands Garden Center." Line 7 contains the loop that will perform the action **alert** for all members of the *roses* array.

```
1. <HTML>
2. <BODY>
3. <SCRIPT>
4. roses = new Array ("Floribunda", "English Rose", "Dog Rose")
5. roses["Latin name"] = "rosa"
6. roses["Stockist"] = "Newlands Garden Centre"

7. for (i in roses) {alert (roses[i])}

8. </SCRIPT>
9. </BODY>
10. </HTML>
```

The *break* Command

In the code below (Program 3-29 on the website), the reader is asked to multiply 10 by 10. So long as he or she does not answer "100," the question will be asked again—a maximum of 10 times. Lines 7 and 8 limit the number of times the loop executes; the variable *counter* is incremented each time through the loop, and line 7 allows the loop to continue so long as *counter* is smaller than 10. Line 10 checks whether the reader's answer is correct. If it is not, the loop goes into another cycle. However, if the answer is correct, the command **break** in line 11 terminates the loop, preventing the question from being asked again.

```
1. <HTML>
2. <BODY>
3. <SCRIPT>

4. counter = 0
5. correctAnswer = 100
6. readerAnswer = ""

7. while (counter < 10) {
8. counter ++
9. readerAnswer = prompt ("What is 10 multiplied by 10?", "")
```

```
10.  if (readerAnswer == correctAnswer) {
11.  alert ("Correct answer!"); break}
12.  }

13.  </SCRIPT>
14.  </BODY>
15.  </HTML>
```

The *continue* Command

The **continue** command also allows us to break out of a loop, but in a limited way.
When **continue** is executed, it forces any remaining instructions inside the loop to be
ignored and the loop to skip to the next cycle immediately.

In the example below (Program 3-30 on the website), the reader is asked to enter
a vowel. If he or she enters a letter (line 7) that is not a vowel (this is checked in lines
8 through 12), the **continue** command (line 13) will cause any further instructions within
the loop (that is, line 14) to be ignored. The loop will immediately begin again at line 6.
In this way, the instruction to display the message "Oops—an error!" (line 14) is
ignored.

If the letter entered is not a vowel, line 14 will be processed, and the error message will be displayed before the reader is again asked to enter a vowel.

```
1.   <HTML>
2.   <BODY>
3.   <SCRIPT>

4.   readerAnswer = ""
5.   score = 0

6.   for (i = 1; i <= 5; i++) {
7.   readerAnswer = prompt ("Enter a vowel (lower case)", "")
8.   if (readerAnswer == "a"
9.   || readerAnswer == "e"
10.  || readerAnswer == "i"
11.  || readerAnswer == "o"
12.  || readerAnswer == "u")
13.  {score ++; continue}
14.  alert ("Oops -- an error!")
15.  }
16.  alert ("You scored " + score)

17.  </SCRIPT>
18.  </BODY>
19.  </HTML>
```

Text Processing

We often need to analyze text rather more deeply than simply comparing it to see if it matches some other text, as in this example:

```
if (answer == "aluminum") {alert ("Correct answer!")}
```

Sometimes we need to know whether a portion of text is included within another portion. The answer "Yes, it is" is logically equivalent to "yes"—yet textually it is very different. The first answer has an uppercase "Y" and some additional words. A simple matching will not work. Analyzing text is explored in detail in Chapter 7, "Interpreting User Input."

However, the present section introduces some of JavaScript's basic text-handling facilities.

How to Do It

Take the following string of text contained in a variable *message*:

```
message = "Hello there"
```

JavaScript offers a number of facilities enabling us to manipulate and analyze this text. For example:

```
message.toUpperCase ()
```

will convert the text to uppercase, and

```
message.toLowerCase ()
```

to lowercase.

There are a variety of other ways of formatting the text. For example:

```
message.italics ()
message.blink ()
message.big ()
```

and so on. These may be combined in appropriate ways, such as:

```
message.bold ().strike ()
```

to give bold strike-through text.

These functions should be used in conjunction with **document.write**, introduced in Chapter 4; they will not work with **alert**.

Other facilities enable us to analyze the text. For example, the value of:

```
message.length
```

will be 11—that is, 10 letters and the space in between. The following code:

```
message.substring (0,8)
```

will retrieve characters of the string starting at the first character (character 0 is the first character; the numbering starts at 0, not 1) and ending with the character *before* character 8. In the case of our example, the result is "Hello th".

The following code:

```
message.indexOf ("r")
```

retrieves the position of the character specified. The letter "r" appears as character 9 in our string (starting at 0). The code:

```
message.charAt (6)
```

returns the character located at position 6 (again, starting at 0); in this case, it's the letter "t." Finally,

```
message.lastIndexOf ("e")
```

will return the position of the last occurrence of the letter "e"—in this case, position 10.

Using Arithmetic Operators

We need arithmetic operators to enable us to add value to data and information provided by our readers. At the simplest level, we may need to calculate a total from a series of online transactions—multiplying the cost per item by the number required. However, we may also want to engage in much more complex calculations and to communicate the results to our readers.

How to Do It

JavaScript offers a range of arithmetic operators. We can use the normal operators available on any calculator:

```
xyz = 2 + 4 * 5
```

and we can use brackets to specify how calculations should be performed:

```
xyz = (2 + 4) * 5
```

In the example below (Program 3-31 on the website), **alert (abc)** will display "22," and **alert (xyz)** will display "30."

```
<HTML>
<BODY>
<SCRIPT>

abc = 2 + 4 * 5
xyz = (2 + 4) * 5

alert (abc)
alert (xyz)
```

```
</SCRIPT>
</BODY>
</HTML>
```

We can assign values to variables using the following code. The variable *abc* is initially set to the value 10. The variable is then modified using the arithmetic operators. The result of each modification is shown below the operator.

```
abc = 10
abc -= 2
    result = 8
abc += 4
    result = 12
abc *= 2
    result = 24
abc /= 4
    result = 6
abc ++
    result = 7
abc --
    result = 6
abc %= 4    [divides the left number by the right number and returns the
remainder]
    result = 2
```

Here is Program (3-32 on the website) to illustrate this process:

```
<HTML>
<BODY>
<SCRIPT>

abc = 10
abc -= 2
alert (abc)
abc += 4
alert (abc)
abc *= 2
alert (abc)
abc /= 4
alert (abc)
abc ++
alert (abc)
abc --
alert (abc)
abc %= 4
alert (abc)
```

```
</SCRIPT>
</BODY>
</HTML>
```

We can test the value of numbers using the following:

== [equals]

!= [does not equal]

> [greater than]

>= [greater than or equal to]

< [smaller than]

<= [smaller than or equal to]

COMMUNICATING THE RESULTS TO *Your Readers*

hapter 2 introduced ways of obtaining input from our readers, either in the form of information explicitly given to us (in response to questions and options we have presented to them) or as knowledge of the actions performed by them (gathered by event handlers). In Chapter 3 we examined techniques we can use to add value to this information.

In this chapter, we explore how we can communicate the results of this processing—that is, communicate the added value—to our readers. JavaScript offers us a range of possibilities. We can, for example, generate and display new Web pages entirely within the reader's browser without the need to download a new page from our server. Or we can open a new window and either display a preexisting Web page or dynamically generate and display a new one. We can do the same with frames.

We can also display the results of processing information in text boxes and text areas, or display a message in the status bar at the bottom of the screen, without needing to reload the Web page. We can make the reader's browser go to other Web pages, specifying a particular URL, or tell it to return to a previously visited page, then go forward again.

> **NOTE** JavaScript 1.2 offers a range of exciting techniques to enhance these basic display processes. "Dynamic HTML" allows us, for example, to write text to different areas of the screen each with its own display style. Layers of text and images can be overlayed, moved, resized, or made to disappear and reappear, creating complex animation effects. Dynamic HTML is introduced in Chapter 9.

We can dynamically create forms and e-mail the contents to ourselves—useful, for example, for an online questionnaire. We can preprocess the results, subjecting them to some analysis and/or summarizing process, before they are e-mailed to us. We can do all this, admittedly with some limitations, within our Web page and without the need for CGI programming.

Generating New Web Pages "On the Fly"

We can program our Web pages to write more Web pages, themselves composed of HTML and JavaScript code, and incorporating variable values. At the simplest level, we can, for instance, customize our pages so that they welcome each reader with his or her name and the current date. We can retrieve the reader's name if it has been stored in a cookie from a previous visit. We can also write Web pages that use the results of the sorts of processing we explored in Chapter 3.

As we have seen, it is easy to communicate this sort of information to our readers using alert message boxes. However, there are many occasions when a Web page is preferable. For example, we are not subject to the format limitations of an alert message or the need for the reader to click OK to clear the message box before he or she can proceed.

How to Do It

The following code (Program 4-1 on the website) will write text to the current window. The JavaScript commands can be in the HEAD or BODY of the document.

```
<HTML>
<BODY>

Hello there.

<SCRIPT>

document.write ("I hope you are well.")

</SCRIPT>

Welcome to my page.

</BODY>
</HEAD>
```

This code will write "Hello there. I hope you are well. Welcome to my page." in the current window.

We can include HTML within the **document.write** commands. For example (Program 4-2 on the website):

```
<HTML>
<BODY>
<SCRIPT>
```

```
document.write ("<H1>Welcome</H1><H2>to my page</H2><HR><B>This page is designed to
...</B>")
</SCRIPT>
</BODY>
</HTML>
```

 If text written using **document.write** fails to appear, try inserting <BR> at the end of the **document.write** text as follows:

```
document.write ("I hope you are well.<BR>")
```

In some versions of JavaScript on some platforms, this may be necessary if the text is to be displayed. Other forms of break in HTML (for example, <P> and <HR>) also work.

It is possible to concatenate text, as long as each chunk is enclosed in quotes and is added correctly using the + sign:

```
document.write ("<H1>Welcome</H1>"
+ "<H2>to my page</H2><HR>"
+ "<B>This page is designed to ...</B>")
```

This code will result in exactly the same display as the previous code.

Unless concatenating text as shown above, do not include any line breaks in the text appearing within the parenthesis of **document.write**.

 If you get an error message when writing large amounts of text using **document.write**, try splitting the text and concatenating it as shown here. Put each + sign and accompanying chunk of text on a new line, as in the example. The error may sometimes be caused by JavaScript reading only part of the text. It then thinks that you have forgotten the closing quotes and parenthesis.

The ability to concatenate various elements within the **document.write** command is very useful. In particular, it allows us to inject variable values into what we are writing. To take a simple example (Program 4-3 on the website):

```
<HTML>
<BODY>
<SCRIPT>
readerName = prompt ("Tell me your name", "")
document.write ("<H1>Welcome</H1><H2>" + readerName
+ "</H2><HR><B>This page is designed to ...</B>")
</SCRIPT>
</BODY>
</HEAD>
```

This code will ask the reader for his or her name, then display it as part of a new Web page, formatted with the <H2> </H2> HTML tags. The following code (Program 4-4 on the website) will display the current day and time as part of the page:

```
<HTML>
<BODY>
<SCRIPT>
today = new Date ()
document.write ("<H1>Welcome</H1><H2>to my page</H2><HR>Today is " + today)
</SCRIPT>
</BODY>
</HEAD>
```

Complex Web pages can be constructed in this way. Information obtained from readers using the techniques introduced in Chapter 2 can be processed to add value using the techniques discussed in Chapter 3. The results can then be communicated to the reader in the form of a customized Web page that uses variable values as shown above.

It is also possible to collect and use information collected from readers from multiple Web pages (for example, a shopping cart), then process the information and display it in this way. As well as using cookies to hold variable values while pages change, we can also use frames to achieve the same end. This concept is explored further in the section "Writing Information to Frames" later in this chapter.

It is important to note that **document.write** will in fact clear the current screen before it displays text. Consider the following code (Program 4-5 on the website):

```
<HTML>
<BODY>
<FORM>
<INPUT TYPE = "button" VALUE = "Click me"
onClick = "document.write ('Hello <BR> ')">
</FORM>
</BODY>
</HEAD>
```

When the reader clicks the button, the button will disappear and "Hello" will appear in an otherwise blank screen.

The commands **document.clear ()** and **document.close ()** will, as their names suggest, clear the screen and close the current document. They are not necessary if, as shown above, we are simply writing to the current screen. The ability to decide whether to clear the screen before writing new text, or to add new text to existing text, can be useful.

Text and HTML commands within the **document.write** command must be enclosed in quotes. Be careful to use different quotes (double or single) to embed them. This often occurs when you are using event handlers; for example:

```
onClick = "document.write ('Hello there ')"
```

If you have used both double and single quotes and need to use a further layer, use **"** as follows (Program 4-6 on the website):

```
<HTML>
<BODY>
<FORM>
<INPUT TYPE = "button" VALUE = "Make a text box"
onClick = "document.write ('Here is the text box<BR><FORM NAME =
&quot;myForm&quot;><INPUT TYPE=&quot;text&quot; NAME=&quot;myTextBox&quot;></FORM> ')"
</FORM>
</BODY>
</HTML>
```

It is often preferable to call a *function* to avoid overly complex layers of quotes. The example above would be better handled as follows (Program 4-7 on the website):

```
<HTML>
<HEAD>
<SCRIPT>

function showForm () {
document.write ("Here is the text box<BR><FORM NAME = 'myForm '> <INPUT TYPE= 'text '
NAME= 'myTextBox '></FORM>")
}

</SCRIPT>
</HEAD>
<BODY>
<FORM>
<INPUT TYPE = "button" VALUE = "Make a text box"
onClick = "showForm ()">
</FORM>
</BODY>
</HTML>
```

Opening New Windows

If we open a new window, we can write information or load new documents into it without having to unload the previous document (to which the new information may relate). The new window may be sized so that it forms a small extra window that can be moved around the screen, resized, and closed as required by the reader. This is often useful for presenting information that complements information presented in the main screen.

In the case of an advice-giving system (such as those introduced in the latter part of this book), this technique can be used to present additional information to the reader, enabling him or her better to answer a question posed by the system as it pursues its line of reasoning. It would enable a reader to perform an Internet search, for example, and read the resulting documents, without having to unload the original Web page in which the question was asked.

We can also set the focus onto a particular window. This has the effect of bringing the information to the top of the screen if it was hidden behind some other window. In JavaScript 1.2, it is possible to create a window that appears permanently on the top—that is, one that cannot be hidden by any other window.

How to Do It

A window may be opened using the command:

```
myWindow = window.open ()
```

We can, of course, specify a number of things about a new window. For example, we can load a particular page into it by including its URL (this example assumes a document in the same directory as the current one; otherwise, a full URL should be used):

```
myWindow = window.open ("mydoc.html")
```

We can refer to this window by its name, *myWindow*, to write to it:

```
myWindow.document.write ("Hello there")
```

We cannot use this name as a target for a normal HTML hyperlink, however; therefore, the following code will not work:

```
<A HREF = "mydoc.html" TARGET = "myWindow"> Link </A>
```

To refer to the window as an HTML hyperlink target, we need to specify a name as the second parameter of the **window.open** command:

```
myWindow = window.open ("mydoc.html", "window2")
```

The following code will now work:

```
<A HREF = "mydoc.html" TARGET = "window2"> Link </A>
```

A window can have a range of parameters. These are:

First parameter. URL to load in the window.

Second parameter. Name to be used when quoting the window as the target of an HTML hyperlink.

Third parameter. A feature list including any of the following. Note that *yes* can be replaced by *no* to switch off any feature. Alternatively, *1* can be used for *yes* and *0* for *no*.

    toolbar=yes

    location=yes

```
directories=yes
status=yes
menubar=yes
copyhistory=yes
scrollbars=yes
resizable=yes
width=500  [width in pixels]
height=300  [width in pixels]
```

The following code (Program 4-8 on the website) opens a window 500 pixels wide and 300 pixels high. The window will have the properties displayed in the third parameter, the feature list. The first parameter is left empty since we do not want to load any preexisting document into the window.

 If a new window does not appear as you intended, make sure that you have no spaces anywhere in the feature list between the quotes.

```
1. <HTML>
2. <BODY>
3. <SCRIPT>

4. myWindow = window.open
("","window2","location=yes,menubar=yes,height=300,width=500")

5. myWindow.document.write ("<FORM><INPUT TYPE= 'button ' VALUE= 'Close window '
onClick= 'self.close () '></FORM>")

6. </SCRIPT>

7. </BODY>
8. </HTML>
```

Line 5 above displays a button in the new window, which, when clicked, will close the window. Note the command **self.close ()**. This refers to the current window. The same effect would be had by the **window.close ()** command. Do not call the window by name from the window itself. The command **myWindow.document.write ("Hello")** will generate an error message if the command actually appears in the document currently loaded in *myWindow*. As well as referring to windows by name, we can also use the following:

top   [current window]

parent   [parent window of the current frame]

self   [current window]

window   [current window]

We can also set the focus on a particular window. The following code (Program 4-9 on the website) opens a new window. If we click outside the window, it loses focus and becomes hidden behind the main window. Click the button in the main window, however, and the new window will reappear. This is done using the command **myWindow.focus ()** in the button's event handler.

```
<HTML>
<BODY>
<SCRIPT>

myWindow = window.open ("","","height=300,width=500")
myWindow.document.write ("This is myWindow <P> Click outside this window and it will
disappear under the main window <P>")

document.write ("<FORM><INPUT TYPE= 'button ' VALUE= 'Click to put the focus on
myWindow ' onClick= 'myWindow.focus () '></FORM>")

</SCRIPT>

</BODY>
</HTML>
```

We can also write information to the status bar of a window—the narrow area at the very bottom of the screen. This may be suitable for displaying small amounts of text. We can do this by adding "**status = **" to the window name as follows:

```
myWindow.status = "Welcome to my window"
```

This example assumes that we have included a status bar as a feature of *myWindow*.

Writing Information to Text Boxes and Text Areas

Communicating information to readers using text boxes and text areas can be useful in that our Web page does not have to reload to display new updated information. The reader can instantly see the results of the processing of information he or she has given.

Although this can be done using alert message boxes, the information presented in such messages disappears when the reader clears the message box in order to continue. The information is thus not available on screen to the reader, who may want to use it while reading and responding to the Web page.

Without leaving the current page, the reader can enter different information, or make different choices, and instantly be shown the results. For example, he or she could be shown how the total cost would change if different types and/or numbers of products were ordered. Appropriate calculations could be made to take account of discount or to add tax before the results were displayed.

How to Do It

Let's take a very simple example. The code below (Program 4-10 on the website) is similar to an example presented in Chapter 3. The reader is asked to state how many disks he or she would like to purchase. In the original version, the result was displayed as an alert message. However, in this version the results of the calculation are presented in a text box.

```
<HTML>
<BODY onLoad = "pricePerDisk = 50; subTotal = 0; total = 0;
document.orderForm.orderBox.select (); document.orderForm.orderBox.focus ()"
onUnload = "document.orderForm.reset ()">
How many disks do you require?
<FORM NAME = "orderForm">
<INPUT TYPE = "text" NAME = "orderBox" VALUE = 0>
<INPUT TYPE = "text" NAME = "subTotalBox" VALUE = "Subtotal">
<INPUT TYPE = "text" NAME = "totalBox" VALUE = "Total">
<INPUT TYPE = "button"
VALUE = "Submit"
onClick = "subTotal = pricePerDisk * orderForm.orderBox.value; total += subTotal;
this.form.subTotalBox.value = 'Subtotal = ' + subTotal; this.form.totalBox.value =
'Total = ' + total; this.form.orderBox.focus (); this.form.orderBox.select ()">
</FORM>
</BODY>
</HTML>
```

The values of text areas are retrieved in exactly the same way as the text boxes in this example. The example below (Program 4-11 on the website) uses text areas instead of text boxes.

```
<HTML>
<BODY onLoad = "pricePerDisk = 50; subTotal = 0; total = 0;
document.orderForm.orderBox.value = 0; document.orderForm.orderBox.select (); docu-
ment.orderForm.orderBox.focus ()"
onUnload = "document.orderForm.reset ()">
How many disks do you require?
<FORM NAME = "orderForm">
<TEXTAREA NAME="orderBox" COLS=15 ROWS=3> 0 </TEXTAREA><P>
<TEXTAREA NAME="subTotalBox" COLS=15 ROWS=3> Subtotal </TEXTAREA>
<TEXTAREA NAME="totalBox" COLS=15 ROWS=3> Total </TEXTAREA>
<INPUT TYPE = "button"
VALUE = "Submit"
```

```
onClick = "subTotal = pricePerDisk * eval (orderForm.orderBox.value); total +=
subTotal; this.form.subTotalBox.value = 'Subtotal = ' + subTotal;
this.form.totalBox.value = 'Total = ' + total; this.form.orderBox.focus ();
this.form.orderBox.select ()">
</FORM>
</BODY>
</HTML>
```

Note that we have changed part of the code in the Submit button's event handler from:

```
subTotal = pricePerDisk * orderForm.orderBox.value
```

to:

```
subTotal = pricePerDisk * eval (orderForm.orderBox.value)
```

This is because the default value given to a text area is interpreted by JavaScript as a text string, not a number. If the reader were to click the Submit button without first entering a number in the text area, an error message would be displayed as JavaScript attempted to multiply this value by the number stored in the variable *pricePerDisk*. The error message would report that the value of *orderBox* was not a valid number. The **eval** command has the effect of converting the text string to a number.

JavaScript has no problem interpreting reader input to the text area as a number. Nor does it have any problem interpreting the default value of a text box, as in the previous example.

Writing Information to Frames

Normal HTML in one frame can specify the loading of documents in other frames, by means of the TARGET attribute. However, JavaScript allows us to write information dynamically to frames, incorporating not only text and HTML, but also variable values and JavaScript commands.

Frames can also be useful to hold variables while different documents are displayed to the reader. Normally, variables created in a Web page are lost as soon as the page is unloaded. However, different documents can be loaded in and out of one or more frames, yet use common variable values stored in the parent frame. These values can be communicated from and to new documents as they are loaded.

How to Do It

The following file sets up two frames called *frame1* and *frame2*. The document frame1.html is loaded into *frame1*, and frame2.html into *frame2*. This is Program 4-12 on the website.

```
<HTML>
<HEAD>
<TITLE>FRAMES</TITLE>
```

```
</HEAD>
<FRAMESET COLS="25%, *">
<FRAME SRC = "frame1.html" NAME="frame1">
<FRAME SRC="frame2.html" NAME="frame2">
</FRAMESET>
</HTML>
```

The file frame1.html is shown below. This is loaded into *frame1*. Assuming that frame2.html is simply a blank document, the screen will appear as in Figure 4.1.

```
<HTML>
<BODY>
This is frame 1, and this is the
<p><A HREF="link1.html" TARGET="frame2">
First link </A>
<p><A HREF="javascript:void (0)" onClick="parent.frame2.document.write ('Second
link<br> ')"> Second link </A>
<p><A HREF="javascript:void (0)" onClick="parent.frame2.document.clear();
parent.frame2.document.write ('Third link -- note this link clears the frame each
time <br> ')">
Third link </A>
<FORM>
```

Figure 4.1 Two frames.

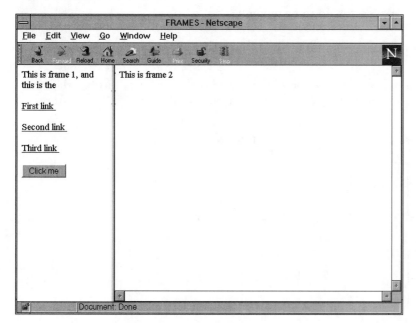

```
<INPUT TYPE="button" VALUE="Click me" onClick="parent.frame2.document.write ('You
clicked!<br> ')">
</FORM>
</BODY>
</HTML>
```

As shown in the first link in the code above, if we simply want to load an existing document into *frame2*, we need only use the name "frame2" in a normal HTML hyperlink:

```
<A HREF="link1.html" TARGET="frame2"> First link </A>
```

However, if we want to write dynamically to this frame using **document.write**, or indeed refer to the frame in any other JavaScript command—for example the Click me button, we need to specify the path to it, which, if we are referring to it from *frame1*, is "parent.frame2".

 Note the use of **javascript:void (0)** in the second and third hyperlinks. This specifies that when the hyperlink is clicked, the JavaScript command command **void (0)** should be executed. This command means "Do nothing!" In other words, we want all the action to take place in the **onClick** event handler, in which we specify what should be written to the targeted frame. We want the HREF attribute to be ignored.

This path is clear if we examine the hierarchical structure of our frames. Figure 4.2 shows this structure.

Figure 4.2 shows that *frame1* and *frame2* can communicate only through their parent. To refer from *frame2* to *frame1*, we would therefore need to specify "parent.frame1."

Figure 4.2 Hierarchical structure of two frames.

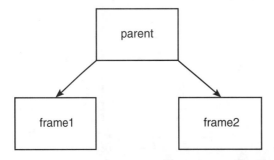

We will now construct a slightly more complex set of frames (Program 4-13 on the website), as shown in Figure 4.3. Figure 4.4 shows the hierarchical structure of this set.

The code below sets up this set of frames:

```
<HTML>
<HEAD>
<TITLE>Frames</TITLE>
</HEAD>
<FRAMESET ROWS="50%, *">
<FRAME SRC = "frame1.html" NAME="frame1">
    <FRAMESET COLS="50%, *">
        <FRAMESET ROWS="50%, *">
            <FRAME SRC = "frame2a.html" NAME ="frame2a">
            <FRAME SRC = "frame2b.html" NAME = "frame2b">
        </FRAMESET>
        <FRAME SRC= "frame3.html" NAME="frame3">
    </FRAMESET>
</FRAMESET>
</HTML>
```

Figure 4.3 A complex set of frames.

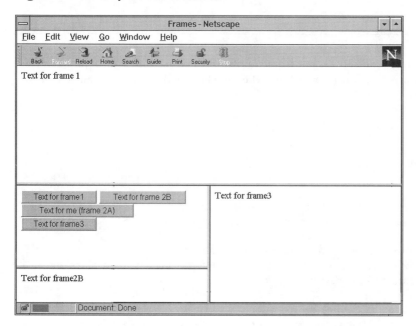

Figure 4.4 Hierarchical structure of a complex set of frames.

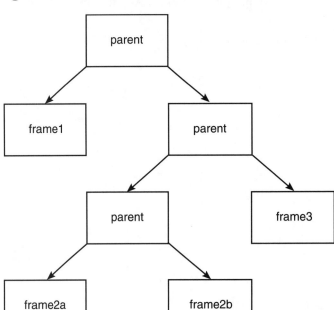

The following code represents frame2a.html, which is loaded into *frame2a*. This document displays four buttons, which, when clicked, will write information to the different frames.

```
<HTML>
<BODY>
<FORM>
<INPUT TYPE="button" VALUE = "Text for frame1"
onClick="parent.parent.parent.frame1.document.write ('Text for frame 1 <BR> ')">

<INPUT TYPE="button" VALUE = "Text for frame 2B"
onClick="parent.frame2b.document.write ('Text for frame2B <BR> ')">

<INPUT TYPE="button" VALUE = "Text for me (frame 2A)"
onClick="self.document.write ('Text for frame 2A <BR> You will have to click the BACK
to get to the buttons again<BR> ')">

<INPUT TYPE="button" VALUE = "Text for frame3"
onClick="parent.parent.frame3.document.write ('Text for frame3 <BR> ')">
```

```
</BODY>
</HTML>
```

As noted previously, for one frame to write to another, it must use the correct path. So, for example, *frame2a* can communicate with *frame1* using the path "parent.parent.parent.frame1". The same frame can communicate with its sibling *frame2b* using "parent.frame2b".

We can set up variables in the parent document. These variables will remain until the parent document is unloaded. We can communicate the values of these variables to and from other frames using the same paths we used for writing information to them.

For example, the parent document in our example below (Program 4-14 on the website) not only creates a set of frames, it also sets up a variable *score*, which it sets to 0:

```
<HTML>
<HEAD>
<TITLE>FRAMES</TITLE>
<SCRIPT>

var score = 0

</SCRIPT>
</HEAD>
<FRAMESET ROWS="50%, *">
<FRAME SRC = "frame1.html" NAME="frame1">
    <FRAMESET COLS="50%, *">
        <FRAMESET ROWS="70%, *">
            <FRAME SRC = "frame2a.html" NAME ="frame2a">
            <FRAME SRC = "frame2b.html" NAME = "frame2b">
        </FRAMESET>
        <FRAME SRC= "frame3.html" NAME="frame3">
    </FRAMESET>
</FRAMESET>
</HTML>
```

The document **frame2a.html**, which is loaded into *frame2b*, is shown below. Note that the **onClick** event handler of a button in this frame can read and/or change the variable *score*, stored in the parent document, by using the correct path:

```
onClick = "parent.parent.parent.score ++"
```

This document displays three buttons, which, when clicked, will display the value of the variable *score* in *frame1* or in an alert box and will increment *score* by 1.

```
<HTML>
<BODY>
<FORM>
<INPUT TYPE="button" VALUE = "Click to show value of score"
onClick="alert ('Score is ' + parent.parent.parent.score)">
```

```
<INPUT TYPE="button" VALUE = "Click to show score in frame 1"
onClick="parent.parent.parent.frame1.document.clear (); parent.parent.frame1.docu-
ment.write ('Score is ' + parent.parent.score + '<BR> ')">

<INPUT TYPE="button" VALUE = "Click to increment score by 1"
onClick="parent.parent.parent.score ++">

</FORM>
</BODY>
</HTML>
```

The variable *score* will remain stored in the parent document while other documents can be loaded and unloaded in and out of the other frames. These new documents can all read and write to the *score* variable as shown in this example.

Loading Documents and Images

JavaScript commands allow us to load documents into windows and frames without the reader having to click a hyperlink. As we saw in Chapter 3, this may be useful if, for example, we want to interrupt the linking process to give further information about a link and give the reader a chance to cancel the action if desired. Loading a new page may also be something we want to do at a certain stage as other JavaScript commands are being executed—for example, in a function.

Images on a Web page may also be changed without the need to reload the page. This technique can be useful in implementing a dynamically changing contents page to a document, for example. Images signifying chapters or sections can be changed either when the reader moves the mouse over them or when the link has been followed. Two images could be stored, one being substituted for the other as required. Both images could contain the same text but differ in color. The effect would be to highlight the selected chapter or section of the document.

How to Do It

Let's look at how this is done. First we'll concentrate on loading documents into windows and frames. We will then explore how we can dynamically load and reload images into our pages. Note that Dynamic HTML, offered in JavaScript 1.2, greatly extends our ability to display and manipulate images to create complex animation effects. Dynamic HTML will be introduced in Chapter 9.

Loading Documents

We can load a document into the current window using the JavaScript command:

```
self.location = "URL"
```

where URL is a valid document address. The commands:

```
window.location = "URL"
```

```
top.location = "URL"
```

will load the document into the current and top window (which may be one and the same). We can also load a document into another window or frame. The code:

```
myWindow.location = "URL"
```

will load the document into the named window. Assuming that we have two frames, *frame1* and *frame2*, a command in *frame1* can load a document into *frame2* using the address of that frame:

```
parent.frame2.location = "URL"
```

We can also navigate using the Netscape **history** object. This object allows us to load Web pages already visited by the reader. The command:

```
history.back ()
```

or

```
history.go (-1)
```

will load the previous document. The command

```
history.forward ()
```

or

```
history.go (1)
```

will load the next document (assuming that there is one in the history list). We can specify documents by their position in the history list. For example:

```
history.go (-4)
history.go (2)
```

and we can specify a string, which will load the nearest document containing the string in its URL. For example:

```
history.go ("home")
```

The following code (Program 4-15 on the website) shows these commands in use in hyperlinks and buttons:

```
<HTML>
<BODY>

<A HREF="javascript:history.go (-1)"> Back </A>

<FORM>
<INPUT TYPE="button" VALUE = "Forward"
onClick = "history.forward ()">
</FORM>
```

```
</BODY>
</HTML>
```

Naturally, the Forward button will only work if there are documents ahead of the currently loaded one in the history list.

Loading Images

JavaScript allows us to change images without reloading the Web page. Assuming that we have created a document including an image, with the code:

```
<IMG SRC = "image1.gif">
```

this image will be automatically indexed so that we can refer to it as:

```
document.images[0]
```

If more images had been included in our document, they would be indexed as:

```
document.images[1]
document.images[2]
```

and so on.

JavaScript allows us to change any image by referring to its index address. The following command:

```
document.images[0].src = "image2.gif"
```

would change the image from image1.gif to image2.gif.

We can preload images so that they will be displayed very quickly when this command is used. We can do this using the following procedure (Program 4-16 on the website):

```
1. <HTML>
2. <BODY onLoad = "picture2 = new Image (100,100); picture2.src = 'image2.gif '">

3. Here is a picture
4. <IMG SRC = "image1.gif" WIDTH=100 HEIGHT=100>

5. <FORM>
6. <INPUT TYPE = "button" VALUE = "Change picture"
7. onClick = "document.images[0].src = picture2.src">
8. </FORM>
9. </BODY>
10. </HTML>
```

Line 2 creates a new **Image** object, 100 pixels wide by 100 pixels high, giving it the name *picture2*. Line 2 then loads the image image2.gif into this object. This is done within the **onLoad** event handler.

The body of the document displays some text (line 3), an image—image1.gif (line 4)—and a form (lines 5 through 8). When the reader clicks the button, the button's event handler changes the value of the first image on the page (**document.images[0]**). The new image image2.gif, already stored in the object *picture2*, is loaded in place of it (line 7).

The **new Image ()** command can be used with empty parentheses if you do not want to specify height and width.

As previously noted, Dynamic HTML, introduced in Chapter 9, offers extended facilities for displaying and manipulating images, and creating complex animation effects.

Sending E-Mails

Generally, the most effective way of automatically e-mailing information from forms is to have it interpreted by a program or script at the server end. However, it is also possible to send e-mail without having such facilities. HTML allows us to send e-mail when a form is submitted, using the ACTION command:

```
<FORM ACTION="mailto:email-address" METHOD="POST">
...
<INPUT TYPE="submit" NAME="my button" VALUE="Submit">
```

However, forms written in normal HTML can send only unprocessed information—choices the reader has made using radio buttons, checkboxes, and so forth, and information typed into text boxes and text areas.

There are drawbacks and limitations to this process. When the e-mail is received, spaces are replaced by other characters so that effort is required to obtain a "clean" copy of the information. There is also a limit to the amount of information that can be sent in this way. Always try a test message before relying on this technique. Only part of a large amount of text may be received.

JavaScript allows us to send information in the same way, but it also allows us to process the information and send the results of this processing in the e-mail. This process is subject to the limitations mentioned above relating to clarity and volume of information received.

Despite these limitations, this technique may be useful in, for example, preprocessing the results of an online questionnaire (perhaps summarizing or conducting some other analysis on the raw data) before e-mailing it.

How to Do It

We can do this using the **document.write** command introduced earlier in this chapter. Just as we can write and display new Web pages incorporating variable values with text, we can write new Web pages incorporating variable values with forms.

The following very simple example assumes that data has been obtained from the reader in the form of an online questionnaire. Let us also assume that using techniques introduced in Chapter 3, we have processed this data and stored the results in the variables *averageRating* and *timeSpent*, reflecting the average rating that the reader gave in our online survey and how long he or she spent completing it.

The following code (Program 4-17 on the website) creates a form with hidden fields containing this information and a visible button asking the reader to submit. We would normally either show the information to be sent (by using visible instead of hidden fields) or tell the reader what is to be e-mailed. For simplicity, the code below assigns a value to the variables *averageRating* and *timeSpent*. In reality, these would have been calculated by the program.

```
<HTML>
<BODY>
<SCRIPT>

averageRating = 85
timeSpent = "12 minutes"

document.write ("<FORM NAME= 'myForm ' ACTION= 'mailto:email-address ' METHOD= 'POST
'> <INPUT TYPE= 'hidden ' NAME= 'Average rating ' VALUE= '"
+ averageRating
+ "'> <INPUT TYPE= 'hidden ' NAME= 'Time spent ' VALUE= '"
+ timeSpent
+ "'> <INPUT TYPE= 'submit ' VALUE= 'Submit '> </FORM>")

</SCRIPT>
</BODY>
</HTML>
```

Server-side JavaScript offers a range of facilities enabling e-mail to be sent automatically. These will be introduced in Chapter 10.

PROGRAMMING YOUR WEB PAGES
to "Think"

In certain cases it is possible to program your Web pages to give their readers advice and make decisions, just as you would if you were interacting *personally* with them. This can be an extremely useful capability. If you are advertising products on the Web, for example, imagine people reading your pages and receiving interactive advice on which product best matches their individual needs and circumstances. Your Web pages could ask them relevant questions and, depending on their individual answers, give them personalized advice and recommendations.

Needless to say, it is *your* advice and recommendations that your pages would be giving! The technique is simply a question of converting relevant parts of your knowledge—your decision-making processes—into a program. There are many examples of computer systems that do precisely this. They store some of the expertise of the person or persons who created them, and they act "intelligently," simulating decisions and advice that would normally be provided by their human counterparts.

Some of these so-called "intelligent" systems are able to simulate parts of the knowledge of humans who are truly expert in their field. Such intelligent systems are known as *expert systems*. Systems that behave less intelligently can still perform useful, routine tasks that would otherwise require human attention. Useful examples of expert and intelligent computer systems can be found at **www.exsysinfo.com/Appnotes/areas.html**. Applications are myriad, with thousands of systems in use in almost every area of human activity, including medicine, business, education, accounting and finance, marketing, manufacturing, agriculture, government, and the military. Specific systems offer decision support in such varied areas as personal tax advice, risk assessment, agricultural crop management, toxicity of chemicals, patient care for student nurses, underwriting assistance, flaw detection in welding, cost/benefit analysis, and credit worthiness analysis.

Other examples of working systems and details of the large volume of research and development can be found by searching the Web using keywords such as "knowledge based systems," "intelligent systems," "intelligent knowledge based systems," and "expert systems."

Examples of the sorts of knowledge that are particularly well suited to this process include the following:

Interpreting complex rules and regulations. For example, advising readers as to whether they qualify for some discount, entitlement, entry to an academic institution, or the like, or on procedures for, say, complaining to a local authority.

Diagnosis and troubleshooting. For example, advising readers on what is wrong with a piece of equipment and what steps they can take to solve the problem.

Identifying/classifying. For example, advising potential customers on a product that best suits their needs, or identifying anything from rock specimens to insects!

The important thing to note is that your Web page will treat each of its readers individually, giving advice tailored to his or her particular needs and circumstances.

Drawing Conclusions

Central to the notion of intelligence is the process of making inferences or drawing conclusions from evidence. If, to take a classic example, we are presented with the statements:

Socrates is a man.
All men are mortal.

we can easily answer the question:

Is Socrates mortal?

Yet we have not been told this fact explicitly; we worked it out from the other two statements. One way of encoding the type of knowledge we used to make this inference is to use the sort of IF...THEN rules introduced in Chapter 3. Such rules can enable us to build into our Web pages the capability to make inferences.

However, inferring that Socrates is mortal is not of much practical use! The good news is that the same basic technique can be used to build Web pages capable of making inferences in areas that are more complex and useful to us. In this way, we can program our Web pages to interact with their readers, making decisions and giving advice based on our own stored knowledge—as though we were ourselves responding in person.

Indeed, you can add considerable value to your Web pages if they can provide their readers with a significant level of interactivity and individual attention that:

Would not otherwise be provided (that is, readers would not otherwise have access to a human sales assistant or advisor) and/or

Release you to do more by handling at least a proportion of queries (some of the more routine, perhaps) that would otherwise require a human's personal attention.

Our first example will advise readers as to whether they are eligible to be admitted for one or more Master courses in librarianship and information management. We'll start with an extract from the admissions handbook. In plain English, this extract reads as follows:

For entry to the M.A. in Library and Information Management (MA LIM), candidates should possess a good first degree plus at least 5 years' approved experience.

For entry to the M.A. in Librarianship (MA Lib), candidates require a good first degree plus at least 1 year's approved experience.

For entry to the M.Sc. in Information Management (MSc IM), candidates require a good degree in a science or social science discipline plus at least 1 year's approved experience.

> **NOTE** It will not escape you that the advice given by our first simple example system could just as easily be provided by presenting the readers of our Web page with a plain paragraph of text. This is because we need to examine basic techniques in an easily intelligible way. Bear in mind that these systems become genuinely useful in the real world when they are required to give advice and make decisions that entail a greater volume and complexity of knowledge. Beyond a certain level of complexity, it becomes more difficult for people to interpret and apply to their own particular circumstances complex rules, regulations, and other information simply by reading them as text. This is why a potential customer may prefer to seek advice from a member of the sales staff rather than simply reading sales and technical documentation.

One way of encoding such knowledge into our Web pages is to translate them into IF...THEN rules. These rules take the form:

IF *some condition(s)* THEN *some conclusion(s)*

To keep things simple, we'll start with just the first part of the regulations:

For entry to the M.A. in Library and Information Management (MA LIM), candidates should possess a good first degree plus at least 5 years' approved experience.

We can encode this material as the following rule:

IF you have a good degree
AND you have at least 5 years' approved experience
THEN you are eligible for the MA LIM
ELSE you are not eligible for the MA LIM

We can translate this into JavaScript using the IF...THEN rules introduced in Chapter 3 as follows (Program 5-1 on the website):

```
1.   <HTML>
2.   <HEAD>
3.   <SCRIPT LANGUAGE="JavaScript">

4.   function eligible () {
5.   if (confirm ("Do you have a good degree?")
6.   && confirm ("Do you have at least 5 years' approved
          experience?")
7.   { return "You are eligible for the MA LIM" }
8.   else { return "You are not eligible for the MA LIM" }
9.   }

10.  </SCRIPT>
11.  </HEAD>

12.  <BODY>
13.  <FORM>
14.  <INPUT TYPE="button" VALUE="Start"
15.      onClick="alert (eligible ())">
16.  </FORM>
17.  </BODY>
18.  </HTML>
```

Recall from Chapter 3 that a function has to be *called* before it actually does anything. The function **eligible** (line 4) is called by the **alert** command when the Start button is clicked (lines 14 and 15). However, before the **alert** command can actually display anything, it must discover the *value* of the function **eligible**. It does this by obeying all the commands that make up this function. Line 5 tells it to display a confirm box asking the reader to confirm whether or not he or she has a good degree (Figure 5.1).

Line 6 asks the second question: whether the reader has at least 5 years' approved experience. If the reader replies "Yes" to both questions, then "You are eligible for the

Figure 5.1 The system's opening question.

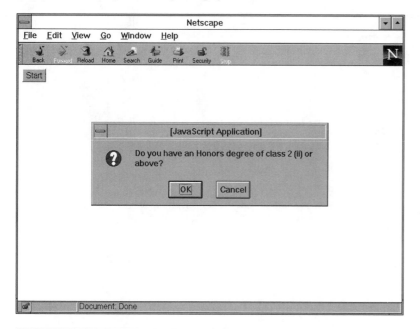

MA LIM" will be returned (line 7) as the value of the function **eligible**. Otherwise, "You are not eligible for the MA LIM" will be returned as its value (line 8).

Now the value of the function **eligible** has been found. The **alert** command knows what to display, and assuming that the reader fulfills both requirements, the message shown in Figure 5.2 will appear. If the reader does *not* fulfill both requirements, the alternative message, "You are not eligible for the MA LIM," will appear.

Complex Problem Solving

We can combine a number of these IF...THEN rules to form more complex chains of reasoning, in which the conclusion of one rule (the THEN part) forms a condition (the IF part) of another rule. We will need to do this if we want our system to be able to encode more complex and sophisticated forms of knowledge.

Recall that our first rule is:

IF you have a good degree
AND you have at least 5 years' approved experience
THEN you are eligible for the MA LIM
ELSE you are not eligible for the MA LIM

Figure 5.2 The system's conclusion.

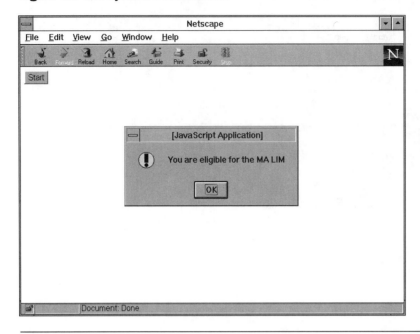

Our system simply asks the readers if they have a good degree and relevant experience. But our readers are unlikely to know exactly what we mean by a "good" degree and "approved" experience.

We can write further rules which will clarify these questions:

IF you have an Honors degree of class 2 (ii) or above
THEN you have a good degree
ELSE you do not have a good degree

IF you have worked in a library or information unit for 5 years or more
OR a significant part of your work for 5 years or more entailed information handling
THEN you have at least 5 years' approved experience
ELSE you do not have at least 5 years' approved experience

Here is the complete set of rules so far. Each line is numbered so that it can be referred to more easily below.

Eligibility rule
1. IF you have a good degree
2. AND you have at least 5 years' approved experience
3. THEN you are eligible for the MA LIM

4. ELSE you are not eligible for the MA LIM

Good degree rule
5. IF you have an Honors degree of class 2 (ii) or above
6. THEN you have a good degree
7. ELSE you do not have a good degree

Approved experience rule
8. IF you have worked in a library or information unit for 5 years or more
9. OR a significant part of your work for 5 years or more entailed information handling
10. THEN you have at least 5 years' approved experience
11. ELSE you do not have at least 5 years' approved experience

Note how the first *condition* of the eligibility rule (line 1) is the same as the *conclusion* of the good degree rule (line 6). Similarly, the second condition of the eligibility rule (line 2) is the same as the conclusion of the approved experience rule (line 10).

Our system will look at the eligibility rule and try to establish whether its conditions are true. If they are, it will assert that its conclusion must therefore be true.

The system therefore tries to prove the first condition of the eligibility rule (line 1). It can do this if it can prove the conclusion of rule 2 (line 6). To do this, it must prove the condition of the good degree rule (line 5). Because there are no further rules it can use to help it decide whether this condition is true, it must ask the reader directly:

"Do you have an Honors degree of class 2 (ii) or above?"

If the reader replies "Yes," the conclusion of the good degree rule (line 6) is proved true. So, the first condition of the eligibility rule (line 1) is also proved true. The next step, therefore, is to try to prove the second condition of the eligibility rule (line 2).

The conclusion of the approved experience rule (line 10) matches this condition, and so the system will try to prove the approved experience rule. It can do this if *either* the first condition (line 8) *or* the second condition (line 9) is true. Because there is no other rule with either of these conditions as its conclusion, the system will ask the reader directly:

"Have you worked in a library or information unit for 5 years or more?"

If the answer is "yes," the approved experience rule has been proved. Thus the eligibility rule has also been proved, and the system will conclude that the reader is indeed eligible for the MA in Library and Information Management. If the answer is "no," the system will try to prove the second, alternative condition of the approved experience rule (line 9):

"Has a significant part of your work for 5 years or more entailed information handling?"

If the answer is "yes," the approved experience rule and therefore the eligibility rule are proved true. If the answer is "no," the approved experience rule and therefore rule 1 are proved untrue and the system will conclude that the reader is *not* eligible for the MA in Library and Information Management.

These rules can be translated fairly easily into JavaScript. Note that each rule is encoded as a function. However, function names are not allowed to contain spaces. We could rename functions as follows:

```
function  you_have_at_least_5_years_approved_experience ()
```

However, this is unnecessarily cumbersome, and it would be preferable to abbreviate the function name. This does not matter, because abbreviating the name will not affect anything the reader will see. But whenever we abbreviate a name, we must make sure we do it *wherever* it appears in our program (in other words, in both conditions and conclusions of rules).

Here is the whole program (Program 5-2 on the website). It uses suitably abbreviated forms of names:

```
<HTML>
<HEAD>
<SCRIPT LANGUAGE = "JavaScript">

function eligible_for_MA_LIM () {
if ( good_degree () == "yes"
&& approved_experience () == "yes" )
{ return "You are eligible for the MA LIM" }
else { return "You are not eligible for the MA LIM" }
}

function good_degree () {
if ( confirm ("Do you have an Honors degree of class 2 (ii) or above?") )
{ return "yes" } else { return "no" }
}

function approved_experience () {
if ( confirm ("Have you worked in a library or information unit for 5 years or more?")
|| confirm ("Has a significant part of your work for 5 years or more entailed information handling?") )
{ return "yes" } else { return "no" }
}

</SCRIPT>
</HEAD>
<BODY>
<FORM>
```

```
<INPUT TYPE="button" VALUE = "Start" onClick="alert (eligible_for_MA_LIM () )">
</FORM>
</BODY>
</HTML>
```

 NOTE A shorter way of writing a rule is to make those rules that are checked in its conditions (the "IF" part) return *true* or *false* (Boolean values) instead of "yes" or "no" (text strings). Thus if the good_degree and approved_experience rules returned *true* instead of "yes" and *false* instead of "no", the eligible_for_MA_LIM rule could be written more economically as:

> if (good_degree () && approved_experience ())
>   { return "You are eligible for the MA LIM" }
>   else { return "You are not eligible for the MA LIM" }

The longer version has been preferred since arguably it is less cryptic and makes the reasoning clearer to follow, particularly to those new to programming.

Making Alternative Recommendations

The rules we have been looking at so far are only a subset of the original, more complex set of regulations. A person may in fact be eligible for more than one course. If this is the case, we want to be able to list all appropriate courses, not stop after the first one!

The admission handbook regulations we have been examining can be encoded into the following rules. Note that the first three rules did not appear in our previous example. They have been added in order to handle the various messages to be displayed to the reader in a slightly tidier way:

> IF you are eligible for the MA LIM
> THEN say "I am glad to say that you are eligible for the MA LIM"
> ELSE say "I am sorry but you are not eligible for the MA LIM"
>
> IF you are eligible for the MA Lib
> THEN say "I am glad to say that you are eligible for the MA Lib"
> ELSE say "I am sorry but you are not eligible for the MA Lib"
>
> IF you are eligible for the MSc IM
> THEN say "I am glad to say that you are eligible for the MSc IM"
> ELSE say "I am sorry but you are not eligible for the MSc IM"
>
> IF you have a good degree
> AND you have at least 5 years' approved experience
> THEN you are eligible for the MA LIM

IF you have a good degree
AND you have at least 1 year's approved experience
THEN you are eligible for the MA Lib

IF you have a good degree
AND your degree is in a science or a social science discipline
AND you have at least 1 year's approved experience
THEN you are eligible for the MSc IM

IF you have an Honors degree of class 2 (ii) or above
THEN you have a good degree

IF you have worked in a library or information unit for 1 year or more
OR a significant part of your work for 1 year or more entailed information handling
THEN you have at least 1 year's approved experience

IF you have worked in a library or information unit for 5 years or more
OR a significant part of your work for 5 years or more entailed information handling
THEN you have at least 5 years' approved experience

These rules can be translated into JavaScript as follows (Program 5-3 on the website). Note that the three top rules will all be placed in a single function, **start**. This will allow us to check eligibility for all three courses by calling one function when the Start button is clicked.

```
<HTML>
<HEAD>
<SCRIPT>

function start () {
if ( eligible_for_MA_LIM () == "yes" )
{ alert ( "I am glad to say that you are eligible for the MA LIM") } else { alert
("I am sorry but you are not eligible for the MA LIM") }
if ( eligible_for_MA_Lib () == "yes" )
{ alert ( "I am glad to say that you are eligible for the MA Lib") } else { alert
("I am sorry but you are not eligible for the MA Lib") }
if ( eligible_for_MSc_IM () == "yes" )
{ alert ( "I am glad to say that you are eligible for the MSc IM") } else { alert
("I am sorry but you are not eligible for the MSc IM") }
}

function eligible_for_MA_LIM () {
if ( good_degree () == "yes" && _5_years_experience () == "yes")
{ return "yes" } else { return "no" }
}
```

```
function eligible_for_MA_Lib () {
if ( good_degree () == "yes" && _1_year_experience() == "yes")
{ return "yes" } else { return "no" }
}

function eligible_for_MSc_IM () {
if ( good_degree () == "yes"
&& degree_discipline () == "science or social science"
&& _1_year_experience () == "yes")
{ return "yes" } else { return "no" }
}

function good_degree () {
if ( confirm ("Do you have an Honors degree of class 2 (ii) or above?") )
{ return "yes" } else { return "no" }
}

function _5_years_experience() {
if ( confirm ("Have you worked in a library or information unit for 5 or more
years?") )
{ return "yes" } else { return "no" }
}

function _1_year_experience() {
if ( confirm ("Have you worked in a library or information unit for 1 or more
years?") )
{ return "yes" } else { return "no" }
}

function degree_discipline () {
if (confirm ("Is your degree in a science or social science discipline?"))
{return "science or social science"}
else {return "no"}
}

</SCRIPT>
</HEAD>
<BODY>
<FORM>
<INPUT TYPE="button" VALUE = "Start" onClick="start ()">
</FORM>
</BODY>
</HTML>
```

Although it works perfectly well, this code is rather clumsy. It will ask the reader:

"Have you worked in a library or information unit for 1 or more years?"

but it will ask *twice*—once when trying to assess eligibility for the MA in Librarianship and again when assessing eligibility for the MSc in Information Management.

We will explore ways of making sure that our Web pages act a little more intelligently by remembering what our readers tell them and not asking them the same question more than once, in "Avoid Asking the Same Question More Than Once." But first, let's examine how to encode more complex sets of rules.

More Complex Rules

Regulations may be more complex than those we have used as an example so far. In fact, here is the full version of the entry requirements for the MA in Library and Information Management:

> For entry to the M.A. in Library and Information Management (MA LIM), candidates should possess
>
> (a) a good first degree plus *at least 5 years' approved experience*; or
>
> (b) a good first degree plus *a recognized qualification in librarianship or information science* plus *at least 2 years' approved experience*; or
>
> (c) an Associateship of the Library Association (A.L.A.) plus *at least 5 years' approved experience* plus *evidence acceptable to the Head of department of a substantial contribution to librarianship or information management.*

More complex regulations like these can be handled in either of two ways. First, we can translate them into an equally complex rule:

```
IF (you have a good degree
    AND you have at least 5 years' approved experience)
OR (you have a good degree
    AND a recognized qualification in librarianship or information science
    AND at least 2 years' approved experience)
OR (you have an Associateship of the Library Association
    AND at least 5 years' approved experience
    AND evidence of a substantial contribution to librarianship or information
        management)
THEN you are eligible for the MA LIM
ELSE you are not eligible for the MA LIM
```

Note the use of parentheses to ensure that the conditions we want to go with each other in fact do so. This rule can be translated into JavaScript as follows:

```
function eligible_for_MA_LIM () {
if (
```

```
(good_degree () == "yes" && _5_years'_experience () == "yes")
|| (good_degree () == "yes" && recognised_qualification () == "yes" &&
_2_years_experience () == "yes")
|| (ALA == "yes" && _5_years'_experience () == "yes" && evidence_of_contribution ()
== "yes")
)
{ return "yes" } else { return "no" }
}
```

Note the extra set of parentheses compared to the "plain English" version of the rules. Remember that JavaScript requires parentheses around the condition of a rule:

```
if ( condition ) ...
```

However, beyond a certain level of complexity, it will be much easier to break a rule into a series of simpler rules. In the case of our example, these could be:

> IF you have a good degree
>> AND you have at least 5 years' approved experience
> THEN you are eligible for the MA LIM
> ELSE you are not eligible for the MA LIM
>
> IF you have a good degree
>> AND recognized qualification in librarianship or information science
>> AND at least 2 years' approved experience
> THEN you are eligible for the MA LIM
> ELSE you are not eligible for the MA LIM
>
> IF you have an Associateship of the Library Association
>> AND at least 5 years' approved experience
>> AND evidence of a substantial contribution to librarianship or information
> management
> THEN you are eligible for the MA LIM
> ELSE you are not eligible for the MA LIM

If these rules are contained within a single function, JavaScript will check them all in sequence. However, recall that as soon as JavaScript obeys a command to return a value (in this case, "yes" or "no"), that value becomes the only value returned by the function. So, if the reader does not qualify for the MA LIM under the first rule, JavaScript will think he or she is not eligible, no matter whether he or she *is* eligible under a subsequent rule. This is not intelligent behavior! For this reason, we need to ·modify the function so that although all the rules return "yes" if the reader is eligible, the function returns "no" only if it has got to the bottom line without *any* of the rules proving successful:

```
function eligibility () {

if (good_degree () == "yes" && _5_years'_experience () == "yes")
```

```
{return "yes"}

if (good_degree () == "yes" && recognised_qualification () == "yes" &&
_2_years'_experience () == "yes")
{return "yes"}

if (ALA == "yes" && _5_years'_experience () == "yes" && evidence_of_contribution ()
== "yes")
{return "yes"}

return "no"
}
```

When processing all the rules in our example so far, our Web page will ask about the reader's qualifications and experience in an unnecessarily long-winded way. If three rules require confirmation that the reader has a "good degree," then the system will ask the same question three times!

We need our pages to be able to remember what their readers have already told them so they can avoid asking the same question more than once.

Avoiding Asking the Same Question More Than Once

To avoid unnecessary repetition of a question, our Web pages need to know (a) that the question has been asked before and (b) what reply the reader gave. We can program this capability into our pages. Before giving the program in full, here is an example of the relevant code applied to just one question:

"Do you have an Honors degree of class 2 (ii) or above?"

Once this question has been asked, we want the system to remember the reader's answer, and to avoid asking the same question again if the information is required in another rule. The following approach will solve this problem. In the interests of clarity, a simple form of the rule has been used instead of the more complex form discussed in the previous section. Each line in the code is numbered to assist in the explanation below. Naturally, the numbers are not part of the code!

```
1.  var good_degree_status = "not known"

2.  function eligible_for_MA_LIM () {
3.  if ( good_degree () == "yes")
4.  { return "yes" } else { return "no" }
5.  }

6.  function good_degree () {
7.  if (good_degree_status == "not known")
8.      {if (confirm ("Do you have an Honors degree of class
            2 (ii) or above?"))
```

```
9.       { good_degree_status = "yes"; return "yes" }
10.      else { good_degree_status = "no"; return "no" }}
11. return good_degree_status }
```

Line 1 creates a variable called *good_degree_status* and sets its value as "not known." When line 3 calls the function **good_degree** (), the first thing this function does (line 7) is to check whether the value of *good_degree_status* is "not known." If it is indeed "not known," lines 8, 9, and 10 are processed. If not—in other words, if its value is either "yes" or "no"—then JavaScript goes straight to line 11.

Lines 7 through 11 read as follows:

7. IF the value of the variable *good_degree_status* is "not known"
8.   THEN
         IF the reader confirms that s/he has an Honors degree of 2(ii) or above
9.   THEN return "yes" as the value of *good_degree_status*
            AND return "yes" as the value of the function **good_degree ()**
10.   OTHERWISE return "no" as the value of *good_degree_status*
            AND return "no" as the value of the function **good_degree ()**
11. Return the value of *good_degree_status* as the value of the function
    good_degree (). Note that if a value has already been returned for this function
    (from line 9 or 10), this last line will not take effect, because the value returned
    first is the *only* value to be returned.

If the reader has already been asked this question, the value of *good_degree_status* cannot be "not known." This is because lines 8, 9, and 10 would have come into operation (and therefore would have changed the value to either "yes" or "no") when the question was asked for the first time.

Coming to line 7 on any subsequent occasion, JavaScript will know that the value of *good_degree_status* is either "yes" or "no." It will therefore skip straight to line 11 (without asking the reader the question again) and return the value ("yes" or "no") to line 3.

Before we see the whole program, let us first deal with another, similar problem. The program will still ask as totally separate questions:

"Have you worked in a library or information unit for 1 or more years?"
"Have you worked in a library or information unit for 2 or more years?"
"Have you worked in a library or information unit for 5 or more years?"

It will ask the second and third questions even if the reader replies "no" to the first. Again, this is hardly intelligent behavior! It will make sense to use the technique we have just been exploring to improve this part of the questioning as well. We can do this by breaking the questions into two parts:

"Have you worked in a library or information unit?"

and, if the reader replies "yes," then:

"For how long have you carried out this work?"

This second question will present the reader with a prompt box into which he or she should type a number (as shown in Figure 5.3).

Once the length of approved experience is stored in a variable, each rule can use this information to work out whether it is sufficient to satisfy its conditions. So, if we set up two variables:

```
var approved_experience_status = "not known"
var duration_experience_status = "not known"
```

we can store the reader's replies in these variables as follows:

```
function approved_experience () {
if (approved_experience_status == "not known")
    {if (confirm ("Have you worked in a library or
    information unit?")
    || confirm ("Has a significant part of your work entailed
    information handling?"))
    {approved_experience_status = "yes"; return "yes"}
    else {approved_experience_status = "no"; return "no"}}
return approved_experience_status
}
```

Figure 5.3 Asking about the reader's experience.

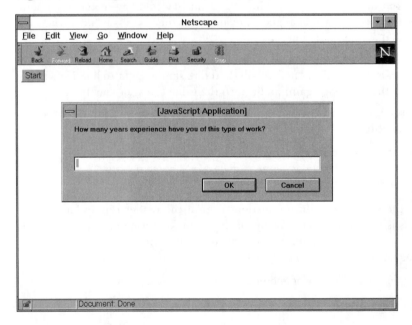

```
function duration_experience () {
if (duration_experience_status == "not known")
{duration_experience_status = prompt ("How many years' experience have you of this
type of work?", " ")}
return duration_experience_status
}
```

Here is the complete code (Program 5-4 on the website). Note that the first few lines of the **start** procedure create the variables and give them their starting values. This is needed if we wish to allow the program to be run repeatedly by clicking the Start button.

```
<HTML>
<HEAD>
<SCRIPT>

function start () {
approved_experience_status = "not known"
duration_experience_status = "not known"
good_degree_status = "not known"
degree_discipline_status = "not known"
if ( eligible_for_MA_LIM () == "yes" )
{ alert ( "I am glad to say that you are eligible for the MA LIM") } else { alert
("I am sorry but you are not eligible for the MA LIM") }
if ( eligible_for_MA_Lib () == "yes" )
{ alert ( "I am glad to say that you are eligible for the MA Lib") } else { alert
("I am sorry but you are not eligible for the MA Lib") }
if ( eligible_for_MSc_IM () == "yes" )
{ alert ( "I am glad to say that you are eligible for the MSc IM") } else { alert
("I am sorry but you are not eligible for the MSc IM") }
}

function eligible_for_MA_LIM () {
if ( good_degree () == "yes" && approved_experience () == "yes" &&
duration_experience () >= 5)
{ return "yes" } else { return "no" }
}

function eligible_for_MA_Lib () {
if ( good_degree () == "yes" && approved_experience () == "yes" &&
duration_experience () >= 1)
{ return "yes" } else { return "no" }
}

function eligible_for_MSc_IM () {
if ( good_degree () == "yes"
&& approved_experience () == "yes"
&& degree_discipline () == "science or social science"
&& duration_experience () >= 1)
```

```
{ return "yes" } else { return "no" }
}

function good_degree () {
if (good_degree_status == "not known")
{if (confirm ("Do you have an Honors degree of class 2 (ii) or above?"))
{good_degree_status = "yes"; return "yes"}
else {good_degree_status = "no"; return "no"}}
return good_degree_status
}

function degree_discipline () {
if (degree_discipline_status == "not known")
{if (confirm ("Is your degree in a science or social science discipline?"))
{degree_discipline_status = "science or social science"; return "science or social
science"}
else {degree_discipline_status = "other"; return "other"}}
return degree_discipline_status
}

function approved_experience () {
if (approved_experience_status == "not known")
{if (confirm ("Have you worked in a library or information unit?")
|| confirm ("Has a significant part of your work entailed information handling?"))
{approved_experience_status = "yes"; return "yes"}
else {approved_experience_status = "no"; return "no"}}
return approved_experience_status
}

function duration_experience () {
if (duration_experience_status == "not known")
{duration_experience_status = prompt ("How many years' experience have you of this
type of work?", " ")}
return duration_experience_status
}

</SCRIPT>
</HEAD>
<BODY>
<FORM>
<INPUT TYPE="button" VALUE="Start" onClick="start ()">
</FORM>
</BODY>
</HTML>
```

Note that if the reader, when asked how many years' experience he or she has, types something other than a number, then if you are using Netscape 3 (JavaScript 1.1) a JavaScript error will be displayed, saying that the value is not a valid number. In Netscape 4 (JavaScript 1.2) the **duration_experience ()** condition of each rule will fail—making the reader ineligible for any of the courses! We will explore ways of validating reader input—in this case, checking that it is a number and reacting appropriately if it is not—in Chapter 7.

Programming Your Pages to Explain Lines of Reasoning

One of the advantages of intelligent and expert systems is their ability to explain, on demand, their lines of reasoning—why they are asking a particular question and how they reached a particular conclusion.

Because they are able to do this, such systems are often extremely useful for training purposes. Novices can interact with the system, comparing their own decisions with those of the expert (or at least more knowledgeable person) encoded in the system. Unlike the human expert, however, the computer system will never tire of explaining its reasoning when presented with numerous example cases.

We'll build an explanation mechanism into our small intelligent system. At first, the system will display a message just before it asks each question, explaining *why* it is asking the question (Figure 5.4). After it has processed all its rules and come up with

Figure 5.4 The system explains why it is asking the question.

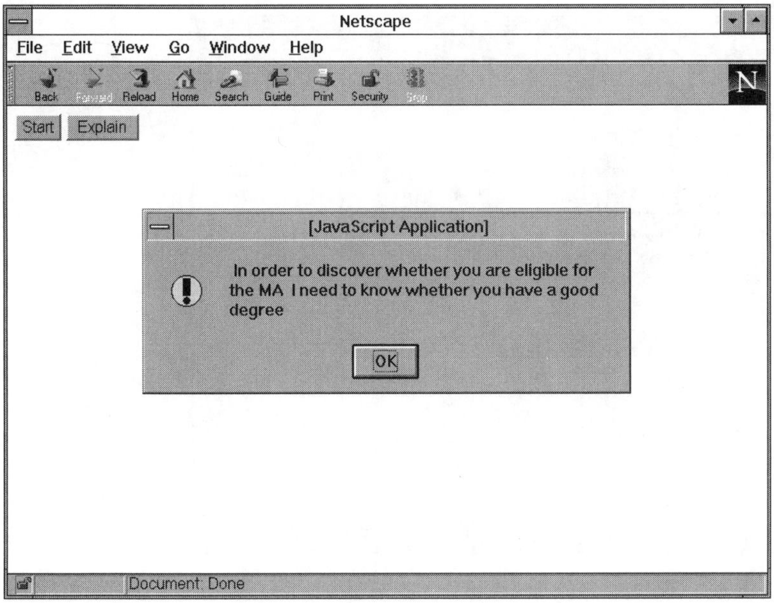

a decision as to whether the reader is or is not eligible for the MA in Library and Information Management, it will explain *how* it reached its conclusion (Figure 5.5).

The latter explanation is optional in that when the system has finished, it displays an Explain button; if and when the Explain button is clicked by the reader, it will display the chain of reasoning that led the system to come to the conclusions it did.

Normally we would want the "why" explanations to be optional, too. In other words, when the reader is presented with a question, as well as "yes" and "no" options there should be a similar "explain" option allowing the reader to request an explanation of why the particular question is being asked. This is more difficult and will be tackled in the second version of the program presented in the section "More User-Friendly Input" later in this chapter.

Here is the code we will use for our explanation (Program 5-5 on the website). In the interests of clarity, we use a simple version of the program—relating only to the MA in Library and Information Management (MA LIM). The new code that keeps track of the system's chain of reasoning is shown in boldface. The *why_trace* variable keeps track of why each question is being asked (in terms of the emerging chain of reasoning). The *how_trace* variable cumulatively keeps track of the evidence on which each particular conclusion has been reached.

Figure 5.5 The system explains how it reached its conclusion.

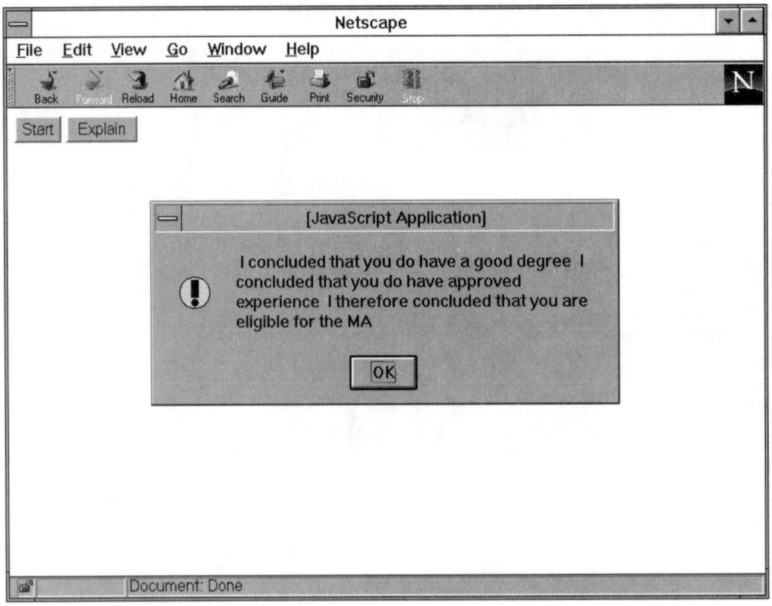

```
<HTML>
<HEAD>
<SCRIPT LANGUAGE="JavaScript">

var why_trace=""
var how_trace=""

function start () {
why_trace=""
how_trace=""
if ( eligible_for_MA_LIM () == "yes" ) { alert ("I am glad to say that you are
eligible for the MA LIM") }
else { alert ("I am sorry that you are not eligible for the MA LIM") }
}

function eligible_for_MA_LIM () {
var old_why_trace = why_trace
var old_how_trace = how_trace
why_trace = why_trace + " In order to discover whether you are eligible for
the MA LIM "
if ( good_degree () == "yes" && approved_experience () == "yes") {
why_trace = old_why_trace
how_trace = how_trace + " I therefore concluded that you are eligible for the
MA LIM ";
return "yes"}
else {how_trace = old_how_trace;
why_trace = old_why_trace
return "no"}
}

function good_degree () {
var old_why_trace = why_trace
var old_how_trace = how_trace
why_trace = why_trace + " I need to know whether you have a good degree "
alert (why_trace)
if (confirm ("Do you have an Honors degree of class 2 (ii) or above?")) {
why_trace = old_why_trace
how_trace = how_trace + " I concluded that you do have a good degree ";
return "yes"}
else {how_trace = old_how_trace;
why_trace = old_why_trace
return "no"}
}

function approved_experience () {
var old_why_trace = why_trace
```

```
var old_how_trace = how_trace
why_trace = why_trace + " I need to know whether you have approved experience "
alert (why_trace)
if ( confirm ("Have you worked in a library or information unit for 5 years or
more?") || confirm ("Has a significant part of your work for 5 years or more
entailed information handling?") ) {
why_trace = old_why_trace
how_trace = how_trace + " I concluded that you do have approved experience ";
return "yes"}
else {how_trace = old_how_trace;
why_trace = old_why_trace
return "no"}
}


</SCRIPT>
</HEAD>
<BODY>
<FORM>
<INPUT TYPE="button" VALUE="Start" onClick="start ()">
<INPUT TYPE="button" VALUE="Explain" onClick="alert (how_trace)">
</FORM>
</BODY>
</HTML>
```

Let us follow JavaScript as it processes the rules to see how it builds its explanation of why a particular question is being asked and how it justifies its conclusions.

We'll join it as it begins to process the **eligible_for_MA_LIM** rule. The first thing it does is to make a copy of whatever is in *why_trace* and *how_trace*. This is so that, if necessary (as explained below), it can revert to the values these variables had before the rule was processed:

```
var old_why_trace = why_trace
var old_how_trace = how_trace
```

Two local variables, *old_why_trace* and *old_how_trace*, are created to store the values of *why_trace* and *how_trace* as they are before the rule is processed. At present, these values are "" and ""—that is, blank—because there is as yet no chain of reasoning built up.

JavaScript then adds the words "In order to discover whether you are eligible for the MA LIM" to whatever is already in the variable *why_trace*.

The next thing JavaScript must do is check out the condition:

```
if ( good_degree () == "yes" && approved_experience () == "yes" )
```

To do this it must process the **good_degree** rule. This rule states that (having similarly made a copy of the entry values of *why_trace* and *how_trace*) the words "I need to know whether you have a good degree" are added to whatever is in *why_trace*. The variable *why_trace* now contains the words:

> *In order to discover whether you are eligible for the MA LIM*
> *I need to know whether you have a good degree*

The **good_degree** rule then instructs JavaScript to ask the reader to confirm:

> *"Do you have an Honors degree of class 2 (ii) or above?"*

If the reader clicks the Why ask radio button, the contents of *why_trace* will be displayed.

So long as JavaScript is following a chain of reasoning, *why_trace* will be built up cumulatively so that if the reader asks why a particular question is being asked, the "why" explanations from all the rules in the chain will be cumulatively displayed. However, when a particular chain of reasoning has been completed, *why_trace* reverts to the state it was in before that chain of reasoning began to be processed. In this way, any "why" explanations that are in fact irrelevant to the particular question being asked are removed.

```
why_trace = old_why_trace
```

A similar procedure applies to the "how" explanation of how a conclusion is reached. The contents of *how_trace* are added to by each rule—but only if that rule has been successfully proved. So, if the reader confirms that he or she has "an Honors degree of class 2 (ii) or above," *how_trace* has added to its existing contents (that is, nothing at present) the words "I concluded that you do have a good degree." If the reader goes on also to confirm that he or she has "worked in a library or information unit for 5 years or more," the words "I concluded that you do have approved experience" are added.

Because both its conditions are now satisfied, the **eligible_for_MA_LIM** rule will now add to *how_trace* the words "I therefore concluded that you are eligible for the MA LIM." If the reader now clicks the Explain button, the contents of *how_trace* will be displayed (as shown in Figure 5.5 on page 104).

However, whenever a rule fails, *how_trace* reverts to the state it was in before the rule was processed:

```
how_trace = old_how_trace
```

In this way, irrelevant "how" explanations are removed.

Negative Explanation

Negative explanation is explanation of why someone is *not* eligible or does *not* qualify for something. This is often the most important type of explanation to be given to the reader.

In the case of our example system, if readers are not eligible for particular courses, they are likely to want to know why—precisely which aspect(s) of their qualifications or experience is not acceptable for entry.

Negative explanation can be added to our current system. As in the previous section, in the interests of clarity we will stick with a simple version of the code. The new code is again shown in boldface. This is Program 5-6 on the website.

```
<HTML>
<HEAD>
<SCRIPT LANGUAGE="JavaScript">

var why_trace=""
var how_trace=""
var how_not_trace=""
var explanation=""

function start () {
why_trace=""
how_trace=""
how_not_trace=""
if ( eligible_for_MA_LIM () == "yes" ) { explanation = how_trace; alert ("I am glad
to say that you are eligible for the MA LIM") }
else { explanation = how_not_trace; alert ("I am sorry that you are not eligible
for the MA LIM") }
}

function eligible_for_MA_LIM () {
var old_why_trace = why_trace
var old_how_trace = how_trace
why_trace = why_trace + " In order to discover whether you are eligible for the MA
LIM "
if ( good_degree () == "yes" && approved_experience () == "yes") {
why_trace = old_why_trace
how_trace = how_trace + " I therefore concluded that you are eligible for the MA LIM
";
return "yes"}
else {how_trace = old_how_trace;
why_trace = old_why_trace;
how_not_trace = how_not_trace + "Therefore you are not eligible for the MA LIM
because you need both a good degree and approved experience"
return "no"}
}

function good_degree () {
var old_why_trace = why_trace
var old_how_trace = how_trace
```

```
why_trace = why_trace + " I need to know whether you have a good degree "
alert (why_trace)
if (confirm ("Do you have an Honors degree of class 2 (ii) or above?")) {
why_trace = old_why_trace
how_trace = how_trace + " I concluded that you do have a good degree ";
return "yes"}
else {how_trace = old_how_trace;
why_trace = old_why_trace;
how_not_trace = how_not_trace +  " You do not have an honors degree of class
2(ii) or above "
return "no"}
}


function approved_experience () {
var old_why_trace = why_trace
var old_how_trace = how_trace
why_trace = why_trace + " I need to know whether you have approved experience "
alert (why_trace)
if ( confirm ("Have you worked in a library or information unit for 5 years or
more?") || confirm ("Has a significant part of your work for 5 years or more
entailed information handling?") ) {
why_trace = old_why_trace
how_trace = how_trace + " I concluded that you do have approved experience ";
return "yes"}
else {how_trace = old_how_trace;
why_trace = old_why_trace;
how_not_trace = how_not_trace +  "You do not have the level of required experi-
ence "
return "no"}
}

</SCRIPT>
</HEAD>
<BODY>
<FORM>
<INPUT TYPE="button" VALUE="Start" onClick="start ()">
<INPUT TYPE="button" VALUE="Explain" onClick="alert (explanation)">
</FORM>
</BODY>
</HTML>
```

Note that if the reader is found to be eligible, the positive explanation will be automatically displayed when the Explain button is clicked. If he or she is *not* eligible, the negative explanation will be displayed instead (Figure 5.6). This is achieved by creating another variable *explanation* and filling it with whichever of *how_trace* or *how_not_trace* is appropriate in the start rule, after the system has decided whether or not the reader is eligible.

Figure 5.6 Displaying a negative explanation.

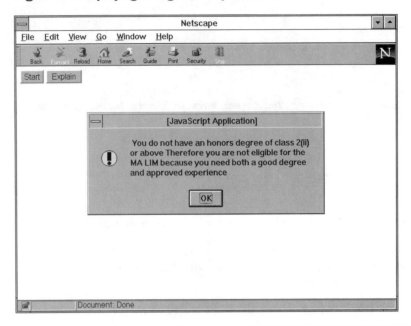

More User-Friendly Explanations

We still have a problem with enabling our readers, before answering a particular question, to ask for an explanation of the reasoning giving rise to the question. At present, we display an intrusive alert message saying why the question is going to be asked. Only when the reader clicks OK will the system go on to pose the question. Figure 5.7 shows the alert box.

To make this "why" facility optional, as in the case of the "how" and "how not" explanations discussed in the previous section, requires a fairly substantial change in the architecture of our system (although the basic reasoning mechanism will remain the same). We explore these changes in the next section.

However, a compromise would be to write the "why" explanation for each question to a frame, thus allowing the reader either to read or to ignore it before answering each question, as shown in Figure 5.8.

As in previous sections, we will use a simple version of the code. This means that negative explanation (in which the system will explain why a reader is *not* eligible if the conclusion is negative) is not implemented. In this way, the essentials of frame-based explanation, as opposed to the previous type of explanation based on alert boxes, are illustrated more clearly.

Figure 5.7 Processing stops until OK is clicked.

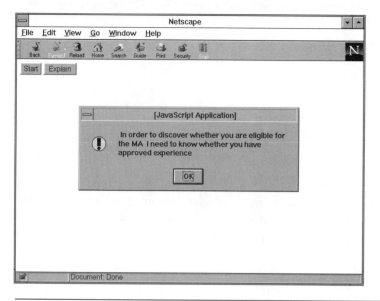

Figure 5.8 Explanation displayed in a frame.

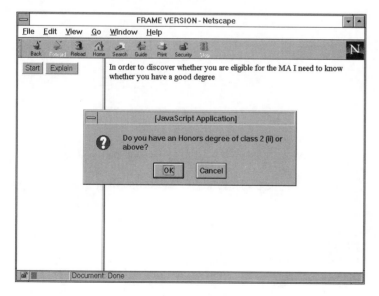

This example is Program 5-7 on the website. First comes the document that creates the frames. This is the document that we will load into the browser to start the program. We will call it start.html.

```
<HTML>
<HEAD>
<TITLE>FRAME VERSION</TITLE>
</HEAD>
<FRAMESET COLS="25%, *">
<FRAME SRC = "doc1.html" NAME="frame1">
<FRAME SRC="dummy.html" NAME="frame2">
</FRAMESET>
</HTML>
```

Note that start.html states that doc1.html should be loaded into *frame1*, and dummy.html into *frame2*. The file dummy.html is empty . Its only function is to display an empty *frame2*—awaiting the "why" explanations when a question is asked.

Here are the contents of the file dummy.html:

```
<HTML>
<BODY>
</BODY>
</HTML>
```

Here is the file doc1.html. New code is in bold.

```
<HTML>
<HEAD>
<SCRIPT LANGUAGE="JavaScript">

var why_trace=""
var how_trace=""

function start () {
why_trace=""
how_trace=""
if ( eligible_for_MA_LIM () == "yes" ) { alert ("I am glad to say that you are
eligible for the MA LIM") }
else { alert ("I am sorry that you are not eligible for the MA LIM") }
}

function eligible_for_MA_LIM () {
var old_why_trace = why_trace
var old_how_trace = how_trace
why_trace = why_trace + " In order to discover whether you are eligible for the MA
LIM "
```

```
if ( good_degree () == "yes" && approved_experience () == "yes") {
why_trace = old_why_trace
how_trace = how_trace + " I therefore concluded that you are eligible for the MA LIM
";
return "yes"}
else {how_trace = old_how_trace;
why_trace = old_why_trace
return "no"}
}


function good_degree () {
var old_why_trace = why_trace
var old_how_trace = how_trace
why_trace = why_trace + " I need to know whether you have a good degree "
parent.frame2.document.clear ();
parent.frame2.document.write (why_trace + "<br>")
if (confirm ("Do you have an Honors degree of class 2 (ii) or above?")) {
why_trace = old_why_trace
how_trace = how_trace + " I concluded that you do have a good degree ";
return "yes"}
else {how_trace = old_how_trace;
why_trace = old_why_trace
return "no"}
}


function approved_experience () {
var old_why_trace = why_trace
var old_how_trace = how_trace
why_trace = why_trace + " I need to know whether you have approved experience "
parent.frame2.document.clear ();
parent.frame2.document.write (why_trace + "<br>")
if ( library_worked_5_years () == "yes" || info_handling_5_years () == "yes"  ) {
why_trace = old_why_trace
how_trace = how_trace + " I concluded that you do have approved experience ";
return "yes"}
else {how_trace = old_how_trace;
why_trace = old_why_trace
return "no"}
}


function library_worked_5_years () {
var old_why_trace = why_trace
var old_how_trace = how_trace
why_trace = why_trace + " I need to know whether you have 5 years or more experience
of library/information work "
```

```
parent.frame2.document.clear ();
parent.frame2.document.write (why_trace + "<br>")
if (confirm ("Have you worked in a library or information unit for 5 years or
more?")) {
why_trace = old_why_trace
how_trace = how_trace + " You told me that you have 5 or more years library/informa-
tion work experience ";
return "yes"}
else {how_trace = old_how_trace;
why_trace = old_why_trace
return "no"}
}

function info_handling_5_years () {
var old_why_trace = why_trace
var old_how_trace = how_trace
why_trace = why_trace + " I need to know whether a significant part of your work for
5 years or more entailed information handling "
parent.frame2.document.clear ();
parent.frame2.document.write (why_trace + "<br>")
if (confirm ("Has a significant part of your work for 5 years or more entailed
information handling?")) {
why_trace = old_why_trace
how_trace = how_trace + " You told me that a significant part of your work for 5
years or more entailed information handling ";
return "yes"}
else {how_trace = old_how_trace;
why_trace = old_why_trace
return "no"}
}

</SCRIPT>
</HEAD>
<BODY>
<FORM>
<INPUT TYPE="button" VALUE="Start" onClick="start ()">
<INPUT TYPE="button" VALUE="Explain"
onClick="parent.frame2.document.clear ();
parent.frame2.document.write (how_trace + '<br>')">
</FORM>
</BODY>
</HTML>
```

As previously mentioned, negative explanation is not included in this version of
the program. Therefore, the Explain button to ask how the system came to its conclusion will display the system's line of reasoning only if the reader is indeed eligible for

the MA LIM. To enable the system to explain why a reader is *not* eligible, see the technique explained in the section "Negative Explanation" earlier in this chapter.

More User-Friendly Input

Displaying in a frame an explanation of why each particular question is being asked, as implemented in the previous section, is only a partial solution. It would be better if we could make such "why" explanations optional, displayed only if the reader clicks a Why ask? button.

However, more important, we may want to offer the reader a series of options along with each question. We may want to allow him or her to follow hyperlinks to additional information sources that may help answer the question.

For example, when our system asks, "Has a significant part of your work for 5 years or more entailed information handling?" the reader may be uncertain what is meant by *information handling*. We may therefore want to make the phrase *information handling* into a hyperlink that, when clicked, displays explanatory information.

In other words, we may want to present the reader with a question, but not at the same time disable other normal browser functions. We want to do this while still retaining our basic reasoning mechanism allowing rules to be linked together to form complex chains of reasoning:

1. IF A is true
2.   AND B is true
3. THEN C is true
4. ELSE C is not true

5. IF D is true
6.   OR E is true
7. THEN A is true
8. ELSE A is not true

9. IF F is true
10. THEN B is true
11. ELSE B is not true

However, we will need to modify parts of the code surrounding this basic mechanism. Our problem is caused by the fact that once JavaScript begins to process a chain of reasoning like this, it does not stop until it reaches its conclusion. Using the example above, once JavaScript begins to process the first rule (line 1), it will not stop until it has proved that C is or is not true (line 3 or 4). Displaying a prompt or confirm box—for example, at line 5, asking the reader to state whether or not D is true—will *temporarily* suspend JavaScript's activity, but only until the reader has clicked OK or Cancel. Until the reader does this, the remaining chain of reasoning is stacked up just waiting to resume.

Assuming that we do *not* wish to use a confirm or prompt box, let us translate this into a simplified version of our prototype system:

Eligibility rule
1 IF you have a good degree
2. AND you have approved experience
3. THEN you are eligible for the MA in Library and Information Management
4. ELSE you are not eligible for the MA in Library and Information Management

Good degree rule
5. Display a form asking whether the reader has an honors degree of class 2 (ii) or above
6. IF the value of the form is "Yes"
7. THEN you have a good degree
8. ELSE you do not have a good degree

Approved experience rule
9. Display a form asking whether the reader has worked for 5 years or more in a library or information unit
10. IF the value of the form is "Yes"
11. THEN you have approved experience
12. ELSE you do not have approved experience

JavaScript will begin by trying to prove line 1. To do this, it needs to prove line 7. Therefore, it must process lines 5 and 6. If line 7 is true, line 1 is true, and JavaScript will go on to investigate line 2, and so on.

However, the point is that JavaScript will not stop at lines 5 and 9. It will not wait for the reader to read the questions, never mind answer them or click any hyperlinks for further information.

What's worse, JavaScript will reach its conclusion as to whether a reader is or is not eligible despite the fact that he or she has not been given the chance to answer any questions! This conclusion will *always* be that the reader is *not* eligible, because JavaScript has no evidence that either a good degree or approved experience is possessed.

What we must do is arrange things so that each time we want to ask the reader a question, JavaScript has in fact come to the *end* of its chain of reasoning and has therefore released the browser's normal functions. We can do this by allowing JavaScript to cycle repeatedly through its chain of reasoning, with each cycle resulting in a question asked to the reader. The reader's action of answering the question will trigger the next cycle, and so on until there are no more questions left to ask the reader. Only at this point will JavaScript display its conclusions.

JavaScript will work repeatedly through the following cycle:

1. Go through the entire chain of reasoning to establish a question the reader needs to be asked.
2. Ask the reader that question, then draw any conclusions that depend on the answer.

The point is that it is the reader's action of answering each question (line 2) that triggers the start of a new cycle (line 1). Each time the reader answers a question, the answer is stored so that it does not appear on the list of questions yet to be answered. When there are no more outstanding questions, the whole process is completed.

Here is the pseudo-code we will subsequently translate into JavaScript:

Create variables
eligibility_status="unknown"
experience_status="unknown"
degree_status="unknown"
next question to be asked=""

Cycle rule
RUN the *eligible* rule
IF *next question to be asked* is empty, then display the value of *eligibility_status*
    (this means that the program has reached its conclusion)
ELSE ask the question stored in *next question to be asked*

Eligible rule
IF the *degree* rule returns "yes"
    AND the *approved_experience* rule returns "yes"
THEN *eligibility_status* = "yes"
ELSE *eligibility_status* = "no"

Degree rule
IF *degree_status*="unknown"
    THEN *next_question_to_be_asked* = "Have you an honors degree of 2 (ii) or
      above?"
      AND return "unknown" as the value of the *degree* rule
IF *degree_status*="yes"
    THEN return "yes" as the value of the *degree* rule
IF *degree_status*="no"
    THEN return "no" as the value of the *degree* rule

Approved experience rule
IF *approved_experience_status*="unknown"
    THEN *next_question_to_be_asked*="Have you worked in a library/information
      unit for at least 5 years?"
      AND return "unknown" as the value of the *approved_experience* rule

IF *approved_experience_status*="yes"
    THEN return "yes" as the value of the *approved_experience* rule
IF *approved_experience_status*="no"
    THEN return "no" as the value of the *approved_experience* rule

Note that if we instruct JavaScript to process the **cycle** rule, it will go through the entire chain of reasoning and end up with the variable *next_question_to_be_asked* containing "Have you worked in a library/information unit for at least 5 years?" and a partial conclusion that the reader is not eligible (because he or she has not yet answered any question).

Note that the **degree** rule gave *next_question_to_be_asked* the value "Have you an honors degree of 2 (ii) or above?" However, the **approved experience** rule overwrote this with "Have you worked in a library/information unit for at least 5 years?" which is the value of *next_question_to_be_asked* at the end of the first cycle. Next time through the cycle, because the question "Have you worked in a library/information unit for at least 5 years?" was answered in the first cycle (and therefore the value of *approved_experience_status* is not "unknown"), the **approved experience** rule will *not* this time overwrite the value of *next_question_to_be_asked*. Therefore, at the end of the second cycle, its value will be "Have you an honors degree of 2 (ii) or above?" This happens in each cycle until there are no more questions to be asked—at which time *next_question_to_be_asked* will be empty, thus fulfilling the condition of the second line of the **cycle** rule and ending the program.

It is the reader's action of answering the question that triggers each new cycle. We program this by including a call to process the **cycle** rule within the **onClick** event handler of the radio button the user will click to record his or her answer. Similarly, the "why" explanation is triggered by including it in the **onClick** event handler of the radio button labeled "Why ask?"

At the end of each cycle (prior to the reader instigating another cycle by clicking on an answer to the particular question being posed), normal browser functions are enabled. Therefore, hyperlinks and buttons to other information sources can be followed.

In our program, clicking on the Why ask? radio button calls the function **information_window ()**:

```
onClick='parent.frame1.information_window ()'
```

This function opens a new browser window and writes the contents of *why_trace* and a hyperlink labeled "More information" (as shown in Figure 5.9).

In the code below, this hyperlink is to the Alta Vista Internet search engine.

> **NOTE** Internet search engines allow you to search for documents containing keywords you specify. We explore ways of adding value to the process of keyword searching in Chapters 6 and 7.

Figure 5.9 A more flexible form of explanation.

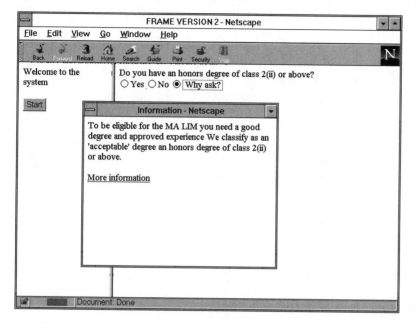

This window will behave like a normal browser window, into which you can write text, hyperlinks, and so on using **document.write** or into which you can load documents.

```
function information_window () {
new_window = window.open
("","Information","menubar=yes,scrollbars=yes,width=600,height=300")
new_window.document.clear ()
new_window.focus ()
new_window.document.write ("<HEAD><TITLE>Information</TITLE></HEAD><BODY>" + why_trace
+ "<br><A HREF='http://www.altavista.digital.com/'>More information</A><br></BODY>")
}
```

This is Program 5-8 on the website. Here is the top level document start.html.

```
<HTML>
<HEAD>
<TITLE>FRAME VERSION 2</TITLE>
</HEAD>
<FRAMESET COLS="25%, *">
<FRAME SRC = "doc1.html" NAME="frame1">
<FRAME SRC="dummy.html" NAME="frame2">
</FRAMESET>
</HTML>
```

The file dummy.html is a blank document:

```
<HTML>
<BODY>
</BODY>
</HTML>
```

Here are the contents of doc1.html:

```
<HTML>
<HEAD>
<SCRIPT LANGUAGE="JavaScript">

var experience_status = "unknown"
var good_degree_status = "unknown"
var do_list = "start"
var why_trace=""
var how_trace=""
var how_not_trace=""
var eligibility_status=""

function cycle () {
eligibility ()
if (do_list == "") {
parent.frame2.document.clear ()
if (eligibility_status == "yes") {parent.frame2.document.write (how_trace + "<br>")}
if (eligibility_status == "") {parent.frame2.document.write (how_not_trace + "<br>")}
}
else {ask_about (do_list) }
}

function ask_about (item) {
if (item != "") {
parent.frame2.document.clear ();
parent.frame2.document.write ("<FORM>" + item + "<br><INPUT TYPE='radio' NAME='rb1'
onClick='parent.frame1.record_answer (&quot;" + item + "&quot;, &quot;yes&quot;);
parent.frame1.cycle ()' >Yes <INPUT TYPE='radio' NAME='rb1'
onClick='parent.frame1.record_answer (&quot;" + item + "&quot;, &quot;no&quot;);
parent.frame1.cycle ()' >No <INPUT TYPE='radio' NAME='rb2' onClick='parent.frame1
.information_window ()'> Why ask? </FORM><br>")} }

function record_answer (item, item2) {
answer = item2
if (item == "Do you have an honors degree of class 2(ii) or above?")
{good_degree_status  = answer}
if (item == "Have you worked in a library or information unit for 5 or more years?")
{ experience_status = answer}
}
```

```
function eligibility () {
why_trace = ""
how_trace = ""
how_not_trace = ""
do_list = ""
eligibility_status = ""
var old_why_trace = why_trace
why_trace = why_trace + " To be eligible for the MA LIM you need a good degree and
approved experience "
if (good_degree () == "yes" && approved_experience () == "yes")
{why_trace=old_why_trace; how_trace = how_trace + "Therefore you are eligible ";
eligibility_status = "yes";
return "yes"}
else {
how_not_trace = how_not_trace + "\nBoth a good degree and approved experience are
required for eligibility. \nTherefore you are not eligible. ";
return "no"}
}


function approved_experience () {
var old_why_trace = why_trace
why_trace = why_trace + " I need to know if you have the required level of relevant
work experience "
if (experience_status == "unknown") {do_list = "Have you worked in a library or
information unit for 5 or more years?"; return "unknown"}
if (experience_status == "yes") {why_trace=old_why_trace; how_trace = how_trace +
"You do have sufficient relevant work experience. "; return "yes"}
if (experience_status == "no") {why_trace=old_why_trace;
how_not_trace = how_not_trace + "\nYou do NOT have enough relevant work experience.
";
return "no"}
}


function good_degree () {
var old_why_trace = why_trace
why_trace = why_trace + " We classify as an 'acceptable' degree an honors degree of
class 2(ii) or above."
if (good_degree_status  == "unknown") {do_list = "Do you have an honors degree of
class 2(ii) or above?"; return "unknown"}
if (good_degree_status  == "yes") {why_trace=old_why_trace; how_trace = how_trace +
"You told me you have a good honors degree. "; return "yes"}
if (good_degree_status  == "no") {why_trace=old_why_trace;
how_not_trace = how_not_trace + "\nYou told me that you do NOT have an honors degree
of class 2(ii) or above. ";
return "no"}
}
```

```
function information_window () {
new_window = window.open
("","Information","menubar=yes,scrollbars=yes,width=600,height=300")
new_window.document.clear ()
new_window.focus ()
new_window.document.write ("<HEAD><TITLE>Information</TITLE></HEAD><BODY>" + why_trace
+ "<P><A HREF='http://www.altavista.digital.com/'>More information</A><P></BODY>")
}

</SCRIPT>
</HEAD>
<BODY>
Welcome to the system
<FORM>
<INPUT TYPE="button" VALUE="Start"
onClick="experience_status = 'unknown';
good_degree_status = 'unknown';
do_list = 'start';
why_trace='';
how_trace='';
how_not_trace='';
eligibility_status='';
cycle ('')">
</FORM>
</BODY>
</HTML>
```

Figure 5.10 The system asks a question.

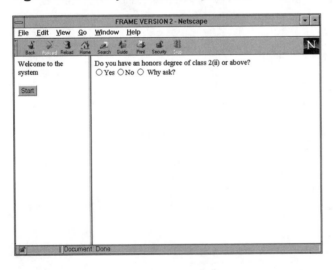

Figure 5.11 The reader asks why it is being asked.

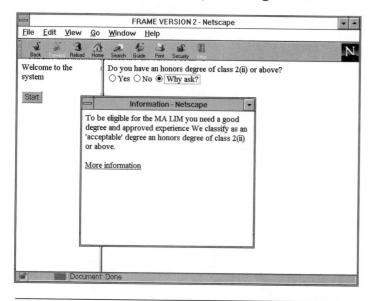

Note that [/n] tells JavaScript to start a new line when displaying text in an alert box. Figures 5.10 through 5.12 illustrate the system in interaction with a reader.

Figure 5.12 The system displays its conclusion.

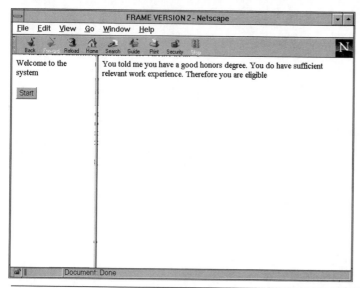

STORING KNOWLEDGE IN

Your Web Pages

In Chapter 5, we saw how certain types of knowledge can be represented as IF... THEN rules. However, concepts can be related in a great number of ways, of which causal relationships of this type are only one. Other types of conceptual relationships can be equally important.

For example, *hierarchical relationships* are central to many areas of our knowledge. Hierarchical relationships are one sort of relationship that can be represented by what are known as *semantic networks*, in which concepts are shown as nodes and relationships between them as labeled arrows, as shown in Figure 6.1. This figure depicts an extract of a classification useful for organizing information about musical instruments. Such a classification could be used to organize a database or catalog of products for customers.

If we ask a music shop assistant for information on a particular instrument, we expect him or her to possess and act upon this knowledge of relationships between concepts. However, unless we directly imbue computer systems with such knowledge, they will behave extremely unintelligently. If a computerized musical instrument catalog or database has information indexed under *violins*, it will not know that this information is relevant to a request for *stringed instruments* unless we tell it.

If a customer is searching for information on *stringed* instruments, information on *violins* and *double basses* is relevant because they are types of stringed instruments. Similarly, if a customer wants information on *saxophones*, he or she would expect information on the various types of saxophones: *alto, baritone,* and *tenor*.

Let us take another example, which will form the basis of our next prototype system. Imagine that we are searching for information on tourism in Europe. We approach our friendly librarian, who assures us that the library possesses no relevant titles on this subject. We would not be impressed if we then went to the library's shelves and found books on tourism in Italy, France, Scotland, and Germany! This

Figure 6.1 Part of a musical instruments classification.

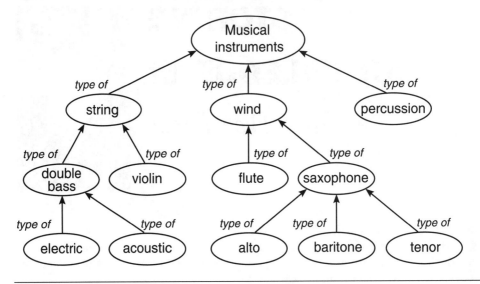

would hardly be intelligent behavior on the part of the librarian. As humans, we implicitly know that information relating to Europe includes information relating to Europe's component countries, which include Italy, France, Scotland, Germany, and others. However, if we want our Web pages to exhibit the sort of intelligence expected of—but not displayed by—our hypothetical librarian, we need to imbue our pages with this type of knowledge.

Semantic Networks

Although we can give computers knowledge of conceptual relationships by using semantic networks, we are a long way away from being able to imbue them with the wide range of conceptual relationships that make up what we might call "common sense."

Nevertheless, providing such knowledge in small, narrowly defined specialist areas can still be useful. Examples include developing intelligent product catalogs for customers or intelligent help systems based on knowledge of conceptual relationships.

We will take as our example the problem of searching for information on the Internet. Search engines such as Alta Vista, Excite, and Yahoo! allow us to search using keywords. If we enter the words *tourism* and *Europe*, the search engine will retrieve all the documents in its index that contain these words. The problem is that many search engines may behave like our hypothetical librarian, not including in the search related words like *hotels, travel, United Kingdom,* and *Scotland.*

In fact, a number of search engines do offer a range of more sophisicated search options. Engines like Alta Vista and Euroferret offer *query expansion facilities* that suggest related words not included in your original search query. These words are suggested because they also occur frequently in documents that are relevant to your query. Such search engines will allow you to select those terms you would like to include in your search.

For our example, we will build a small intelligent system that, when given a keyword representing a topic, will automatically find keywords for all *subordinate* topics. Facilities such as this can operate in a variety of ways. For example, they could work behind the scenes, automatically adding keywords to expand a search. In this way, a search for information on a broad topic will automatically find information also containing its narrower component topics.

However, equally if not more problematic when using an Internet search engine is how to *narrow* the search rather than how to broaden it. In this case, the same mechanism could be used to suggest narrower, more specific keywords to the person wanting the information. He or she could select which terms, if any, should be substituted for the broader term initially entered into the search engine.

It is important to note that the same principles apply to *any* subject domain in which one concept includes other, more specific concepts. The techniques presented here are therefore of extremely wide applicability. However, it must also be noted that, particularly if you are developing Web pages to be processed by client machines as opposed to a server, the most suitable topics will entail small, narrowly defined specialist subject areas. Handling of broader areas of knowledge will require large volumes of data and rapid database access mechanisms.

The subject area we will use to introduce the basic techniques has been selected on the grounds of simplicity and familiarity to the reader. A more realistic example is given after the basic introduction. If asked to find information on Europe, our first system will automatically include information on Europe's component countries—Britain, Germany, and so on—and the components of these countries (England, Northern Ireland, etc.).

If asked for information on Britain, our system will automatically include England, Northern Ireland, Scotland, and Wales. However, the amount of knowledge used by the system is extremely small, consisting at the top level of only Europe and North America and within these only a small number of countries. When asked for information on the world, the system will display the whole of its knowledge (see Figure 6.2).

If asked for information on a continent or country it knows nothing about, the system will display unchanged the name it has been given. This facility would be useful, for example, in the case of an intelligent front end to a Web search engine. The system could check whether it has any knowledge of what it is being asked for. If it has, it can add value to the search by including any subordinate component concepts. If not, it can pass the request unchanged to the search engine.

We can build semantic networks representing this type of hierarchical knowledge by using JavaScript *objects*. We will do this to build our prototype system. First, we concentrate on the mechanism for finding subordinate concepts, then we explore how to use the output of the mechanism to improve searches using a search engine such as Alta Vista.

The hierarchical knowledge we will use in this small demonstration system is as follows:

```
World
        Europe
                Britain
                        England
                        Northern Ireland
                        Scotland
                        Wales
                Germany
        North America
                Canada
                United States
```

In the interests of clarity and simplicity, so that we can concentrate on how the basic mechanism works, our list is very partial. Of the continents, only Europe and North America are included, and Europe is subdivided into only Germany and Britain.

Each element we want to subdivide we represent as an *array* object. This array will have a *name* and a set of *narrower terms*. We can refer to and retrieve these in order to manipulate the hierarchy, as we will see below. The **Europe** object is as follows:

```
Europe["name"] = "Europe"
Europe["narrower terms"][0] = Germany
Europe["narrower terms"][1] = Britain
```

The two narrower terms are also arrays, which means they can themselves be subdivided using the "narrower terms" array. The **Britain** object is as follows:

```
Britain["name"] = "Britain"
Britain["narrower terms"][0] = "England"
```

Figure 6.2 The system's response to the keyword _World_.

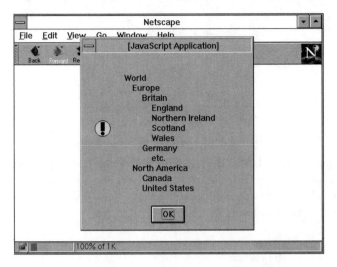

```
Britain["narrower terms"][1] = "Northern Ireland"
Britain["narrower terms"][2] = "Scotland"
Britain["narrower terms"][3] = "Wales"
```

The narrower terms in this case are strings, not arrays, because we do not want to subdivide them further.

We will add a top-level object—**World**—so that we can include the next highest concepts as narrower terms in its array (thus allowing them to be searched for easily):

```
World["name"] = "World"
World["narrower terms"][0] = Europe
World["narrower terms"][1] = North_America
```

Here is our JavaScript code for this part of the program. Although very clear, the following code is not the most economical way of setting up a semantic network. A more economical version will be given in the section "Using a Larger Knowledge Base" later in this chapter.

```
World = new Array ()
Europe = new Array ()
Britain = new Array ()
Germany = new Array ()
North_America = new Array ()

World["narrower terms"] = new Array (Europe, North_America)
Europe["narrower terms"] = new Array (Britain, Germany)
```

```
Britain["narrower terms"] = new Array ("England", "Northern Ireland", "Scotland",
"Wales")
Germany["narrower terms"] = new Array ("etc.")
North_America["narrower terms"] = new Array ("Canada", "United States")

World["name"] = "World"
Europe["name"] = "Europe"
Britain["name"] = "Britain"
Germany["name"] = "Germany"
North_America["name"] = "North America"
```

This knowledge structure is represented in diagrammatic form in Figure 6.3.

Having set up our small hierarchical knowledge structure in this way, we can now write the program that will manipulate it. In pseudo-code, this program runs as follows. This particular example is for a request for information on Europe. It will call the **findSelectedKeywords** rule with the command:

```
findSelectedKeywords ("Europe", keywords)
```

Here is a pseudo-code version of the rules:

> function **findSelectedKeywords** (*term*, *keywords*)
> IF what is passed to this rule in *keywords* has a *name* property
> THEN
>> IF what is passed to this rule in *term* = the *name* property of *keywords*
>> THEN call the **expandKeyword** rule and pass to it what is in *keywords*
> Having done the above, do exactly the same (that is, call the
> **findSelectedKeywords** rule recursively) with each of *keyword*'s narrower terms

> function **expandKeyword** (*keyword*)
> for each of *keyword*'s narrower terms
> IF it has not got an array of narrower terms
> THEN add it to what is already in the variable *list*
> ELSE pass it to the **findSelectedKeywords** rule.

Here is the relevant code:

```
1. function findSelectedKeyword (term, keyword) {
2. if (keyword["name"] != null) {
3. if (term == keyword["name"]) {
4. list += "\n"
5. var tab = ""
6. expandKeyword (keyword, tab)}
7. for (i in keyword["narrower terms"]) {
8. findSelectedKeyword (term, keyword["narrower terms"][i])}}
9. }

10. function expandKeyword (keyword, tab) {
```

Figure 6.3 The knowledge structure.

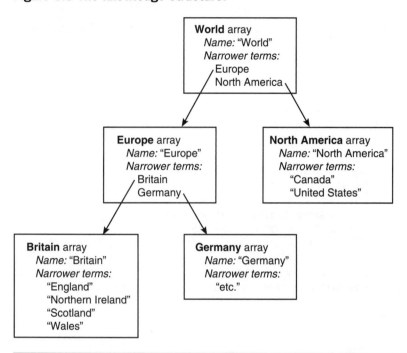

```
11. list += tab + keyword["name"]
12. for (i in keyword["narrower terms"]) {
13. if (keyword["narrower terms"][i]["name"] == null)
14. {list += "\n" + (tab + "    ") + keyword["narrower terms"][i]}
15. else {
16. list += "\n"
17. expandKeyword (keyword["narrower terms"][i], tab + "    ")}}
18. }
```

Note that as the rules are called recursively (line 8 calls line 1, and line 17 calls line 10), the keywords found at each subordinate level in the hierarchy are stored in a variable list. We need to create this variable at the beginning of the program. We also need to add instructions to actually run the program—to ask the reader to type in a keyword, then to pass this keyword to the rules we have written, and finally to display the results to the reader:

```
var list = " "

term = prompt ("Enter a search request", " ")
expand (term, World)
```

```
if (list == "") {list = term}
alert (list)
```

Now here is the complete code (Program 6-1 on the website), followed by a detailed explanation of how it works.

```
<HTML>
<HEAD>
<SCRIPT>

World = new Array ()
Europe = new Array ()
Britain = new Array ()
Germany = new Array ()
North_America = new Array ()

World["narrower terms"] = new Array (Europe, North_America)
Europe["narrower terms"] = new Array (Britain, Germany)
Britain["narrower terms"] = new Array ("England", "Northern Ireland", "Scotland",
"Wales")
Germany["narrower terms"] = new Array ("etc.")
North_America["narrower terms"] = new Array ("Canada", "United States")

World["name"] = "World"
Europe["name"] = "Europe"
Britain["name"] = "Britain"
Germany["name"] = "Germany"
North_America["name"] = "North America"

list = ""

function findSelectedKeyword (term, keyword) {
if (keyword["name"] != null) {
if (term == keyword["name"]) {
list += "\n"
var tab = ""
expandKeyword (keyword, tab)}
for (i in keyword["narrower terms"]) {
findSelectedKeyword (term, keyword["narrower terms"][i])
}}}

function expandKeyword (keyword, tab) {
list += tab + keyword["name"]
for (i in keyword["narrower terms"]) {
if (keyword["narrower terms"][i]["name"] == null)
{list += "\n" + (tab + "      ") + keyword["narrower terms"][i]}
else {
```

```
list += "\n"
expandKeyword (keyword["narrower terms"][i], tab + "        ")}}
}

term = prompt ("Type in country ", " ")
findSelectedKeyword (term, World)
if (list == "") {list = '"' + term + '"'}
alert (list)

</SCRIPT>
</HEAD>
</HTML>
```

Below is a full description of how the program works. As a given rule is processed, it is listed in full with the values that apply to it. As a rule is called recursively (in other words, as it calls itself), it is listed in full again with the new values it has been passed to process. Thus, line 6 of the **findSelectedKeyword** rule below recursively calls the **findSelectedKeyword** rule (itself). The whole rule is therefore listed again (lines 7 through 12) with the new values that apply in this second cycle.

If we start the program off with the following call:

```
findSelectedKeyword ("Europe", World)
```

the program will run as follows. The parts of the pseudo-code that apply at each stage as this particular instance is run are shown in bold. In the interests of clarity, code relating purely to formatting (adding new lines and tab spaces in the *list* variable as it is built up) are not included.

1. **function findSelectedKeyword ("Europe", World)**
2. **IF World["name"] exists — i.e. "World"**
3. **THEN**
4.   IF "Europe" = "World"
5.   THEN expandKeyword (World)
6. **findSelectedKeyword ("Europe", Europe)** then findSelectedKeyword each of World's other narrower terms

7. **function findSelectedKeyword ("Europe", Europe) [called by line 6]**
8. **IF Europe["name"] exists — i.e. "Europe"**
9. **THEN**
10.   **IF "Europe" = "Europe"**
11.   **THEN expandKeyword (Europe)**
12. findSelectedKeyword ("Europe", Britain) then findSelectedKeyword each of Europe's other narrower terms

13. **function expandKeyword (Europe) [called by line 11]**
14. **add Europe["name"] (i.e. "Europe") to list**

15. **for each of Europe's narrower terms (i.e. Britain and Germany)**
16. IF it is not an array with a "name" property
17. THEN add it to list
18. **ELSE expandKeyword it**

19. **function expandKeyword (Britain) [called by line 18]**
20. **add Britain["name"] (i.e. "Britain") to list**
21. **for each of Britain's narrower terms**
22. **IF it is not an array with a "name" property**
23. **THEN add it to list (thus "England," "Northern Ireland," "Scotland," and "Wales" are added to list)**
24. ELSE expandKeyword it

25. **function expandKeyword (Germany) [called by line 15 and 18]**
26. **add Germany["name"] (i.e. "Germany") to list**
27. **for each of Germany's narrower terms**
28. **IF it is not an array with a "name" property**
29. **THEN add it to list (thus "etc." is added to list — recall that we made "etc." Germany's subdivision!)**
30. ELSE expandKeyword it

The example above will result in the screen shown in Figure 6.4.

Adding Advanced Search Capabilities

Let us now extend the system so that instead of displaying information in an alert message, our system automatically conducts a search using the advanced search option of the Internet search engine Alta Vista. Unlike its simple search option which allows free text input, Alta Vista's advanced search option requires the reader to construct requests using correct syntax. The advantage is that complex searches can be constructed in which the searcher exercises considerable control over how the search will be conducted.

Alta Vista's advanced search option accepts the following as valid requests:

- A single keyword

- More than one keyword if they are: enclosed in double quotes to make them a phrase, or connected by one or more of the Boolean operators AND, OR, NEAR, or AND NOT

Thus a request for *tourism in Europe* would not be valid in an advanced search. However, *"tourism in Europe"* would retrieve documents containing this exact phrase. The request *tourism AND Europe* would find documents containing both words, *tourism OR Europe* documents containing either word, and *tourism AND NOT Europe* documents containing *tourism* but not *Europe*. Asking for *tourism NEAR Europe* would find documents in which the words *tourism* and *Europe* appear within 10 words of each other.

Figure 6.4 The system's response to the query *Europe*.

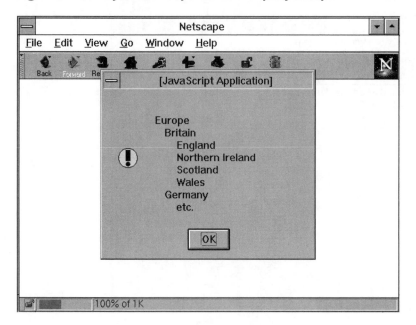

Alta Vista offers a range of other options allowing searches to be specified in a variety of ways. More information on this topic is available from Alta Vista's search pages.

Our small demonstration system will ask the reader to enter a query. If the query is a concept known to the system, it will attempt to "add value" by including the concept's narrower component concepts in the search. It will enclose the concepts in double-quote marks so that, for example, "United States" or "Northern Ireland" will be treated as phrases rather than as separate independent words. It will also connect the keywords using the Boolean operator OR.

Thus a request for *Britain* will result in the following Alta Vista query:

"*Britain*" OR "*England*" OR "*Northern Ireland*" OR "*Scotland*" OR "*Wales*"

Alta Vista will present this query to the reader, as shown in Figure 6.5. The reader may edit the query in the text area as he or she wishes, before clicking Submit to send it to Alta Vista's search engine.

The Alta Vista search results will be displayed as though a search had been conducted from its own search page (Figure 6.6).

Figure 6.5 The expanded query, ready for editing if required.

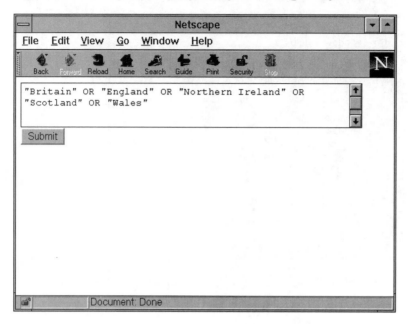

Now here is the code (Program 6-2 on the website), followed by some explanatory notes. Differences between this new version and the previous one are shown in bold.

```
1.  <HTML>
2.  <HEAD>
3.  <SCRIPT>

4.  World = new Array ()
5.  Europe = new Array ()
6.  Britain = new Array ()
7.  Germany = new Array ()
8.  North_America = new Array ()

9.  World["narrower terms"] = new Array (Europe, North_America)
10. Europe["narrower terms"] = new Array (Britain, Germany)
11. Britain["narrower terms"] = new Array ("England", "Northern Ireland", "Scotland",
    "Wales")
12. Germany["narrower terms"] = new Array ("etc.")
13. North_America["narrower terms"] = new Array ("Canada", "United States")

14. World["name"] = "World"
```

Figure 6.6 The Alta Vista search results.

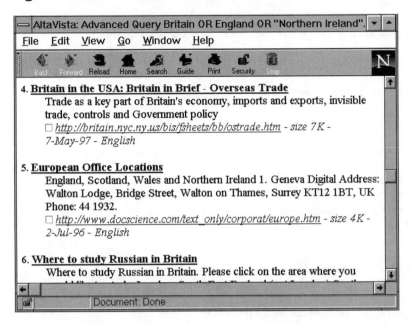

```
AltaVista: Advanced Query Britain OR England OR "Northern Ireland".
File   Edit   View   Go   Window   Help
```

4. Britain in the USA: Britain in Brief - **Overseas Trade**
   Trade as a key part of Britain's economy, imports and exports, invisible
   trade, controls and Government policy
   ☐ *http://britain.nyc.ny.us/bis/fsheets/bb/ostrade.htm - size 7K -*
   7-May-97 - English

5. European Office Locations
   England, Scotland, Wales and Northern Ireland 1. Geneva Digital Address:
   Walton Lodge, Bridge Street, Walton on Thames, Surrey KT12 1BT, UK
   Phone: 44 1932.
   ☐ *http://www.docscience.com/text_only/corporat/europe.htm - size 4K -*
   2-Jul-96 - English

6. Where to study Russian in Britain
   Where to study Russian in Britain. Please click on the area where you

`Document: Done`

```
15. Europe["name"] = "Europe"
16. Britain["name"] = "Britain"
17. Germany["name"] = "Germany"
18. North_America["name"] = "North America"

19. keywordsArray = new Array ()
20. count = 0

21. function findSelectedKeyword (term, keyword) {
22. if (keyword["name"] != null) {
23. if (term == keyword["name"]) {
24. var tab = ""
25. expandKeyword (keyword, tab)}
26. for (i in keyword["narrower terms"]) {
27. findSelectedKeyword (term, keyword["narrower terms"][i])
28. }}}

29. function expandKeyword (keyword, tab) {
30. keywordsArray[count] = '"' + keyword["name"] + '"'
31. count += 1
```

```
32. for (i in keyword["narrower terms"]) {
33. if (keyword["narrower terms"][i]["name"] == null)
34. {
35. keywordsArray[count] = '"' + keyword["narrower terms"][i] + '"'
36. count += 1
37. }
38. else {
39. expandKeyword (keyword["narrower terms"][i], tab + "    ")}
40. }
41. }

42. function processKeywords () {
43. var list = ""
44. for (i in keywordsArray)
45. {if (keywordsArray.length - 1 != i) {list += keywordsArray[i] + " OR "}
46. else {list += keywordsArray[i]}}
47. return list
48. }

49. function sendQuery (query) {
50. fullQuery = "http://alta vista.digital.com/cgi-
bin/query?pg=aq&what=web&kl=&fmt=.&q="
51. + escape (query) + "&r=&d0=21%2FMar%2F86&d1="
52. location.href=fullQuery
53. }

54. term = prompt ("Type in country ", " ")
55. findSelectedKeyword (term, World)
56. if (keywordsArray[0] == null) {keywordsArray[0] = '"' + term + '"'}
57. var query = processKeywords ()

58. document.write ("<FORM NAME='input'><TEXTAREA NAME=q COLS=54 ROWS=3
WRAP=virtual>"
59. + query
60. + "</TEXTAREA><INPUT TYPE='button' VALUE='Submit' onClick = 'sendQuery
(this.form.q.value)'></FORM><br>")

// the next line clears the previous value of "query" from the text area

61. document.input.reset ()

62. </SCRIPT>
63. </HEAD>
64. </HTML>
```

The first lines that are executed are lines 4 through 19, which set up the knowledge base by creating arrays. Line 20 sets up the variable *count* for later use in the

expandKeyword function (lines 29 through 41). Lines 21 through 53 consist of functions, which are therefore not executed until they are called. So, the next commands to be executed are lines 54 through 61. Line 54 displays the input box to the reader, and line 55 passes the keyword(s) typed by the reader to the **findSelectedKeyword** function (lines 21 through 28).

Instead of cumulatively adding the keywords to a *list* variable as in the previous version of the program, the keywords are added to an array object, **keywordsArray** to allow for easy manipulation as we add the Alta Vista syntax. This array is of the form:

```
keywordsArray[1] = "Britain"
keywordsArray[2] = "England"
keywordsArray[3] = "Northern Ireland"
keywordsArray[4] = "Scotland"
keywordsArray[5] = "Wales"
```

This array is built in the **expandKeyword** function (lines 29 through 41), which increases the global variable *count* by 1 each time a keyword is added (lines 31 and 36), thus creating the numbering for the array as it is built. The function **expandKeyword** takes each element of the array and first surrounds it with double quotes, so that any phrase consisting of two or more words will be treated by Alta Vista as a phrase and not as distinct words. The function **processKeywords** combines the keywords using the Boolean operator OR. It checks when the penultimate keyword is being processed so as to make sure not to add OR after the final keyword.

When **findSelectedKeyword** has done its work, line 56 checks whether the system has been able to add any value to the reader's original query. If it has not (that is, if **keywordsArray[0]** is empty), line 56 simply surrounds the original query with double-quotation marks (so that it will obey the syntax required by Alta Vista's advanced search option even if it is a phrase containing spaces). Line 57 processes the query (whether it has had value added to it or not) using the **processKeywords** function, which adds Boolean OR operators if necessary to separate multiple keywords.

The **document.write** command (line 58) displays a text area on the screen and places the query within it, in case the reader wants to alter it in some way. When he or she clicks the Submit button, the function **sendQuery** (lines 49 through 53) is passed the final query (that is, the value of the text area) and combines it into a URL to be sent to the Alta Vista search engine. This particular URL will send the query to the U.S. Alta Vista site. The URL for the European English-language site is shown below.

Note that in the **sendQuery** function, the query becomes **escape (query)**, as shown in line 51. This is necessary if we want to send information in a URL containing certain characters, including ampersands, blank spaces, equal signs, plus signs, or question marks. The **escape** function converts information containing these characters into a form acceptable in a URL. The **unescape** function will change them back again. Thus:

```
escape ("United States")
```

will convert "United States" into:

```
United%20States
```

which can be included in a URL—in our case, a URL containing our request to Alta Vista's search engine. The line:

```
unescape (United%20States)
```

reverses the process.

   Combining the query into a URL like this is a quick way of submitting the query. It assumes a number of choices on the part of the reader—namely, that the search should be a Web search (as opposed to a USENET search), that the start date of the search should be Alta Vista's default (that is, March 21, 1986), and that no ranking order for the retrieved documents should be specified. The URL includes a number of codes specifying such factors. In fact, these codes are the names of input form elements on the Alta Vista search page. These codes, shown in Table 6.1, relate to Alta Vista's page at the time of writing. They may change, but the elements may easily be discovered by loading Alta Vista's page into your browser, then selecting the View Source (or equivalent) option.

   Alternative values may be put after these codes. For example, after the *kl* code indicating that the search should be for documents in a particular language, options include the following, among others:

   "" = any language
   zh = Chinese
   cz = Czech
   da = Danish
   nl = Dutch

Table 6.1 Alta Vista Input Form Elements

Element	Explanation
"http://alta vista.digital.com/cgi-bin/query?pg=aq	
&what=web	Specifies a Web search.
&kl=	Specifies language of documents to be searched for.
&fmt=	Specifies how detailed the document summaries should be.
&q=" + escape (query) + "	The query to go into Alta Vista's Search box.
&r=	Specifies what should go into the Results ranking criteria box.
&d0=21%2FMar%2F86	Start date for the search.
&d1="	End date for the search.

```
en = English
et = Estonian
```

The full list for this code, along with all the others, can be seen by calling up Alta Vista's search page, then selecting View Source (or equivalent) from your browser's menu. Others include:

```
what=web (or Usenet.)
fmt=n.
```

The last option instructs Alta Vista to show only the number of relevant documents retrieved (with no further details). The European English-language site currently also offers the additional options:

```
c (compact form)
d (detailed form).
```

If we want to enter our search in Alta Vista's Results ranking criteria box instead of the main Search box, we can change our URL as follows:

```
"http://alta vista.digital.com/cgi-bin/query?pg=aq&what=web&kl=&fmt=.&q=&r=" + escape
(query) + "&d0=21%2FMar%2F86&d1="
```

The equivalent URL for the European English-language site, specifying that the query should go into the main Search box, would be as follows:

```
"http://www.alta vista.telia.com/cgi-bin/query?mss=gbr%2Fsearch&country=gb&pg=
aq&what=web&kl=XX&q=" + escape (query) + "&r=&d0=21%2FMar%2F86&d1="
```

 TIP Entering the search into the Results ranking criteria box instead of or as well as the main Search box can be effective in that results appear in ranked order according to their relevance to your query. If you enter keywords in the Search box alone, retrieved documents containing your keywords will be presented in no particular order. Entering keywords in the Results ranking criteria box will result in what is known as a "best-match" search. This means that documents in which the keywords appear often and in significant places (such as in the title and early in the document) will be presented first. See Alta Vista's Help link for further information on searching techniques.

Giving the Reader More Options

If we want to allow our readers all the options offered by Alta Vista's main search page (as opposed to making the choices for them as above), we can do this in a variety of ways. The simplest would be to provide a hyperlink to Alta Vista, then instruct the reader to copy the search from the text area on our Web page, click the link to go to Alta Vista's search page, then paste the search into the Search and/or Results ranking criteria boxes.

A slightly more sophisticated approach would be to build into our Web page a form containing a series of select boxes and/or radio buttons reflecting the various options. When the reader clicks Submit, his or her replies are built into the URL in the same way that the query is built in. For example:

```
"http://alta vista.digital.com/cgi-bin/query?pg=aq&what="
+ reader's choice of web or Usenet
+ "&kl=&fmt="
+ reader's choice of format (c, d, n or . )
+ ".&q=&r="
+ escape (query)
+ "&d0="
+ escape (reader's choice of start date e.g. 21/Mar/96)
+ "&d1="
```

Another option is to create our own form using the same names for input elements as used in Alta Vista's own form (shown in Figure 6.7), then submit the form using an <INPUT TYPE="submit"> button. There would then be no need to process any of the reader's options or query text using **escape**. We could then add our own explanatory text to the form as required. It would be necessary to seek Alta Vista's agreement before doing this because, on the negative side, although the search results would be displayed through its own interface, we would in fact be bypassing the main Alta Vista search page and, of course, the advertisements placed there. On the positive side, if our Web page succeeds in adding value to the searching process, this may encourage new searchers to use Alta Vista, or indeed whichever other search engine we select.

Here is the relevant code (Program 6-3 on the website), based on Alta Vista's U.S. site:

```
<HTML>
<HEAD>
<SCRIPT>

World = new Array ()
Europe = new Array ()
Britain = new Array ()
Germany = new Array ()
North_America = new Array ()

World["narrower terms"] = new Array (Europe, North_America)
Europe["narrower terms"] = new Array (Britain, Germany)
```

Figure 6.7 A customized version of Alta Vista's form.

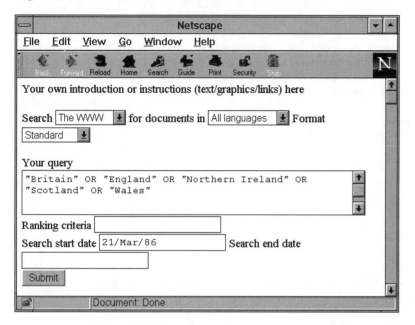

```
Britain["narrower terms"] = new Array ("England", "Northern Ireland", "Scotland",
"Wales")
Germany["narrower terms"] = new Array ("etc.")
North_America["narrower terms"] = new Array ("Canada", "United States")

World["name"] = "World"
Europe["name"] = "Europe"
Britain["name"] = "Britain"
Germany["name"] = "Germany"
North_America["name"] = "North America"

count = 0
keywordsArray = new Array ()

function findSelectedKeyword (term, keyword) {
if (keyword["name"] != null) {
if (term == keyword["name"]) {
var tab = ""
expandKeyword (keyword, tab)}
for (i in keyword["narrower terms"]) {
findSelectedKeyword (term, keyword["narrower terms"][i])
```

```
}}
}

function expandKeyword (keyword, tab) {
keywordsArray[count] = '"' + keyword["name"] + '"'
count += 1
for (i in keyword["narrower terms"]) {
if (keyword["narrower terms"][i]["name"] == null)
{
keywordsArray[count] = '"' + keyword["narrower terms"][i] + '"'
count += 1
}
else {
expandKeyword (keyword["narrower terms"][i], tab + "    ")}
}
}

function processKeywords () {
var list = ""
for (i in keywordsArray)
{if (keywordsArray.length - 1 != i) {list += keywordsArray[i] + " OR "}
else {list += keywordsArray[i]}}
return list
}

term = prompt ("Type in country ", " ")
if (term == null) {term = "Enter your query here"}
findSelectedKeyword (term, World)
if (keywordsArray[0] == null) {keywordsArray[0] = '"' + term + '"'}
var query = processKeywords ()

document.write ("Your own introduction or instructions (text/graphics/links)
here<FORM NAME='input' METHOD=GET ACTION='http://alta vista.digital.com/cgi-
bin/query'><INPUT TYPE=hidden NAME=pg VALUE=aq>Search <SELECT NAME=what><OPTION
VALUE=web SELECTED>The WWW<OPTION VALUE=Usenet>News</SELECT> for documents in <SELECT
NAME=kl><OPTION VALUE='' SELECTED>All languages<OPTION VALUE=en>English<OPTION
VALUE=da>Danish</SELECT> Give me only a precise document count <INPUT TYPE=checkbox
NAME=fmt VALUE=n><P>Your query <br><TEXTAREA NAME=q COLS=54 ROWS=3 WRAP=virtual>"
+ query
+ "</TEXTAREA><br> Ranking criteria <INPUT TYPE=text NAME=r VALUE=' '><br> Search
start date <INPUT TYPE=text NAME=d0 VALUE='21/Mar/86'> Search end date <INPUT
TYPE=text NAME=d1 VALUE=' '><br><INPUT TYPE=submit NAME='search'
VALUE=Submit></FORM><br>")
// next line clears the previous value of "query" from the text area

document.input.reset ()
```

```
</SCRIPT>
</HEAD>
</HTML>
```

Our prototype accepts only single keywords or phrases from the reader. To handle more complex queries—for example, "economic aspects" AND ("tourism" OR "leisure")—we would need to perform a more sophisticated analysis of the query.

Linguistic and other forms of analysis of readers' input are introduced in Chapter 7.

Using a Larger Knowledge Base

The larger your Web pages, the more slowly they will download to each reader's computer. The amount of code your readers' computers can handle has finite limitations. For these reasons, client-side JavaScript—that is, JavaScript interpreted by your readers' browsers as opposed to server-side JavaScript (discussed in Chapter 10)—is not well suited to applications requiring access to very large knowledge bases.

The most suitable client-side applications entail narrow, specialist areas of knowledge or problems that can be broken down into discrete sections, each of which entails a narrow, well-defined, and relatively small amount of specialist knowledge. In the latter case, Web pages corresponding to the different elements of the problem, each containing its own narrow specialist knowledge, can be loaded in turn. This process can be managed by, for example, maintaining global variables relevant to coordinating the different elements of the problem in the parent of a series of frames (see Chapter 4) into which the individual pages may be loaded. Alternatively, cookies could be used (see Chapter 3) to hold global data while various pages are loaded into the browser. Relevant server-side techniques are introduced in Chapter 10.

As well as selecting applications carefully, it is also useful to pay attention to economical coding so that your knowledge base does not take up more space than it has to. Indeed, in this chapter, we examine a more economical way of creating a semantic network-based knowledge base of concepts. At the same time, we explore a new, narrower area of knowledge more suited to realistic applications than was our previous example.

This new system will do exactly what our previous World system did in the sense that it will, when asked for information on a concept, automatically also retrieve information on that concept's narrower, component concepts. Our new subject relates to house plants. The basic knowledge is as follows:

```
plants
        house plants
                foliage plants
                        Coleus
                                Flame nettle
                                Brilliancy
```

                              Pink rainbow
                              Sunset
                Ivy
                              English ivy
                                    Cristata
                                    Golden snow
                                    Glacia
                                    Little diamond
                              Canary ivy
                                    Varigata
                                    Gloire de Marengo
                                    Harlequin
              Fig
                              Mistletoe fig
                              Fiddle leaf fig
                              Creeping fig
                              Rubber plant
                              Weeping fig
              Dracaena
                              Fragrant
                                    Linden
                                    Victoria
                              Madagascar dragon tree
                                    Tricolor
                                    Colorama
        flowering plants
                    African violet
                              Winter dream
                              Rapsodie Venus
                              Ballet Eva
                              Coral Caper
                              Blue nimbus

A more economical knowledge representation is achieved by using matching arrays. For example, using the approach employed *previously*, we would represent the first part of this "plant" knowledge relatively *uneconomically* as follows:

```
plants = new Array ()
housePlants = new Array ()
foliagePlants = new Array ()
etc.


plants["narrower terms"] = new Array (housePlants)
```

```
housePlants["narrower terms"] = new Array (foliagePlants, floweringPlants)
foliagePlants["narrower terms"] = new Array (Coleus, Ivy, Fig, Dracaena)
etc.

plants["name"] = "plants"
housePlants["name"] = "house plants"
foliagePlants["name"] = "foliage plants"
etc.
```

Representing the whole knowledge base in this way would entail some 39 commands. However, it can be represented more economically, using only 14 commands—plus an additional function. This function (the **create** function shown below) has six commands, but is reusable, thus displaying an increasing economy of scale in the case of larger knowledge bases, unlike our original knowledge representation. To illustrate this, let us assume for one moment that each plant has just *one* narrower term. We will extend this to include multiple terms shortly. We can represent this knowledge by using two arrays as follows:

```
plants[0] = "house plants"
plants[1] = "foliage plants"
plants[2] = "Coleus"
plants[3] = "Flame nettle"
etc.

narrowerTerms[0] = "foliage plants"
narrowerTerms[1] = "Coleus"
narrowerTerms[2] = "Flame nettle"
etc.
```

Thus **plant[0]** possesses the narrower term **narrowerTerms[0]**, **plant[1]** possesses **narrowerTerms[1]**, **plant[2] narrowerTerms[2]**, and so on. So we can retrieve information about the narrower terms of, say, "Coleus" by asking:

(a) Find the array number of "Coleus" in the plants array [2]
(b) Look up the same array number [2] in the narrowerTerms array.

This would retrieve "Flame nettle."

In fact, each plant has more than one narrower term. So all we need to do is, instead of typing in *one* narrower term for each plant, create an *array* of narrower terms.

```
plants[0] = "house plants"
plants[1] = "foliage plants"
plants[2] = "Coleus"
plants[3] = "Flame nettle"
plants[4] = "Brilliancy"
plants[5] = "Pink rainbow"
etc.
```

```
narrowerTerms[0][0] = "foliage plants"
narrowerTerms[0][1] = "flowering plants"

narrowerTerms[1][0] = "Coleus"
narrowerTerms[1][1] = "Ivy"
narrowerTerms[1][2] = "Fig"
narrowerTerms[1][3] = "Dracaena"

narrowerTerms[2][0] = "Flame nettle"
narrowerTerms[2][1] = "Brilliancy"
narrowerTerms[2][2] = "Pink rainbow"
```

etc.

These arrays are economically created by using a "master" array of all plant names, and allocating each an array number. The first (House plants") will be allocated the first number **plants[0]**, "foliage plants" the second **plants[1]**, and so on.

```
plants = new Array ("house plants", "foliage plants", "Coleus", "Flame nettle",
"Brilliancy", "Pink rainbow", "Sunset", "Ivy","English ivy", "Cristata", "Golden
snow", "Glacia", "Little diamond", "Canary ivy", "Varigata", "Gloire de Marengo",
"Harlequin", "Fig", "Mistletoe fig", "Fiddle leaf fig", "Creeping fig", "Rubber
plant", "Weeping fig", "Dracaena", "Fragrant", "Victoria", "Linden", "Madagascar
dragon tree", "Tricolo", "Colorama", "flowering plants", "African violet", "Winter
dream", "Rapsodie Venus", "Ballet Eva", "Coral Caper", "Blue nimbus")
```

Next we need to create the array to hold each plant's narrower terms

```
narrowerTerms = new Array ()
```

and then a function that will do the hard work for us. If we call this function with a command such as:

```
create ("house plants", "foliage plants", "flowering plants")
```

it will result in the **narrowerTerms** array's receiving the values:

```
narrowerTerms[0][0] = "foliage plants"
narrowerTerms[0][1] = "flowering plants"
```

If we call the function with:

```
create ("Fig", "Mistletoe fig", "Fiddle leaf fig", "Creeping fig", "Rubber plant",
"Weeping fig")
```

the following entries will be made to the **narrowerTerms** array:

```
narrowerTerms[17][0] = "Victoria"
narrowerTerms[17][1] = "Linden"
narrowerTerms[17][2] = "Mistletoe fig"
narrowerTerms[17][3] = "Fiddle leaf fig"
```

```
narrowerTerms[17][4] = "Creeping fig"
narrowerTerms[17][5] = "Rubber plant"
narrowerTerms[17][6] = "Weeping fig"
```

Here is the function. *NT* is short for "narrower terms" and is used in the function to avoid confusion with the array named **narrowerTerms**:

```
function create (plantName, NT) {
for (i in plants) {
if (plants[i] == plantName) {
    if (NT != null) {
    narrowerTerms[i] = new Array
    for (j = 1; j < create.arguments.length; j++) {
    narrowerTerms[i][(j-1)] = create.arguments[j]}}}
}}
```

We will use this function to create our arrays of narrower terms.

```
create ("house plants", "foliage plants", "flowering plants")
create ("foliage plants", "Coleus", "Ivy", "Fig", "Dracaena")
create ("Coleus", "Flame nettle", "Brilliancy", "Pink rainbow", "Sunset")
create ("Ivy","English ivy", "Canary ivy")
create ("English ivy", "Cristata", "Golden snow", "Glacia", "Little diamond")
create ("Canary ivy", "Varigata", "Gloire de Marengo", "Harlequin")
create ("Fig", "Mistletoe fig", "Fiddle leaf fig", "Creeping fig", "Rubber plant",
"Weeping fig")
create ("Dracaena", "Fragrant", "Madagascar dragon tree")
create ("Fragrant","Victoria", "Linden")
create ("Madagascar dragon tree", "Tricolo", "Colorama")
create ("flowering plants", "African violet")
create ("African violet", "Winter dream", "Rapsodie Venus", "Ballet Eva", "Coral
Caper", "Blue nimbus")
```

Now here is the code in full (Program 6-4 on the website).

```
<HTML>
<HEAD>
<SCRIPT>

plants = new Array ("house plants", "foliage plants", "Coleus", "Flame nettle",
"Brilliancy", "Pink rainbow", "Sunset", "Ivy","English ivy", "Cristata", "Golden
snow", "Glacia", "Little diamond", "Canary ivy", "Varigata", "Gloire de Marengo",
"Harlequin", "Fig", "Mistletoe fig", "Fiddle leaf fig", "Creeping fig", "Rubber
plant", "Weeping fig", "Dracaena", "Fragrant","Victoria", "Linden", "Madagascar drag-
on tree", "Tricolo", "Colorama", "flowering plants", "African violet", "Winter
dream", "Rapsodie Venus", "Ballet Eva", "Coral Caper", "Blue nimbus")

narrowerTerms = new Array ()
```

```
function create (object, NT) {
for (i in plants) {
if (plants[i] == object) {
    if (NT != null) {
    narrowerTerms[i] = new Array
    for (j = 1; j < create.arguments.length; j++) {
    narrowerTerms[i][(j-1)] = create.arguments[j]}}}
}}

create ("house plants", "foliage plants", "flowering plants")
create ("foliage plants", "Coleus", "Ivy", "Fig", "Dracaena")
create ("Coleus", "Flame nettle", "Brilliancy", "Pink rainbow", "Sunset")
create ("Ivy","English ivy", "Canary ivy")
create ("English ivy", "Cristata", "Golden snow", "Glacia", "Little diamond")
create ("Canary ivy", "Varigata", "Gloire de Marengo", "Harlequin")
create ("Fig", "Mistletoe fig", "Fiddle leaf fig", "Creeping fig", "Rubber plant",
"Weeping fig")
create ("Dracaena", "Fragrant", "Madagascar dragon tree")
create ("Fragrant","Victoria", "Linden")
create ("Madagascar dragon tree", "Tricolo", "Colorama")
create ("flowering plants", "African violet")
create ("African violet", "Winter dream", "Rapsodie Venus", "Ballet Eva", "Coral
Caper", "Blue nimbus")

function expandKeyword (keyword, tab) {
for (i in plants) {
if (plants[i] == keyword)
{document.write (tab + keyword + "<br>")
if (narrowerTerms[i] != null) {
tab += "     "
expandNarrowerTerms (i, tab)}
}}
}

function expandNarrowerTerms (location, tab) {
for (i in narrowerTerms[location]) {
expandKeyword (narrowerTerms[location][i], tab)
}
}

plantName = prompt ("Enter the plant name", "")
expandKeyword (plantName, "")

</SCRIPT>
</HEAD>
</HTML>
```

Figure 6.8 Response to the query *flowering plants*.

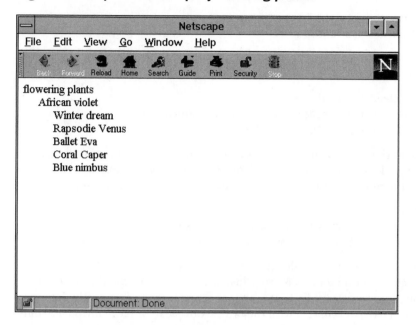

Note that in the **expandKeyword** function, " " adds a space to the text string written by **document.write**. Figure 6.8 shows the system in action.

Inheritance

We now know how to instruct our Web pages to make use of the fact that a concept can include subordinate concepts. So "United Kingdom" includes "England," "Northern Ireland," "Scotland," and "Wales," and "foliage plants" includes "Coleus," "Ivy," "Fig," and "Dracaena." However, such hierarchical relationships can also work in the other direction, in that narrower subordinate concepts can "inherit" characteristics of their superordinate "parent" concepts.

Imagine that someone tells you about a bird you have never heard of. You instantly know that, unless it is a very unusual bird, it will have two wings and a beak. Because you know nothing of this particular bird, you are making a deduction based on your knowledge about birds in general.

We can program computers to make similar deductions using rules of the form:

```
IF creature X is a bird
    AND birds have 2 wings and a beak
THEN creature X also has 2 wings and a beak
```

A more generalized form of the rule would be:

```
IF X is a Y
    AND Y has characteristic Z
THEN X also has characteristic Z
```

We can enable our Web pages to make deductions, using similar rules, in a variety of subject areas. Take the following:

```
IF book X is about "JavaScript"
    AND "JavaScript" is a subdivision of "Computer Programming"
THEN book X is also about "Computer Programming"
```

A rule such as this could be used to enable a document to inherit index terms from its parent concept. Thus a request for a book on "Computer programming" would also retrieve one on the more specific topic "JavaScript." Here is another example:

```
IF plant X is a house plant
    AND watering instructions for house plants are as follows...
THEN watering instructions for plant X are as follows...
```

It is important to be able to allow for exceptions. For instance, plant X may be unusual and require nonstandard watering instructions. To take another example, a penguin is a bird and birds can fly—but a penguin cannot fly. In fact, in the interests of simplicity and clarity, we will stay with the birds example in order to introduce some basic techniques.

Putting Inheritance to Use

We will create a small database of birds. Figure 6.9 shows the options presented to the reader. If the bird *redwing* and the characteristic *main locomotion* are selected, *flies* will be displayed, as shown in Figure 6.10.

However, if *penguin* and *main locomotion* are selected, *swims* will be displayed. There's nothing too remarkable about this; however, the interesting point is that in the case of *redwing*, our system deduced the fact of its locomotion from its knowledge of birds in general. In the case of *penguin*, information relating to an exception overrode this inheritance.

We could of course have achieved similar answers if we had laboriously stored *all* information relating to each type of bird in the database entry for that bird. However, this would mean duplicating in the entry for each type of bird information that is common to all birds (that they have two wings, a beak, etc.). Similarly, we would need to store information common to all or most thrushes (that they have a particular characteristic coloring) in the entry for each type of thrush. This is not a problem in a database the size of our extremely small illustration. However, it does become a problem if we want to create more realistically sized databases containing genuinely useful information.

Figure 6.9 Bird characteristics screen.

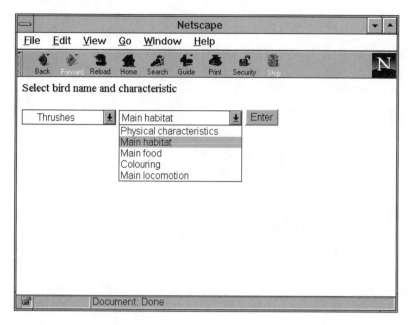

To illustrate the difference and to introduce basic techniques, consider how we might represent knowledge if we were not to take advantage of inheritance. We might create our database as follows:

bird

physical characteristics: *2 wings, beak, 2 legs, warm blooded*
main locomotion: *flies*

landbird

type of: *bird*
physical characteristics: *2 wings, beak, 2 legs, warm blooded*
main locomotion: *flies*
main food: *insects and berries*
main habitat: *land*

seabird

type of: *bird*
physical characteristics: *2 wings, beak, 2 legs, warm blooded*
main locomotion: *flies*
main food: *fish, crustacea*
main habitat: *sea*

Figure 6.10 The main locomotion of the redwing.

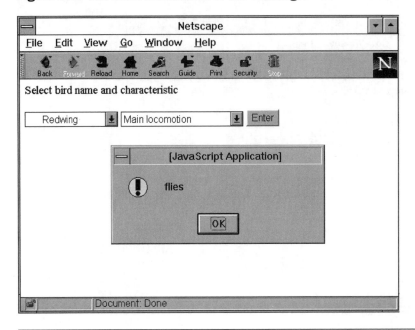

thrush

type of: *landbird*

coloring: *cream breast flecked with brown dots*

physical characteristics: *2 wings, beak, 2 legs, warm blooded*

main locomotion: *flies*

main food: *insects and berries*

main habitat: *land*

mistle thrush

type of: *thrush*

coloring: *cream breast flecked with brown dots*

physical characteristics: *2 wings, beak, 2 legs, warm blooded*

main locomotion: *flies*

main food: *insects and berries*

main habitat: *land*

song thrush

type of: *thrush*

coloring: *cream breast flecked with brown dots*

physical characteristics: *2 wings, beak, 2 legs, warm blooded*

main locomotion: *flies*
main food: *insects and berries*
main habitat: *land*

redwing
type of: *thrush*
coloring: *creamy eye stripes, bright russet flanks*
physical characteristics: *2 wings, beak, 2 legs, warm blooded*
main locomotion: *flies*
main food: *insects and berries*
main habitat: *land*

penguin
type of: *seabird*
physical characteristics: *2 wings, beak, 2 legs, warm blooded*
main locomotion: *swims*
main food: *fish, crustacea*
main habitat: *sea*

It would make sense to store more general information relating to birds in general only once—in the *birds* entry—and information relating to landbirds in general only once—in the *landbirds* entry. We can then give our Web pages some rules of deduction so that they can figure out for themselves, say, the main food of a redwing. They will do this by knowing that a redwing is a thrush, that a thrush is a landbird, and that a landbird eats insects and berries.

Here is a more economical representation of the same knowledge:

bird
physical characteristics: *2 wings, beak, 2 legs, warm blooded*
main locomotion: *flies*

landbird
type of: *bird*
main food: *insects and berries*
main habitat: *land*

seabird
type of: *bird*
main food: *fish, crustacea*
main habitat: *sea*

thrush
type of: *landbird*
coloring: *cream breast flecked with brown dots*

mistle thrush
type of: *thrush*

song thrush
type of: *thrush*

redwing
type of: *thrush*
coloring: *creamy eye stripes, bright russet flanks*

penguin
type of: *seabird*
main locomotion: *swims*

Now here is the code to create this knowledge in JavaScript. The following code is not the most economical way of coding the knowledge. It has been chosen because it is particularly clear. A more economical coding is introduced in the section "A More Economical Approach to Inheritance" later in this chapter.

```
bird = new Array ("physical characteristics", "main locomotion")
landbird = new Array ("type of", "main food", "main habitat")
seabird = new Array ("type of", "main food", "main habitat")
thrush = new Array ("type of", "colouring")
mistle_thrush = new Array ("type of")
song_thrush = new Array ("type of")
redwing = new Array ("type of", "colouring")
penguin = new Array ("type of", "main locomotion", "colouring")

bird["physical characteristics"] = "beak, wings, 2 legs, warm blooded"
bird["main locomotion"] = "flies"

landbird["type of"] = bird
landbird["main habitat"] = "land"
landbird["main food"] = "insects, berries"

seabird["type of"] = bird
seabird["main habitat"] = "sea"
seabird["main food"] = "fish, crustacea"

thrush["type of"] = landbird
thrush["colouring"] = "cream breast flecked with brown dots"

mistle_thrush["type of"] = thrush

song_thrush["type of"] = thrush

redwing["type of"] = thrush
```

```
redwing["colouring"] = "creamy eye stripes, bright russet flanks"

penguin["type of"] = seabird
penguin["main locomotion"] = "swims"
penguin["colouring"] = "black and white"
```

Now here is the rule of deduction. The rule is recursive and in plain English reads:

> IF the bird (e.g., redwing) has the feature (e.g., main locomotion) as one of its own array properties
> THEN store the feature in the variable "list"
> ELSE use this rule to check if the creature's "parent" (i.e., thrush) has the feature.

Here is a full listing of the function as it works recursively. It is listed in full for each of its recursive cycles. Let us assume that we are asking about the redwing's main form of locomotion. The function will be processed as follows. Lines that apply in any given cycle are shown in bold. Nonbold type can therefore be ignored as you read through the procedure:

> IF redwing has the feature main locomotion as one of its own array properties (it does not)
> THEN store the feature in the variable "list"
> **ELSE use this rule to check if thrush (redwing's "parent") has the feature main locomotion.**
> When this has all been done, return what is in the variable "list" (nothing yet).

> IF thrush has the feature main locomotion as one of its own array properties (it does not)
> THEN store the feature in the variable "list"
> **ELSE use this rule to check if landbird (thrush's "parent") has the feature main locomotion.**
> When this has all been done, return what is in the variable "list" (nothing yet).

> **IF landbird has the feature main locomotion as one of its own array properties (it does)**
> **THEN store the feature (i.e., "flies") in the variable "list"**
> ELSE use this rule to check if bird (landbird's "parent") has the feature main locomotion.
> **When this has all been done, return what is in the variable "list" (i.e., "flies").**

Consider the same function when responding to a request about the penguin's main locomotion. In this case, the function will not be called recursively, because it successfully finds the answer in the main IF part of the rule and does not get as far as the ELSE part:

> **IF penguin has the feature main locomotion as one of its own array properties (it does)**

THEN store the feature (i.e., "swims") in the variable "list"
ELSE use this rule to check if seabird (penguin's "parent") has the feature main locomotion.
When this has all been done, return what is in the variable "list" (i.e., "swims").

Thus the inheritance mechanism is overridden if the characteristic being searched for can be found directly, without our having to search for it higher in the hierarchy of birds. Exceptions to the rule can therefore be included simply by stating the exception in the entry for the particular bird or species to which it applies.

Here is the JavaScript code for the function:

```
function possesses (name, feature) {
list = null
if (name[feature] != null) {list = name[feature]}
else {if (name["type of"] != null) {possesses (name["type of"], feature)}}
return list
}
```

Now here is the code in full (Program 6-5 on the website). We have used a select list to gather information about the reader's request for information.

```
<HTML>
<HEAD>
<SCRIPT LANGUAGE="JavaScript">

bird = new Array ("physical characteristics", "main locomotion")
landbird = new Array ("type of", "main food", "main habitat")
seabird = new Array ("type of", "main food", "main habitat")
thrush = new Array ("type of", "colouring")
mistle_thrush = new Array ("type of")
song_thrush = new Array ("type of")
redwing = new Array ("type of", "colouring")
penguin = new Array ("type of", "main locomotion", "colouring")

bird["physical characteristics"] = "beak, wings, 2 legs, warm blooded"
bird["main locomotion"] = "flies"

landbird["type of"] = bird
landbird["main habitat"] = "land"
landbird["main food"] = "insects, berries"

seabird["type of"] = bird
seabird["main habitat"] = "sea"
seabird["main food"] = "fish, crustacea"

thrush["type of"] = landbird
```

```
thrush["colouring"] = "cream breast flecked with brown dots"

mistle_thrush["type of"] = thrush

song_thrush["type of"] = thrush

redwing["type of"] = thrush
redwing["colouring"] = "creamy eye stripes, bright russet flanks"

penguin["type of"] = seabird
penguin["main locomotion"] = "swims"
penguin["colouring"] = "black and white"

function possesses (name, feature) {
list = null
if (name[feature] != null) {list = name[feature]}
else {if (name["type of"] != null) {possesses (name["type of"], feature)}}
return list
}

speciesArray = new Array (bird,landbird,thrush,mistle_thrush,song_thrush, redwing,
seabird, penguin)
characteristicsArray = new Array ("physical characteristics", "main habitat", "main
food", "colouring", "main locomotion")

</SCRIPT>
</HEAD>
<BODY>

Select bird name and characteristic
<FORM NAME="myForm">
<SELECT NAME="species">
<OPTION> Birds
<OPTION>   Land birds
<OPTION>      Thrushes
<OPTION>       Mistle Thrush
<OPTION>       Song Thrush
<OPTION>       Redwing
<OPTION>   Seabirds
<OPTION>     Penguin
</SELECT>
<SELECT NAME="characteristics">
<OPTION> Physical characteristics
<OPTION> Main habitat
<OPTION> Main food
<OPTION> Colouring
```

```
<OPTION> Main locomotion
</SELECT>
<INPUT TYPE="button" VALUE="Enter"
onClick="answer = possesses (speciesArray[myForm.species.selectedIndex],
characteristicsArray[myForm.characteristics.selectedIndex]);
if (answer == null) {answer='This depends on the particular species. Please select a
more specific category from the box to the left'};alert (answer)">
</FORM>
</BODY>
</HTML>
```

Note that we have used <SELECT> options to ask the reader which bird and which characteristic he or she wants to know about. In order to find out which choices the reader has made and to pass them to the **possesses** function, we used two arrays, one for each question. These are **speciesArray** and **characteristicsArray**. The order in which the items appear in the arrays is the same as the order in which they appear in the select lists; therefore, the array number of each is the same as its corresponding <OPTION> number in the <SELECT> object. So, if the reader selects options 2 and 4 from the two lists, items 2 and 4 from the corresponding arrays will be passed to the **possesses** function.

A More Economical Approach to Inheritance

As mentioned in the section "Using a Larger Knowledge Base," earlier in this chapter, it can be important—especially in client-side as opposed to server-side programming— to make code as economical as possible if applications are to load and run quickly.

The following example demonstrates a more economical form of coding, as well as illustrating the application of inheritance to another subject area. Recall that in the "Using a Larger Knowledge Base" section, we used matching arrays to reduce the volume of code necessary for setting up the knowledge base. The example here will also use matching arrays. The knowledge base relates to an imaginary business: the Mild Corporation. This corporation has a Head Office and four divisions. Two of the divisions, Technical Support and Information Services, are located with the Head Office.

We will set up a small database allowing our readers to ask for, say, the locations of the Head Office or the Sales division, the name of the director of Information Services, or for a list of the activities of the Technical Services division. It is important to note that inheritance is used to infer information not explicitly stored. For example, if we ask for the location of Technical Support, inheritance is used to infer that because Technical Support is not listed as having a location of its own and because it is directly subordinate to the Head Office, it shares the location of the Head Office.

Here is the small knowledge base:

Mild Corporation Head Office
Location: *688 West Avenue*

Director: *Mary J. Cheney*
Information services: *Room 310*
Activities: *Main administration; information services; technical support*

Sales Division
Location: *455 West Earl Street*
Director: *Hugh H. Gallagher*
Activities: *Marketing; sales; promotions; events*

Manufacturing Division
Location: *488–507 North Avenue*
Director: *Lawrence F. Sprague*
Information services: *Hick Annex Floor 2*
Activities: *Main production for entire product range*

Technical Support
Director: *Anne G. Carlson*
Activities: *Computing support; equipment maintenance*

Information Services
Director: *Donna W. Scott*
Activities: *Enquiry services to all divisions; information distribution; research support*

Now here is the full code (Program 6-6 on the website):

```
1.  <HEAD>
2.  <SCRIPT>

3.  list = new Array ("Mild Corporation Head Office", "Sales Division", "Manufacturing
Division", "Technical Support", "Information Services")
detailsArray = new Array ("Location", "Director", "Information services",
"Activities")

4.  NT = new Array ()
5.  propertiesArray = new Array ()
6.  propertiesArray[0] = new Array ()
7.  propertiesArray[1] = new Array ()
8.  propertiesArray[2] = new Array ()
9.  propertiesArray[3] = new Array ()
10. propertiesArray[4] = new Array ()

11. function create (object, narrowerTerms) {
12. for (i in list) {
13. if (list[i] == object) {
14. if (narrowerTerms != null) {
15. NT[i] = new Array ()
```

```
16. for (j = 1; j < create.arguments.length; j++) {
17. NT[i][(j-1)] = create.arguments[j]}}}
18. }}

19. function createProperties (object, propertyName, propertyValue) {
20. for (i in list) {
21. if (list[i] == object) {
22. if (propertyName != null) {
23. propertiesArray[i][propertyName] = propertyValue}}
24. }}

25. create ("Mild Corporation Head Office", "Sales division", "Manufacturing
Division", "Technical Support", "Information Services")
26. createProperties ("Mild Corporation Head Office", "Location", "688 West Avenue")
27. createProperties ("Mild Corporation Head Office", "Director", "Mary J. Cheney")
28. createProperties ("Mild Corporation Head Office", "Information services", "Room
310")
29. createProperties ("Mild Corporation Head Office", "Activities", "Main administra-
tion; information services; technical support")
30. createProperties ("Sales Division", "Location", "455 West Earl Street")
31. createProperties ("Sales Division", "Director", "Hugh H. Gallagher")
32. createProperties ("Sales Division", "Activities", "Marketing; sales; promotions;
events")
33. createProperties ("Manufacturing Division", "Location", "488-507 North Avenue")
34. createProperties ("Manufacturing Division", "Director", "Lawrence F. Sprague")
35. createProperties ("Manufacturing Division", "Information services", "Hick Annex
Floor 2")
36. createProperties ("Manufacturing Division", "Activities", "Main production for
entire product range")
37. createProperties ("Technical Support", "Director", "Anne G. Carlson")
38. createProperties ("Technical Support", "Activities", "Computing support; equip-
ment maintenance")
39. createProperties ("Information Services", "Director", "Donna W. Scott")
40. createProperties ("Information Services", "Activities", "Enquiry services to all
divisions; information distribution; research support")

41. function expand1 (term) {
42. alert (term)
43. for (i in list) {
44. if (list[i] == term) {expand (i)}
45. }}

46. function expand (listLocation) {
47. for (i in NT[listLocation]) {
48. expand1 (NT[listLocation][i])}
49. }
```

```
50. function retrieve (thing, property) {
51. if ( ( x = has (thing, property) ) != "no") {return x}
52. else {if (inherits (thing, property) != "no") {return x}}
53. return thing + " does not have property " + property
54. }

55. function has (thing, property) {
56. for (i in list) {
57. if (propertiesArray[i] != null) {
58. if (list[i] == thing && propertiesArray[i][property] != null)
59. {return propertiesArray[i][property] }
60. }}
61. return "no"
62. }

63. function inherits (thing, property) {
64. for (i in list) {if (NT[i] != null) {
65. for (j in NT[i]) {
66. if (NT[i][j] == thing && (x = retrieve (list[i], property) != "no")) {
67. if (propertiesArray[i][property] != null) {
68. return propertiesArray[i][property]} }
69. }}}
70. return "no"
71. }

72. </SCRIPT>
73. </HEAD>

74. <BODY>
75. <H1> Mild Corporation </H1><HR>
76. Select Division name and information required
77. <FORM NAME="myForm">
78. <SELECT NAME="divisions">
79. <OPTION> Head Office
80. <OPTION>   Sales
81. <OPTION>   Manufacturing
82. <OPTION>   Technical Support
83. <OPTION>   Information Services
84. </SELECT>
85. <SELECT NAME="characteristics">
86. <OPTION> Location
87. <OPTION> Director
88. <OPTION> Information services
89. <OPTION> Activities
90. </SELECT>
91. <INPUT TYPE="button" VALUE="Enter"
```

```
92. onClick="answer = retrieve (list[myForm.divisions.selectedIndex],
detailsArray[myForm.characteristics.selectedIndex]);
93. if (answer == null) {answer='Please contact the division direct for this informa-
tion'};alert (answer)">
94. </FORM>
95. </BODY>
96. </HTML>
```

As with the birds system, the reader is invited to select the Head Office or some division of the organization, along with the particular details required (see Figure 6.11), and is shown the resulting information in an alert box.

Line 3 sets up the *list* array as follows:

list[0] = "Mild Corporation Head Office"
list[1] = "Sales Division"
list[2] = "Manufacturing Division"

and so on. Lines 11 through 18 create the NT array containing details of divisions subordinate to the head office:

NT[0][0] = "Sales Division"

Figure 6.11 Information on the Mild Corporation.

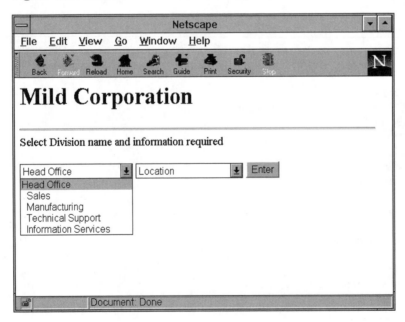

```
NT[0][1] = "Manufacturing Division"
NT[0][2] = "Technical Support"
```

and so on. Lines 19 through 24 create the propertiesArray:

```
propertiesArray[0]["Location"] = "688 West Avenue"
propertiesArray[0]["Director"] = "Mary J. Cheney"
etc.

propertiesArray[1]["Location"] = "455 West Earl Street"
propertiesArray[1]["Director"] = "Hugh H. Gallagher"
etc.

propertiesArray[2]["Location"] = "488–507 North Avenue"
propertiesArray[2]["Director"] = "Lawrence F. Sprague"
```

and so on. As we did in the house plants system earlier in this chapter, we can use matching arrays to retrieve information as follows. Let us assume that we want to know the location of the Sales Division. The procedure would be:

(a) Find the array number of "Sales Division" in the list array [1]
(b) Look up the same array number [1] in the propertiesArray array.
(c) Look up the "Location" property of propertiesArray[1]

This would retrieve "455 West Earl Street."

The function **retrieve** (lines 50 through 54) basically says:

Thing (e.g. Technical Support) possesses *property* (e.g. Location)
IF *property* (Location) is a direct characteristic of *thing* (Technical Support)
OR
    thing (Technical Support) is a narrower term to *something else* (Head Office)
    AND *property* (Location) is possessed by this *something else* (Head Office)

The function **has** (lines 55 through 62) checks whether the part of the organization being asked about actually has the characteristic listed as one of its features. For example, the Sales Division *does* have its own location (line 30). However, Technical Support, although it has a director (line 37) and activities (line 38), does *not* have its own location. Therefore, line 52 of the **retrieve** function calls the **inherits** function (lines 63 through 71).

The **inherit** function checks whether the part of the organization being asked about is in the narrower terms array of some other part of the organization. Technical Support is in the narrower terms array of Head Office (line 25 uses the **create** function to build this array). Therefore the location of Head Office is returned as the location of Technical Support.

If we want more economy of code, we could replace the following lines of the program:

```
propertiesArray[0] = new Array ()
propertiesArray[1] = new Array ()
propertiesArray[2] = new Array ()
propertiesArray[3] = new Array ()
propertiesArray[4] = new Array ()
```

with an additional command in the **createProperties** function. This function checks whether an array already exists for the particular campus being processed. If one does not, it creates one. The command appears in line 3 of the **createProperties** function below:

```
1. function createProperties (object, propertyName, propertyValue) {
2. for (i in list) {
3. if (propertiesArray[i] == null) {propertiesArray[i] = new Array ()}
4. if (list[i] == object) {
5. if (propertyName != null) {
6. propertiesArray[i][propertyName] = propertyValue}}}
7. }
```

Probabilities

In Chapter 5, we examined systems capable of making judgments and giving advice based on IF...THEN rules. Using the plants theme introduced earlier, we can imagine a "plant doctor" system that aims to diagnose plant problems, using rules of the type:

> IF leaves are brown
> AND roots are rotting
> THEN possible cause is overwatering

However, often things are not quite so clear cut, on the part of both the reader and the expert providing the knowledge used by the system. Some problems, such as diagnosing plant problems, are more subtle. They entail weighing evidence and working out the relative likelihood of a number of possible solutions. Evidence may be cumulative. The more symptoms of a particular problem that are present and the more strongly they are present, the more likely that particular problem is to be the source of the trouble.

It is therefore useful if we can build into our Web pages the ability to cope with the following:

- Different strengths of evidence (for example, rotting roots may be more indicative of overwatering than brown leaves)
- Differing levels of certainty (for example, the plant's leaves are "quite" as opposed to "very" brown)

- Cumulating evidence (the more symptoms and the stronger their presence the more likely the particular diagnosis)

- Competing conclusions (from the evidence, there may be a number of possible solutions, each with a different level of likelihood)

Much has been written about the usefulness and problems of using the calculation of probabilities in the design of intelligent advisory systems. One widely employed approach is based on Bayes' Theorem. We will use this technique in our next small demonstration system. This technique has the advantage that it is relatively straightforward to implement. However, this is just one approach, and it does have important limitations.

To use Bayes' Theorem, we first need to know the *prior odds* of whatever hypothesis we are dealing with. Imagine that our hypothesis is that our plant has been overwatered. The prior odds of this hypothesis relate to the degree to which overwatering may be expected to occur in the normal course of events. Imagine that approximately 25 out of every 100 ailing plants brought into a garden center for advice are suffering from overwatering. If we assumed that this sort of level was typical of the population, the prior odds of overwatering would be 25/75.

Typically, we do not have such statistics at hand, so we have to use our experience and judgment to come up with a reasonable figure. We want our system to make decisions similar to those a human expert would make. At the end of the day, the most profitable approach may be to try out different figures not only relating to the prior odds but also to other parameters used in the calculation, such as the logical sufficiency and logical necessity factors described below. This process can entail trial-and-error rather than more scientific calculation!

Next, we require some figures to reflect differing strengths of evidence. For example, even if the leaves of our plant are 100 percent brown, this fact alone does not *guarantee* that overwatering is the problem. On the other hand, if the leaves are 100 percent free from brownness, we cannot completely discount overwatering as a possible cause of the plant's problems. We need to assess how important each symptom is in suggesting a particular problem. We can do this by attaching to each symptom two numbers.

The first number is called the *logical sufficiency factor*. This factor specifies the maximum effect of the symptom in concluding that the particular problem is present—in other words, how much more likely the diagnosis would be if the symptom were maximally present. The second number is the *logical necessity factor*. This factor specifies the maximum effect if the symptom is completely absent. For example, we may decide that if the leaves are 100 percent brown, this would double the likelihood of overwatering being the problem. However, if there is no sign of brownness on the leaves, this may make a diagnosis of overwatering only a quarter as likely. Rotting roots, however, may be much more symptomatic of overwatering, making its likelihood in our opinion three times more certain if strongly present and reducing the likelihood by 50 percent if absent.

Our formula states that for a particular hypothesis (in this case a diagnosis):

The odds in favor of the hypothesis = the prior odds of the hypothesis × the logical sufficiency factor (LS) if the evidence is positive or the logical necessity factor (LN) if the evidence is negative.

We also need to be able to take account of cumulating evidence. The likelihood of overwatering increases as more and more evidence is built up from different sources. The formula is able to include cumulating evidence as follows:

Odds in favor = prior odds × first LS or LN × second LS or LN × third LS or LN etc.

The formula so far gives us the odds in favor of our hypothesis. We can then translate odds into probabilities using the formula:

Probability = odds in favor ÷ (1 + odds in favor)

Finally, we need to take account of different degrees of presence or absence of the symptoms. For example, the person using our system may report that a given symptom is very much or only slightly present. We need to convert such estimates into numbers. So, for example, we may offer our reader a choice between:

A great deal   Quite a lot   A bit   Not at all

then translate these "behind the scenes" into numbers such as:

0.9   0.6   0.3   –1

We can add this level of presence or absence into our formula as follows. First, we need to calculate a revised logical sufficiency factor (LS) if the evidence is positive or a logical necessity factor (LN) if the evidence is negative. We can do this using the formula:

New LS or LN = original LS or LN × degree of presence + (1 – degree of presence)

Let us take an example. The knowledge for our small demonstration system is as follows. For clarity and simplicity, it consists of just two hypotheses: that the plant is suffering from *overwatering* or from *excessive cold*. There are three symptoms: *brown leaves, dark roots,* and *floppy stem*.

Figure 6.12 shows the knowledge base.

Figure 6.13 shows the input screen. The user is asked to indicate the degree of presence of each symptom.

Here is the full code (Program 6-7 on the website). Note that economy of coding has been sacrificed for clarity and explicitness:

```
1. <HTML>
2. <HEAD>
3. <SCRIPT>
```

```
4. certainty = new Array ()
5. certainty['brown leaves'] = -1
6. certainty['roots rotting'] = -1

7. newLSorLN = new Array ()

8. waterLogged = new Array ()
9. waterLogged["prior odds"] = .3

10. waterLogged["symptoms"] = new Array ()
11. waterLogged["symptoms"]["brown leaves"] = new Array ()
12. waterLogged["symptoms"]["roots rotting"] = new Array ()

13. waterLogged["symptoms"]["brown leaves"]["LS"] = 7.3
14. waterLogged["symptoms"]["brown leaves"]["LN"] = 0.9
15. waterLogged["symptoms"]["roots rotting"]["LS"] = 8.7
16. waterLogged["symptoms"]["roots rotting"]["LN"] = 0.7

17. tooCold = new Array ()
18. tooCold["prior odds"] = .4

19. tooCold["symptoms"] = new Array ()
```

Figure 6.12 Knowledge base for the plant diagnosis system.

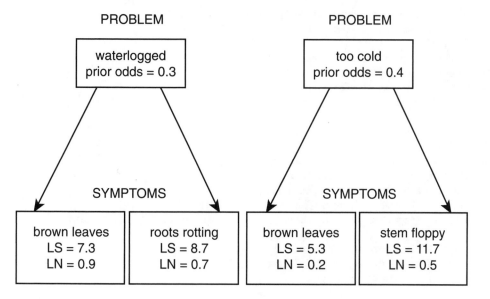

Figure 6.13 Input screen for the plant diagnosis.

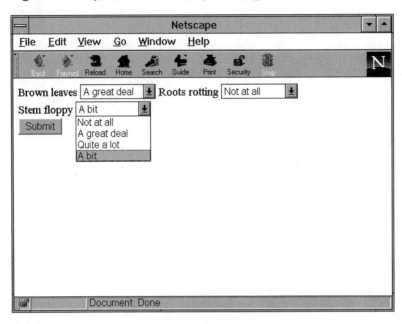

```
20. tooCold["symptoms"]["brown leaves"] = new Array ()
21. tooCold["symptoms"]["stem floppy"] = new Array ()

22. tooCold["symptoms"]["brown leaves"]["LS"] = 5.3
23. tooCold["symptoms"]["brown leaves"]["LN"] = 0.2
24. tooCold["symptoms"]["stem floppy"]["LS"] = 11.7
25. tooCold["symptoms"]["stem floppy"]["LN"] = 0.5

26. function probabilityOf (diagnosis) {
27. for (i in diagnosis["symptoms"]) {
28. diagnosis["symptoms"][i]["certainty"] = certainty[i]
29. if (diagnosis["symptoms"][i]["certainty"] > 0)
30. {var LSorLN = diagnosis["symptoms"][i]["LS"] * 10}
31. else {var LSorLN = diagnosis["symptoms"][i]["LN"] * 10;
32. diagnosis["symptoms"][i]["certainty"] = diagnosis["symptoms"][i]["certainty"] * -
1}
33. newLSorLN[i] = LSorLN * diagnosis["symptoms"][i]["certainty"]
34. + (1 - diagnosis["symptoms"][i]["certainty"])
35. newLSorLN[i] = newLSorLN[i]/10}
36. var oddsInFavour = diagnosis["prior odds"]
37. for (i in newLSorLN) {
```

```
38. oddsInFavour = oddsInFavour * newLSorLN[i]}
39. var prob = oddsInFavour / (1 + oddsInFavour)
40. return prob
41. }

42. </SCRIPT>
43. </HEAD>
44. <BODY>
45. <FORM NAME = "myForm">
46. Brown leaves
47. <SELECT NAME = "select1">
48. <OPTION VALUE = "-1">Not at all
59. <OPTION VALUE = ".9">A great deal
50. <OPTION VALUE = ".6">Quite a lot
51. <OPTION VALUE = ".3">A bit
52. </SELECT>
53. Roots rotting
54. <SELECT NAME = "select2">
55. <OPTION VALUE = "-1">Not at all
56. <OPTION VALUE = ".9">A great deal
57. <OPTION VALUE = ".6">Quite a lot
58. <OPTION VALUE = ".3">A bit
69. </SELECT>
60. <br>
61. Stem floppy
62. <SELECT NAME = "select3">
63. <OPTION VALUE = "-1">Not at all
64. <OPTION VALUE = ".9">A great deal
65. <OPTION VALUE = ".6">Quite a lot
66. <OPTION VALUE = ".3">A bit
67. </SELECT>
68. <br>
69. <INPUT TYPE = "button" VALUE = "Submit"
70. onClick = "certainty['brown leaves'] =
this.form.select1[this.form.select1.selectedIndex].value;
71. certainty['roots rotting'] =
this.form.select2[this.form.select2.selectedIndex].value;
72. certainty['stem floppy'] =
this.form.select3[this.form.select3.selectedIndex].value;
73. document.write ('Probability of being waterlogged = ' +
74. Math.round (100 * probabilityOf (waterLogged))/100  +
75. '<br>Probability of being too cold = ' +
76. Math.round (100 * probabilityOf (tooCold))/100 + '<BR>')">
77. </FORM>
78. </BODY>
79. </HTML>
```

Lines 4 through 25 set up the knowledge base. Each problem (that is, being waterlogged or too cold) is represented as an array with the property *symptoms*. This property is itself an array containing details of the symptoms (for example, brown leaves). Each symptom is itself an array, with LS (logical sufficiency) and LN (logical necessity) properties.

The level of certainty that each symptom is present in the particular plant being asked about ("Not at all," "A bit," Quite a lot," or "A great deal") is stored in the **certainty** array, set up in lines 4 through 6. Before the reader has been asked to indicate the certainty of the symptoms, the certainties are set at "Not at all," that is, *–1* (lines 5 and 6).

Lines 45 through 77 present the form shown in Figure 6.13. When the button is clicked, the estimates given by the reader (for example, that the leaves are "quite" brown) are translated into numbers and stored in the **certainty** array. For example:

```
certainty["brown leaves"] = .9
```

The calculations are performed in the **probabilityOf** function (lines 26 through 41). Lines 29 through 31 check (for each possible problem) whether the certainty value supplied by the reader for each symptom is negative or positive. If it is positive, the LS figure is selected for the calculation. If it is negative, the LN figure is selected. The selected figure is stored in the variable *LSorLN*—so named because it may store either the LS or the LN, depending on whether the certainty is positive or negative.

 The LS or LN is multiplied by 10 (lines 30 and 31) in order to convert the decimal value to a whole number—required by the calculation that follows if it is to be performed correctly. This value is then divided by 10 to convert it back to a decimal in line 35.

Line 32 converts the certainty figure, if it is negative, into a positive number by multiplying it by –1. Again, this is to enable the calculation to be performed correctly.

Lines 33 through 35 calculate the revised LS (if the evidence is positive) or LN (if the evidence is negative) using the formula:

New LS or LN = original LS or LN × degree of presence + (1 – degree of presence)

Lines 36 through 38 calculate the odds in favor:

Odds in favor = prior odds × first LS or LN × second LS or LN × third LS or LN etc.

Line 39 converts the odds into a probability:

Probability = odds in favor ÷ (1 + odds in favor)

which is returned by the function (line 40). The values are then rounded to avoid long decimal numbers (lines 74 and 76) as they are written to the screen (lines 73 through 76).

Figure 6.14 shows the result.

Figure 6.14 The system's diagnosis.

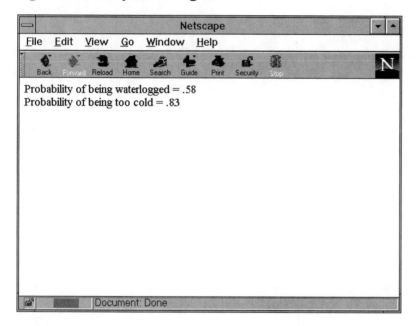

INTERPRETING
User Input

W e have used the information provided by the readers of our Web pages in a variety of ways: to perform calculations, to make decisions, and to give advice. However, the ways in which we have analyzed (as opposed to used) this information have been fairly basic.

At the simplest level, we have used the **confirm** command to obtain a "yes" or "no" response to some proposition:

```
if (confirm ("Would you like more information?")
    {someFunction ()} else {someOtherFunction ()}
```

We have also implemented simple testing to see if the information matches one or more answers we have prestored:

```
answer = prompt ("Would you like more information?")
if (answer == "yes") {someFunction ()}
    else {someOtherFunction ()}
```

Whether we use text boxes, multiple-choice options, or other types of reader input, the level of analysis is basic: we are simply matching the reader's answer with a prestored answer. However, it may often be necessary to analyze reader input a little more deeply.

To take a very simple example, the rule:

```
answer = prompt ("Would you like more information?")
if (answer == "yes") {someFunction ()}
    else {someOtherFunction ()}
```

will not work if the reader replies "Yes" (with an uppercase letter) or "yes please" (with additional text).

We may also want to perform some calculation that depends on the reader's entering the number of items he or she wants to order. For example:

```
order = prompt ("How many items would you like?")
pricePerItem = 50
totalCost = order * pricePerItem
```

If the reader enters "Five" instead of a number, the calculation cannot be performed.

There are occasions on which we require the reader to enter free text, as opposed to selecting from a list of options. For this reason, it is important to be able to analyze this input more deeply than we have done so far. The following sections introduce ways of analyzing more fully responses and information provided by our readers.

Validating Reader Input

Numerical operators in JavaScript allow us to perform simple validating procedures on information provided by the readers of our pages. We can, for example, check that a number falls within a specified range and generate an appropriate message if what the reader enters is outside the range (see Figure 7.1).

Figure 7.1 Validating reader input.

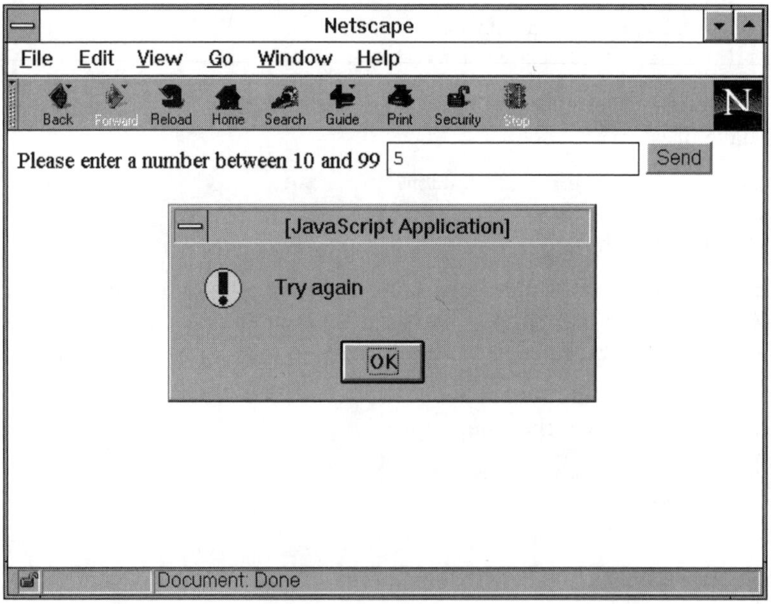

The following code (Program 7-1 on the website) will check input in this way. If we want, we can put the instructions in a button's event handler within a form as follows:

```
<HTML>
<BODY>

<FORM NAME = "myForm">
Please enter a number between 10 and 99
<INPUT TYPE = "text" NAME = "myTextBox">
<INPUT TYPE = "button" VALUE = "Send"
onClick = "if (myForm.myTextBox.value < 10
|| myForm.myTextBox.value > 99)
{alert ('Try again');
myForm.myTextBox.select ();
myForm.myTextBox.focus ()}">
</FORM>

</BODY>
</HTML>
```

Generally, this type of function can be more neatly managed using a function as follows (Program 7-2 on the website):

```
<HTML>
<HEAD>
<SCRIPT>

function validate (textBox) {
if (textBox.value < 10 || textBox.value > 99)
{alert ('Try again');
textBox.select ();
textBox.focus ()}
}

</SCRIPT>
</HEAD>
<BODY>

<FORM NAME = "myForm">
Please enter a number between 10 and 99
<INPUT TYPE = "text" NAME = "myTextBox">
<INPUT TYPE = "button" VALUE = "Click me"
onClick = "validate (myForm.myTextBox)">
</FORM>

</BODY>
</HTML>
```

However, if a reader types a letter instead of a number—for example, the letter O instead of a 0 (zero) or the letter l (lowercase "L") instead of a numeral 1, the checking procedure will not work. We therefore need to build in a check so that we can display an appropriate message such as "Please enter only numbers." We can do this using a function such as the following (Program 7-3 on the website):

```
1.  <HTML>
2.  <HEAD>
3.  <SCRIPT>

4.  function validate (textBox) {
5.  if (!isNumber (textBox.value)) {
6.  alert ("Please enter only a single number");
7.  textBox.select ();
8.  textBox.focus ()}
9.  }

10. function isNumber (item) {
11. numeric = "0123456789"
12. for (var i = 0; i < numeric.length; i++) {
13. if (item == numeric.charAt (i)) {return true}
14. }
15. return false
16. }

17. </SCRIPT>
18. </HEAD>
19. <BODY>

20. <FORM NAME = "myForm">
21. Please enter a single number
22. <INPUT TYPE = "text" NAME = "myTextBox">
23. <INPUT TYPE = "button" VALUE = "Send"
24. onClick = "validate (myForm.myTextBox)">
25. </FORM>

26. </BODY>
27. </HTML>
```

When the **validate** function is passed the value typed into the text box as the reader clicks Send (line 23), line 5 calls the **isNumber** function to check whether the value is in fact a number.

The **isNumber** function (lines 10 through 16) takes the number (which it translates into the variable *item*, line 10), and checks it against each digit of the variable *numeric* (0123456789). This checking is done in lines 12 through 14. When it matches a digit in *numeric*, the function returns the value *true*. If it fails to match any of the digits in *numeric*, it returns *false*. If **isNumber** fails to return *true*—in other words, if the value passed to it does not match any of the digits of *numeric*—an alert message will be displayed (line 6).

This works fine for single numbers. However, it will not distinguish between a number of more than one digit and one or more letters; the same alert message will appear. Clearly, we need to tell JavaScript how to identify a number no matter how many digits it has. Then we can display different alert messages appropriate to the mistake, such as "Please enter only numbers" if the reader includes letters or other unwanted characters and "The number is outside the range required" if the reader enters a number lower than 10 or greater than 99.

Here is the code that will allow JavaScript to identify a number of any length. Note that the **isNumber** function is the same as before.

```
1.  function areAllNumbers (item) {
2.  for (j = 0; j < item.length; j++) {
3.  if (!isNumber (item.charAt (j))) {return false}
4.  }
5.  return true
6.  }

7.  function isNumber (item) {
8.  numeric = "0123456789"
9.  for (var i = 0; i < numeric.length; i++) {
10. if (item == numeric.charAt (i)) {return true}
11. }
12. return false
13. }
```

This time, we simply apply the **isNumber** function to each digit making up the number in *item*. If any should fail to match one of *numeric*'s digits, the **areAllNumbers** function returns *false*. Lines 2 through 4 pass to the **isNumber** function each character of the value typed in by the reader. If any of these characters cannot be matched with one of *numeric*'s digits, **isNumber** returns *false* (line 12), and therefore the **areAllNumbers** function also returns *false* (line 3).

Now here is the complete code, including appropriate alert messages. This is Program 7-4 on the website.

```
<HTML>
<HEAD>
<SCRIPT>

function validate (textBox) {
if (areAllNumbers (textBox.value)) {
if (textBox.value < 10 || textBox.value > 99) {
alert ("The number is outside the required range");
```

```
textBox.select ();textBox.focus ()}
}
else {
alert ("Please enter only numbers");
textBox.select ();
textBox.focus ()}
}

function areAllNumbers (item) {
for (j = 0; j < item.length; j++) {
if (!isNumber (item.charAt (j))) {return false}
}
return true
}

function isNumber (item) {
numeric = "0123456789"
for (var i = 0; i < numeric.length; i++) {
if (item == numeric.charAt (i)) {return true}
}
return false
}

</SCRIPT>
</HEAD>
<BODY>

<FORM NAME = "myForm">
Please enter a number between 10 and 99
<INPUT TYPE = "text" NAME = "myTextBox">
<INPUT TYPE = "button" VALUE = "Click me"
onClick = "validate (myForm.myTextBox)">
</FORM>

</BODY>
</HTML>
```

Figures 7.2 and 7.3 show the system in action.

Fuzzy Matching

Testing whether a reader's answer falls within a particular numerical range entails a degree of "fuzziness." We do not specify what the number must be, only that it must be less than 100 and greater than 9. However, we may also want to inject an element of "fuzziness," as well as numbers, into the analysis of text.

Imagine, for example, interactive training materials that we want to offer via the Web. We may ask the reader a question about, say, metals, for which we require the

Figure 7.2 Checking that input is numerical.

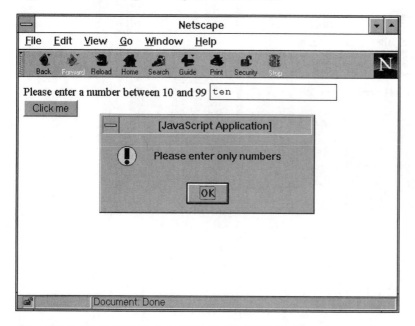

answer "aluminum." However, for various reasons, we may not want to offer a list of choices (using radio buttons, list boxes, etc.)—for example, we may not want to suggest possible answers to the reader and thus allow the possibility of a lucky guess. We therefore require the reader to enter free text into a text box.

However, with the input of free text there is always the possibility of mistyping, misspelling, and misunderstanding. The reader may enter *aluminium* (non-U.S. spelling), *Aluminum* (with an uppercase "A"), or even *The answer is aluminum* (inserting additional text).

If our code says:

```
if (answer == "aluminum") {score ++}
```

the reader would score nothing because his or her answer does not match the correct one.

We can to some extent cope with this type of problem by building an element of "fuzziness" into our analysis procedure. One way of doing this is to use the sort of wildcards employed by search engines such as Alta Vista. Searching for *comput** will find documents containing the words *computing, computer, computers, compute, computed, computation*, and *computational*.

Figure 7.3 Checking that input is within a specified range.

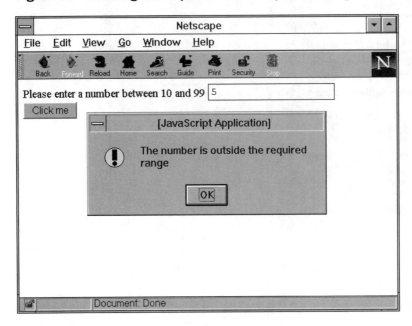

We can do the same, specifying that the correct answer to our question is *alum*m*. In this case, both U.K. and U.S. spellings would match and be accepted as correct. Here is the procedure we will use, first in pseudo-code. The names of functions are in bold type. In the case of our example, the variable *correctAnswer* (line 1) would be passed the value "alum*m" when the function is called.

1. function **fuzzy_match** (*correctAnswer, readerAnswer*)
2. IF *correctAnswer* character 1 **match**es *readerAnswer* character 1
3.   AND the rest of *correctAnswer* **fuzzy_match**es the rest of *readerAnswer*
4. OR *correctAnswer* character 1 **match**es *readerAnswer* character 1
5.   AND *correctAnswer* **fuzzy_match**es the rest of *readerAnswer*
6. THEN *correctAnswer* successfully **fuzzy match**es *readerAnswer*

7. function **match** (*characterA, characterB*)
8. IF *characterA* = *characterB*
9. OR *characterA* = "*"
10. THEN *characterA* successfully **match**es *characterB*

Here is the same pseudo-code, but this time the variables are filled in for an actual query. Let's imagine that we want to **fuzzy_match** "cat" with "cat." Obviously, the match will be successful, but it may be instructive to see how it works. "Cat" is used because it is much clearer to show the entire workings of the procedures with a word of only three characters. The wildcard will be introduced after this first simple example.

If we call the function with the command:

```
fuzzy_match ("cat", "cat")
```

the procedure will work as follows. As in previous examples of recursion (in which a function calls itself with different values), the same function is listed out each time it is called, showing the different contents of the values passed to it. The parts of the function that apply at the time to the particular example are shown in bold. Nonbold code can therefore be ignored as you read through the flow of the program.

1. **function fuzzy_match ("cat", "cat")**
2. **IF "c" matches "c" [it does; see lines 7–10]**
3.   **AND "at" fuzzy_matches "at" [it does; see lines 11–16]**
4. OR "c" matches "c"
5.   AND "cat" fuzzy_matches "at"
6. **THEN "cat" successfully fuzzy matches "cat"**

7. **function match ("c", "c")**
8. **IF "c" = "c"**
9. OR "c" = "*"
10. **THEN "c" successfully matches "c"**

11. **function fuzzy_match ("at", "at")**
12. **IF "a" matches "a" [it does; see lines 17–20]**
13.   **AND "t" fuzzy_matches "t" [it does; see lines 21–26]**
14. OR "a" matches "a"
15.   AND "at" fuzzy_matches "t"
16. **THEN "cat" successfully fuzzy matches "cat"**

17. **function match ("a", "a")**
18. **IF "a" = "a"**
19. OR "a" = "*"
20. **THEN "a" successfully matches "a"**

21. **function fuzzy_match ("t", "t")**
22. **IF "t" matches "t" [it does; see lines 27–30]**
23.   **AND "" fuzzy_matches "" [it does; see text after line 30]**
24. OR "t" matches "t"
25.   AND "t" fuzzy_matches ""
26. **THEN "t" successfully fuzzy matches "t"**

27. **function match ("t", "t")**
28. **IF "t" = "t"**
29. OR "t" = "*"
30. **THEN "t" successfully matches "t"**

Not shown in this simplified pseudo-code is a line in the **fuzzy_match** function that tells the function that it has reached the end of its task and to return *true* if both items passed to it are blank. Thus if we try to **fuzzy_match** "" and "" the function will stop and return *true*.

Now let us examine the pseudo-code to see how the wildcard is able to match any one or more characters. We will keep the example short and simple and call the function with the command:

```
fuzzy_match ("c*", "cat")
```

Here is how the procedure works. As usual, code that applies to the particular example as it runs through each stage is shown in bold.

1. **function fuzzy_match ("c*", "cat")**
2. **IF "c" matches "c" [it does; see lines 7–10]**
3.   **AND "*" fuzzy_matches "at" [it does; see lines 11–16]**
4. OR "c" matches "c"
5.   AND "c*" fuzzy_matches "at"
6. **THEN "c*" successfully fuzzy matches "cat"**

7. **function match ("c", "c")**
8. **IF "c" = "c"**
9. OR "c" = "*"
10. **THEN "c" successfully matches "c"**

11. **function fuzzy_match ("*", "at")**
12. IF "*" matches "a"
13.   AND "" fuzzy_matches "t" [it does not]
14. **OR "*" matches "a" [it does; see lines 17–20]**
15.   **AND "*" fuzzy_matches "t" [it does; see lines 21–26]**
16. **THEN "*" successfully fuzzy matches "at"**

17. **function match ("*", "a")**
18. IF "*" = "a"
19. **OR "*" = "*"**
20. **THEN "*" successfully matches "a"**

21. **function fuzzy_match ("*", "t")**
22. **IF "*" matches "t" [it does; see lines 27–30]**
23.   **AND "" fuzzy_matches "" [it does; see note text line 30]**
24. OR "*" matches "t"

25.   AND "*" fuzzy_matches ""
26. **THEN "*" successfully fuzzy matches "t"**

27. **function match ("*", "t")**
28. **IF "*" = "t"**
29. **OR "*" = "*"**
30. **THEN "*" successfully matches "t"**

As in the previous example, a line in the real code (not shown in this simplified version) tells the function to stop processing and return *true* if both items passed to it are blank. This is line 5 in the code shown below.

The code below (Program 7-5 on the website) asks the reader to "Name the family to which both cheetah and lion belong," requiring the answer "cat" or "cats." To illustrate the wildcard's ability to match more than one character, we will set the template to match anything beginning with "c." This template appears in the **onClick** event handler of the button in the body of the document below (line 23).

```
1.   <HTML>
2.   <HEAD>
3.   <SCRIPT>

4.   function fuzzy_match (A, B) {
5.   if (A.length < 1 && B.length < 1) {return true}
6.   else {
7.   if ((match (A.substring (0,1), B.substring (0,1)) &&
8.   fuzzy_match (A.substring (1, A.length), B.substring (1, B.length)))
9.   || (B.length>0 && match (A.substring (0,1), B.substring (0,1))
10.  && fuzzy_match (A, B.substring (1, B.length))))
11.  {return true} else {return false}
12.  }
13.  }

14.  function match (X,Y) {
15.  if (X==Y||X=="*") {return true} else {return false} }
16.  </SCRIPT>

17.  </HEAD>
18.  <BODY>
19.  Name the family to which both cheetah and lion belong

20.  <FORM NAME = "myForm">
21.  <INPUT TYPE = "text" NAME = "myTextBox">
22.  <INPUT TYPE = "button" VALUE = "Submit"
23.  onClick = "if (fuzzy_match ('c*', myForm.myTextBox.value)) {alert ('Correct!')}
else {alert ('No - try again!')}">
24.  </FORM>
```

```
</BODY>
</HTML>
```

The workings of this example are shown below using the real code instead of the pseudo-code. Note how the second line of the **fuzzy_match** function tells the function to return *true* if the two values passed to it are blank. The function is repeatedly called recursively; each time shorter values are passed to it as the earlier characters are "knocked off" after checking. Thus the function receives "cat," "cat" in the first cycle, "at," "at" in the second, "t," "t" in the third, and "", "" in the third. At this stage, the values are blank, and the function returns *true*.

We will call the function with the command:

```
fuzzy_match ("cat", "cat")
```

Now here is the code with all values filled in.

```
function fuzzy_match ("cat", "cat") {
if ("cat".length < 1 && "cat".length < 1) {return true}
else {
if ((match ("c", "c") &&
fuzzy_match ("at", "at"))
|| ("cat".length>0 && match ("c", "c")
&& fuzzy_match ("cat", "at")))
{return true}
else {return false}}
}


function fuzzy_match ("at", "at") {
if ("at".length < 1 && "at".length < 1) {return true}
else {
if ((match ("a", "a") &&
fuzzy_match ("t", "t"))
|| ("at".length>0 && match ("a", "a")
&& fuzzy_match ("at", "t")))
{return true}
else {return false}}
}


function fuzzy_match ("t", "t") {
if ("t".length < 1 && "t".length < 1) {return true}
else {
if ((match ("t", "t") &&
fuzzy_match ("", ""))
|| ("t".length>0 && match ("t", "t")
&& fuzzy_match ("t", "")))
{return true}
```

```
else {return false}}
}

function fuzzy_match ("", "") {
if ("".length < 1 && "".length < 1) {return true}
else {
if ((match ("", "") &&
fuzzy_match ("", ""))
|| ("".length>0 && match ("", "")
&& fuzzy_match ("", "")))
{return true} else {return false}}
}
```

Here is the same code, but this time we use the wildcard. We will call the function with the command:

```
fuzzy_match ("c*", "cat")
```

Here is the code:

```
function fuzzy_match ("c*", "cat") {
if ("c*".length < 1 && "cat".length < 1) {return true}
else {
if ((match ("c", "c") &&
fuzzy_match ("*","at"))
|| ("cat".length>0 && match ("c", "c")
&& fuzzy_match ("c*", "at")))
{return true}
else {return false}}
}

function fuzzy_match ("*","at") {
if ("*".length < 1 && "at".length < 1) {return true}
else {
if ((match ("*","a") &&
fuzzy_match ("","t"))
|| ("at".length>0 && match ("*","a")
&& fuzzy_match ("*","t")))
{return true}
else {return false}}
}

function fuzzy_match ("*","t") {
if ("*".length < 1 && "t".length < 1) {return true}
else {
if ((match ("*","t") &&
fuzzy_match ("", ""))
|| ("t".length>0 && match ("*","t")
```

```
&& fuzzy_match ("*", "")))
{return true}
else {return false}}
}


function fuzzy_match ("", "") {
if ("".length < 1 && "".length < 1) {return true}
else {
if ((match ("", "") &&
fuzzy_match ("", ""))
|| ("".length>0 && match ("", "")
&& fuzzy_match ("", "")))
{return true} else {return false}}
}
```

The code above does not accept leading or trailing blanks. In other words, if we supply the template "alumin*m", then " aluminium" (starting with a blank) or "aluminium " (ending with a blank) would not match. Nor is it case insensitive. So "Aluminum" would not be accepted as a match because it has an uppercase "A."

The version of the program shown below will handle leading and/or trailing blanks and will accept upper- or lowercase answers (or mixtures of the two). To make it case insensitive, we need to add the two lines shown in bold to the first function:

```
function fuzzy_match (A, B) {
A = A.toLowerCase ()
B = B.toLowerCase ()
if (A.length < 1 && B.length < 1) {return true}
else {
if ((match (A.substring (0,1), B.substring (0,1)) &&
fuzzy_match (A.substring (1, A.length), B.substring (1, B.length)))
|| (B.length>0 && match (A.substring (0,1), B.substring (0,1))
&& fuzzy_match (A, B.substring (1, B.length))))
{return true} else {return false}
}
}
```

We can approach the problem of stripping leading and trailing blanks in two ways. First, we can write a function to do precisely this, as shown below (Program 7-6 on the website):

```
<HTML>
<HEAD>
<SCRIPT>

function stripBlanks (item) {
var wordStarted = "no"
var transformedItem = ""
```

```
for (var i = item.length; i > 0; i—) {
if (wordStarted == "yes")
{transformedItem += item.charAt (i-1)}
else {
     if (item.charAt (i-1) != " ") {
     wordStarted = "yes";
     transformedItem += item.charAt (i-1)} } }
newItem = transformedItem
transformedItem = ""
wordStarted = "no"

for (var i = newItem.length; i > 0; i—) {
if (wordStarted == "yes") {transformedItem += newItem.charAt (i-1)}
else {
     if (newItem.charAt (i-1) != " ") {
     wordStarted = "yes";
     transformedItem += newItem.charAt (i-1)} } }
return transformedItem
}

alert (stripBlanks (prompt ("Input text for leading and trailing blanks to be
stripped", "")))

</SCRIPT>
</HEAD>
</HTML>
```

The word(s) we type into the prompt box will be passed to the function **stripBlanks**, which will strip leading and trailing blanks. If the function is called as follows, for example:

```
stripBlanks ("     hello     ")
```

it will return "hello."

A second approach is shown in the following code. It goes a stage further by allowing blanks and/or text to precede or follow an answer. So "The answer is aluminum I think" would match the template "alum*m," as indeed would "I think the answer is Aluminium."

The code works by adding the wildcard * to the beginning and end of the template in a new function, **fuzzy_match_1**:

```
function fuzzy_match_1 (A) {
A = "*" + A + "*"
}
```

The wildcards match spaces or text appearing before and after the reader's answer. But what if there are no spaces or text before or after the reader's answer? What if he or she simply types "aluminum"? The answer is to include in the **fuzzy_match_1** function a second command that adds a space to the beginning and end of the reader's answer:

```
function fuzzy_match_1 (A, B) {
A = "*" + A + "*"
B = " " + B + " "
}
```

Thus if the reader types "aluminum", the **fuzzy_match_1** function will convert this to " aluminum ," which will successfully match the template "alum*m", also converted by the **fuzzy_match_1** function to "*alum*m*". However, if the reader types "I think the answer is aluminum" the template will still match. Now here is the full code (Program 7-7 on the website):

```
<HTML>
<HEAD>
<SCRIPT>

function fuzzy_match_1 (A, B) {
A = "*" + A + "*"
B = " " + B + " "
return fuzzy_match (A,B)
}

function fuzzy_match (A, B) {
A = A.toLowerCase ()
B = B.toLowerCase ()
if (A.length < 1 && B.length < 1) {return true}
else {
if ((match (A.substring (0,1), B.substring (0,1)) &&
fuzzy_match (A.substring (1, A.length), B.substring (1, B.length)))
|| (B.length>0 && match (A.substring (0,1), B.substring (0,1))
&& fuzzy_match (A, B.substring (1, B.length))))
{return true} else {return false}}
}

function match (X,Y) {
if (X==Y||X=="*") {return true} else {return false}
}

</SCRIPT>
</HEAD>
<BODY>
Which metal has the third lightest weight?
```

```
<FORM NAME = "myForm">
<INPUT TYPE = "text" NAME = "myTextBox">
<INPUT TYPE = "button" VALUE = "Submit"
      onClick = "if (fuzzy_match_1 ('alum*m', myForm.myTextBox.value)) {alert
('Correct!')} else {alert ('No - try again!')}">
</FORM>

</BODY>
</HTML>
```

Figure 7.4 shows the system in action.

Pattern Matching

More extensive linguistic pattern matching can be achieved using *templates*. Although it has little in common with serious modern natural-language processing techniques, ELIZA still finds its way at least into the historical elements of computing and psychology courses. ELIZA is an early program written by Joseph Weizenbaum designed to engage its user in conversation. The following is a slightly adapted extract from a frequently quoted example interaction. See if you can guess which of participants (A or B) is ELIZA and which is the human:

Figure 7.4 Fuzzy answer matching.

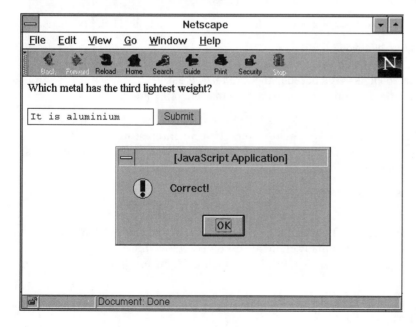

A: Men are all alike.

B: In what way?

A: They're always bugging us about something or other.

B: Can you think of a specific example?

A: Well, my boyfriend made me come here.

B: Your boyfriend made you come here?

A: He says I'm depressed much of the time.

B: I am sorry to hear that you are depressed.

A: It's true. I am unhappy.

B: Do you think coming here will help you not to be unhappy?

A: I need some help. That much seems certain.

B: What would it mean to you if you got some help?

A: Perhaps I could learn to get along with my mother.

B: Tell me more about your family.

You probably guessed that B is the computer program. Although it uses a number of additional facilities that allow it, for example, to associate the word "mother" with "family" in the example above, the basic structure used by ELIZA is a database of *templates* of the type:

INPUT: I am <1> to <2> you
OUTPUT: I appreciate the fact that you are <1> to <2> me
INPUT: My favorite <1> is <2> because <3>
OUTPUT: <2> is not a bad <1>, but I wouldn't say <3>

where <1> <2> and <3> are variables allowing interactions of the type:

A: I am glad to meet you.
B: I appreciate the fact that you are glad to meet me.
A: My favorite band is Oasis because they are really great.
B: Oasis is not a bad band, but I wouldn't say they are really great.

Naturally, a lot of templates and possible alternative answers to the same pattern would be needed to enable a system to interact in an interesting way. Also, some "catch-all" outputs would be needed to cope with examples in which no pattern matches, such as the following:

That's interesting—tell me more.
Please change the subject.

ELIZA is a bit of fun. But pattern matching using templates does have more serious uses. Templates are one of many elements used in certain "information extraction" techniques designed to summarize text automatically. Black and Johnson* report an

---

*A practical evaluation of two rule-based automatic abstracting techniques. *Expert Systems for Information Management* 1 (3) 1988, pp. 159–177.

approach called the "indicator phrase technique" in which text is processed to see if it matches a template such as the following:

"The"
    [skip from 0 to 3 words]
"result(s)" or "conclusion(s)" or "finding(s)"
    [score 3 points if this element is present]
"of this" or "of the" or "in this"
    [skip from 0 to 3 words]
"study"
    [score 2 points if this element is present]
    [skip from 0 to 3 words]
"confirm(s)" or "suggest(s)" or "show(s)"
    [score 3 points if this element is present]
"that"
    [score 1 point if this element is present]

A sentence such as:

"The results of this study into automatic indexing confirm that ..."

would score 9 as indicating the main theme of the article from which it is taken (see Figure 7.5). A sentence such as:

"The results of this study are also available at http:www.xyz.ac.uk/indexing.html"

would score only 5 (see Figure 7.6), so the first one would be preferred.

Figure 7.5 Score for the first sentence.

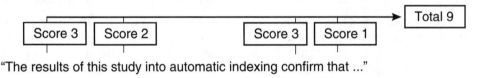

"The results of this study into automatic indexing confirm that ..."

Figure 7.6 Score for the second sentence.

"The results of this study are also available at http://www.xyz.ac.uk/indexing.html"

However, the point is that this processing is enabled by the use of a template against which text is matched. Similar pattern matching could also be used, for example, to clarify queries to a database or search engine using templates such as the following:

INPUT: <1> information on <2> and <3> or <4>
OUTPUT: Say whether you mean ("<2>" AND "<3>") OR "<4>")
   or "<2>" AND ("<3>" OR "<4>")

This would enable an interaction such as:

A: I'm interested in information on cognitive styles and learning strategies or learning styles
B: Say whether you mean
      ("cognitive styles" AND "learning styles") OR "learning strategies"
   or
      "cognitive styles" AND ("learning styles" OR "learning strategies")

The problem with this form of template-based pattern matching is that the level of linguistic analysis of the words being processed is extremely shallow and is restricted to their surface *form* rather than their deeper *meaning*. The result is that the designer of the system must second guess, to a great extent, the precise form of words the user is likely to use—or at least a limited number of possible likely alternatives.

More serious language-processing systems make sophisticated attempts to analyze text at deeper levels, such as syntax, semantics, discourse, and pragmatics. A range of these forms of analysis are available in commercial information retrieval engines that work over intranets and the Internet. We will explore the analysis of text at a *syntactic* (grammatical) level in the next section. Although not semantic, such analysis is deeper than the template-matching processing we have explored so far, because it takes account of the grammatical roles of different words making up text to be processed.

However, it may be instructive to explore a simple form of template-based pattern matching of the sort used in ELIZA. Here are the example templates we will implement. They are extremely simplistic and serve only to illustrate the basic technique. Considerable ingenuity would be required to create templates capable of producing more interesting interactions.

INPUT: I <1> you <2>
OUTPUT: Why do you <1> I <2>?
INPUT: <1> computers <2>
OUTPUT: Do you know a lot about information technology?
INPUT: My <1> is <2> because <3> me <4>
OUTPUT: The fact that <3> you <4> is a good reason for your <1> being <2> I guess
INPUT: <1> *[This will match if all the previous templates fail]*
OUTPUT: Please change the subject

Here is the code (Program 7-8 on the website). The following version is case sensitive and also sensitive to spaces—in other words, it requires an exact match between text entered by the reader and an appropriate template. A catchall template:

```
templatesA[4]="1"
templatesB[4]="Please change the subject"
```

matches any text. This should always be the last template so that it is called upon only if all other templates fail to match.

```
<HTML>
<HEAD>
<TITLE> Talk to me </TITLE>
</HEAD>
<BODY>
<SCRIPT>

list = new Array ()
templatesA = new Array ()
templatesB = new Array ()
var output = ""

templatesA[1]="I 1 you 2"
templatesB[1]="Why do you 1 I 2?"
templatesA[2]="1 computers 2"
templatesB[2]="Do you know a lot about information technology?"
templatesA[3]="My 1 is 2 because 3 me 4"
templatesB[3]="The fact that 3 you 4 is a good reason for your 1 being 2 I guess"
templatesA[4]="1"
templatesB[4]="Please change the subject"

function isNumber (item) {
numeric = "0123456789"
for (var i = 0; i < numeric.length; i++)
if (item == numeric.charAt (i)) {return true}
return false
}

function checkList (list) {
if (list == null) {return ""} else {return list}
}

function fuzzy_output (A) {
for (var i = 0; i < A.length; i++)
if (isNumber (A.charAt (i))) {output += list[A.charAt (i)]}
else {output += A.charAt (i)}
```

```
document.myForm.outputBox.value = output
}


function fuzzy_match (A, B) {
if (A.length < 1 && B.length < 1) {return true}
else {
if ((match (A.substring (0,1), B.substring (0,1)) &&
fuzzy_match (A.substring (1, A.length), B.substring (1, B.length)))
|| (B.length>0 && match (A.substring (0,1), B.substring (0,1))
&& fuzzy_match (A, B.substring (1, B.length))))
{if (isNumber (A.substring (0,1))) {
list[A.substring (0,1)] = B.substring (0,1) +
checkList (list[A.substring (0,1)])}
return true} else {return false}}
}

function match (X,Y) {
if (X==Y) {return true}
if (isNumber (X)) {return true}
return false
}

function start (input) {
for (i in templatesA) {
if (fuzzy_match (templatesA[i], input))
{fuzzy_output (templatesB[i]); return true}
}
return false }

</SCRIPT></P>
Talk to me
<FORM NAME = "myForm"> Input <br>
<INPUT TYPE = "text" NAME = "inputBox" SIZE = 70>
<INPUT TYPE = "button" VALUE = "Send" onClick = "start (myForm.inputBox.value);
myForm.inputBox.focus (); myForm.inputBox.select (); output = ''; list = new Array
()">
<p> Output <br>
<INPUT TYPE = "text" NAME = "outputBox" SIZE = 70>
</FORM>

</BODY>
</HTML>
```

The program will work with sentences such as:

My favorite color is green because it reminds me of the countryside which will result in the output:

The fact that it reminds you of the countryside is a good reason for your favorite color being green

Try these matching sentences (the third will match the "catchall" template):

I think that you ask too much
I have to use computers in my work
My next job can wait because it bores me

 JavaScript 1.2 is less tolerant than 1.1 of heavy amounts of recursion. So, while a long sentence entailing several matches (such as the first "My favorite color ..." example) works fine in Navigator 3, Navigator 4 will display an error message that says "Too much recursion." The problem arises because recursive matching is being applied to each *letter* of the sentence rather than to each *word*. Version 2 of the program, shown below, overcomes this problem by matching words rather than letters.

The examples are very contrived, and the system is brittle in that it requires exact matches, including case and spaces. Thus while the phrase "I like you very much" successfully matches template 1, the phrase "I like you" will not; the template requires one or more characters after the word "you."

 Recall that the section "Fuzzy Matching" in this chapter introduced techniques for handling upper- and lowercase input and input containing extra spaces. These would allow the system to be more flexible.

Figures 7.7 and 7.8 illustrate the system in action.

Basically, this system is a version of the **fuzzy_match** function we explored in the section "Fuzzy Matching." It differs in that it treats numbers as wildcards (represented in the earlier program as *). Each wildcard (each number) matches one or more words such that the *rest* of the sentence also matches the rest of the template. Whatever portion of text matches each wildcard (each number) is reproduced in the output at the point in the output template at which the same number occurs.

As explained in the Note, this program uses a lot of recursion because each letter of the sentence generates its own recursive cycle. Whereas Navigator 3 is happy with this, Navigator 4—probably quite sensibly!—is less tolerant.

Figure 7.7 Template 2 successfully matches.

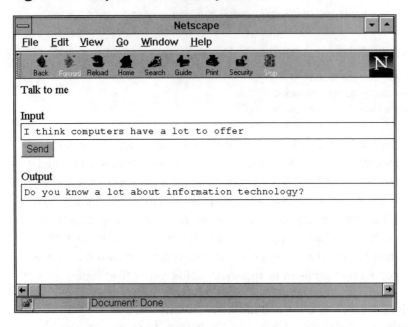

The problem can be overcome by matching words rather than letters. This method greatly reduces the amount of recursion required. Matching words can be done by writing a function to convert letters into words and performing the fuzzy matching on these words. However, JavaScript 1.2 offers a number of useful commands that enable us to do this more easily. We will use these commands in the following version, which therefore requires JavaScript 1.2 (Netscape Navigator 4).

This version (Program 7-9 on the website) also requires exact matching of case and spaces. Here is the code. Changes to the previous version appear in bold.

```
1.   <HTML>
2.   <HEAD>
3.   <TITLE> Talk to me </TITLE>
4.   </HEAD>
5.   <BODY>
6.   <SCRIPT>

7.   list = new Array ()
8.   templatesA = new Array ()
9.   templatesB = new Array ()
10.  var output = ""
```

Figure 7.8 Template 3 successfully matches.

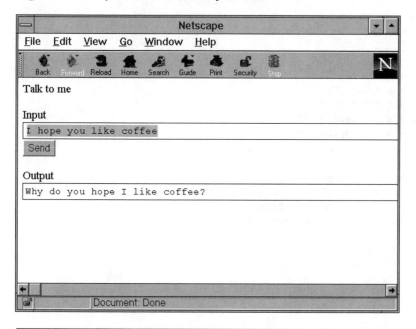

```
11. templatesA[1]="I 1 you 2"
12. templatesB[1]="Why do you 1 I 2?"
13. templatesA[2]="1 computers 2"
14. templatesB[2]="Do you know a lot about information technology?"
15. templatesA[3]="My 1 is 2 because 3 me 4"
16. templatesB[3]="The fact that 3 you 4 is a good reason for your 1 being 2 I
guess"
17. templatesA[4]="1"
18. templatesB[4]="Please change the subject"

19. function isNumber (item) {
20. numeric = "0123456789"
21. for (var i = 0; i < numeric.length; i++)
22. if (item == numeric.charAt (i)) {return true}
23. return false
24. }

25. function checkList (list) {
26. if (list == null) {return ""} else {return list}
27. }

28. function fuzzy_output (A) {
```

```
29. for (var i = 0; i < A.length; i++)
30. if (isNumber (A.charAt (i))) {output += list[A.charAt (i)]}
31. else {output += A.charAt (i)}
32. document.myForm.outputBox.value = output
33. }


34. function fuzzy_match (A, B) {
35. var arrayA = A.split (",")
36. var arrayB = B.split (",")
37. var Afirst = arrayA.splice (0,1)
38. var Bfirst = arrayB.splice (0,1)
39. if (A.length < 1 && B.length < 1) {return true}
40. else {
41. if ((match (Afirst, Bfirst) &&
42. fuzzy_match (arrayA.toString (), arrayB.toString ()))
43. || (B.length>0 && match (Afirst, Bfirst)
44. && fuzzy_match (A, arrayB.toString ())))
45. {if (isNumber (Afirst)) {
46. list[Afirst] = Bfirst + " " +
47. checkList (list[Afirst])}
48. return true} else {return false}}
49. }


50. function match (X,Y) {
51. if (X==Y) {return true}
52. if (isNumber (X)) {return true}
53. return false
54. }


55. function start (input) {
56. input = input.split (" ")
57. input = input.toString ()
58. for (i in templatesA) {
59. templatesA[i] = templatesA[i].split (" ")
60. templatesA[i] = templatesA[i].toString ()
61. if (fuzzy_match (templatesA[i], input))
62. {fuzzy_output (templatesB[i]); return true}
63. }
64. return false }


65. </SCRIPT></P>
66. Talk to me
67. <FORM NAME = "myForm"> Input <br>
68. <INPUT TYPE = "text" NAME = "inputBox" SIZE = 70>
69. <INPUT TYPE = "button" VALUE = "Send" onClick = "start (myForm.inputBox.value);
myForm.inputBox.focus (); myForm.inputBox.select (); output = ''; list = new Array
()">
```

```
70.  <p> Output <br>
71.  <INPUT TYPE = "text" NAME = "outputBox" SIZE = 70>
72.  </FORM>

73.  </BODY>
74.  </HTML>
```

Lines 56 and 57 change the string of text typed in by the reader into a string in which the words are separated by commas instead of spaces. This is to make the format of the strings compatible with the format produced by the **toString** commands in lines 42 and 44 in the **fuzzy_match** function.

Line 56 uses the **split** command to convert the string to an array, in which each word separated by a space " " becomes an element. Line 57 changes the array back into a string but with the words separated by commas instead of spaces. Lines 59 and 60 do exactly the same to each template in turn as an attempt is made to match it with the input sentence.

Thus two comma-separated strings are passed to the **fuzzy_match** function as *A* and *B*. Lines 35 and 36 split each string into an array, each word in the string becoming an element in the array. Lines 37 and 38 use the **splice** command to extract the first element of each array. The arguments of this command specify that JavaScript should begin at array element 0 (the first element) and extract 1 element. Thus the value of *Afirst* will be the first element of **arrayA**, and the value of *Bfirst* will be the value of the first element of **arrayB**.

Note that this procedure changes the value of **arrayA** and **arrayB**. They now contain what they contained before, minus the extracted first element. So, assuming that the values passed as *A* and *B* to the **fuzzy_match** function were:

"I,1,you,2"
"I,think,that,you,are,asking,too,much"

here are the values of the variables and arrays by the time JavaScript gets to line 39:

Afirst = "I"
arrayA[0] = "1"
arrayA[1] = "you"
arrayA[2] = "2"

Bfirst = "I"
arrayB[0] = "think"
arrayB[1] = "that"
arrayB[2] = "you"
arrayB[3] = "are"
arrayB[4] = "asking"
arrayB[5] = "too"
arrayB[6] = "much

The program then behaves in exactly the same way as the previous version, except for changing the arrays back into strings when **fuzzy_match** is called recursively each time (lines 42 and 44).

Syntactical Analysis

Using syntactical analysis, we can identify the various roles played by different words in a sentence. So, for example, in the sentence:

The man bought a red apple.

we have a *noun phrase* consisting of a *determiner* ("the") and a *noun* ("man"), followed by a *verb phrase* consisting of a *verb* ("bought"), and another noun phrase this time consisting of a determiner ("a"), an adjective ("red"), and a noun ("apple"). It is possible to specify a set of rules that will allow us to tell whether a particular sequence of words is or is not a correctly constructed sentence. If our rules are as follows:

A sentence can consist of:
    a noun phrase followed by a verb phrase.
A noun phrase can consist of:
    a determiner [optional] followed by an adjective [optional] followed by a noun
A verb phrase can consist of:
    a verb followed by a noun phrase.

we can tell that a sentence such as:

The man red apple

or

The man bought a red

are not valid sentences.

Grammar rules able to handle realistically complex natural language are a lot more complex than our simple example, but the principles are the same.

We tend to think of syntax, or grammar, as applying to natural language. However, syntax can apply to other forms of language. Computer programs, for example, require that code obey the syntax of the particular computer language being used. So, for example,

```
<FORM NAME = "myForm"
```

is *not* valid because HTML syntax demands a closing bracket (**>**). Similarly, in the use of the Alta Vista Internet search engine advanced search interface, a request requires correct syntax. So, whereas

```
("learning styles" OR "learning strategies" ) AND "computer based learning"
```

is a valid query,

```
("learning styles" OR learning strategies) AND "computer based learning"
```

is not because the words *learning strategies* are neither enclosed in double quotes to make them into a phrase nor connected using one of the legal operators AND, OR, AND NOT, or NEAR.

Syntactical rules can apply to a wide range of activities, and we will explore a more useful application shortly. However, for our first example, we will stick with natural language. We will use the very simple rules presented above. Their purpose is not to supply a complex set of rules capable of handling sophisticated natural-language constructions, but rather to provide a clear and simple example of how we can implement this technique. We can translate the rules into pseudo-code as follows:

> IF the text consists of a noun phrase followed by a verb phrase
> THEN it forms a sentence
>
> IF the text consists of a determiner [optional] followed by an adjective [optional]
> followed by a noun
> THEN it forms a noun phrase
>
> IF the text consists of a verb followed by a noun phrase
> THEN it forms a verb phrase

Now we need to add some rules to specify what are valid determiners, nouns, adjectives, and verbs, which we can do as follows. We will do this for a very small number of words. A large database of such words would of course be required to handle realistically complex text, even if restricted to a narrow subject topic.

> IF the text = "the" or "a"
> THEN it is a determiner
>
> IF the text = "man" or "dog"
> THEN it is a noun
>
> IF the text = "bites"
> THEN it is a verb

The following code shows how the *sentence*, *noun phrase*, *noun*, and *verb phrase* rules are implemented:

```
1.   function sentence (input) {
2.   var i = 1
3.   while (i <= input.length) {
4.   var A = input.substring (0,i)
5.   var B = input.substring (i+1, input.length)
6.   if (noun_phrase (A) && v_phrase (B)) {return true}
7.   i++
8.   }
```

```
9.  return false }

10. function noun_phrase (input) {
11. var i = 1
12. while (i <= input.length) {
13. var A = input.substring (0,i)
14. var B = input.substring (i+1, input.length)
15. if ((determiner (A) && noun (B))
16. || noun (input)) {return true}
17. i++
18. }
19. return false }

24. function noun (input) {
25. if (input == "man" || input == "dog") {
26. return true}
27. return false }

28. function v_phrase (input) {
29. var i = 1
30. while (i<= input.length) {
31. var A = input.substring (0,i)
32. var B = input.substring (i+1, input.length)
33. if (verb (A) && noun_phrase (B)) {return true}
34. i++
35. }
36. return false }
```

Lines 3 through 8 repeatedly break the input sentence into two pieces represented by variables A (line 4) and B (line 5). This cycle begins with A representing the first character of the sentence and B representing the rest. In each cycle through this repeated procedure, a character is added from the sentence to A, the remainder (B) obviously being shortened by the loss of that character.

Let us take as an example the sentence "man bites dog." Here are the values of the variables A and B in the **sentence** function, in each cycle:

A = m
B = an bites dog

A = ma
B = n bites dog

A = man
B = bites dog

When A and B reach these values, A will satisfy the **noun_phrase** rule (which states that either a noun on its own or a noun preceded by a determiner successfully constitutes a noun phrase—lines 15 and 16). The first part of the **sentence** rule, which requires that *A* must be a noun phrase (line 6), is satisfied, so the next part of the **sentence** rule is checked out: *B* must be a verb phrase (line 6).

The value of *B* (which is now "bites dog") is passed to the **verb_phrase** rule. This sets up its own *A* and *B* variables (lines 31 and 32) and a similar repetitive process takes place within this function. Here are the values of *A* and *B* within the **verb_phrase** rule in each cycle:

A = b
B = ites dog

A = bi
B = tes dog

A = bit
B = es dog

A = bite
B = s dog

A = bites
B = dog

At this stage, *A* will satisfy the **verb** rule not shown here, and thus also the first condition of the **verb_phrase** rule (line 33). The second condition of the **verb_phrase** rule—namely, that *B* is a noun phrase (line 33)—is therefore next to be tried.

The process continues in this fashion until the entire sentence matches the rules, in which case the function returns *true*, or fails to match the rules, in which case it returns *false*.

Now here is the full code (Program 7-10 on the Website). This version of the program is case and space sensitive.

```
<HTML>
<HEAD>
<SCRIPT>

function sentence (input) {
var i = 1
while (i <= input.length) {
var A = input.substring (0,i)
var B = input.substring (i+1, input.length)
if (noun_phrase (A) && v_phrase (B)) {return true}
i++
}
return false }

function noun_phrase (input) {
```

```
var i = 1
while (i <= input.length) {
var A = input.substring (0,i)
var B = input.substring (i+1, input.length)
if ((determiner (A) && noun (B))
|| noun (input)) {return true}
i++
}
return false }

function v_phrase (input) {
var i = 1
while (i<= input.length) {
var A = input.substring (0,i)
var B = input.substring (i+1, input.length)
if (verb (A) && noun_phrase (B)) {return true}
i++
}
return false }

function determiner (input) {
if (input == "the" || input == "a") {
return true}
return false }

function noun (input) {
if (input == "man" || input == "dog") {
return true}
return false }

function verb (input) {
if (input == "bites") {
return true}
return false }

if (sentence (prompt ("Enter your sentence", "")))
{alert ("This is a valid sentence")} else {alert ("This is not a valid sentence")}

</SCRIPT>
</HEAD>
</HTML>
```

These simple grammar rules will accept as valid sentences such as:

the man bites the dog
a dog bites a man

a dog bites the man
man bites dog

and so on, but will correctly reject as invalid sentences such as:

the man bites
the dog bites
dog the man bites
bites dog the man

Note that the matching is extremely brittle. Adding a space before or after a sentence, or putting more than one space between words, will cause the match to fail and the sentence to be rejected as invalid. Techniques introduced in the section "Fuzzy Matching" earlier in this chapter could be used to make the system more flexible.

As previously mentioned, the notion of syntax extends to more than natural language. Our next example provides a component for an intelligent "front end" to an Internet search engine like Alta Vista or indeed an interactive tutorial system designed to teach keyword searching.

> **NOTE** Search engines find all the documents in their indexes that contain the words you specify. An "intelligent front end" is an additional interface to such a search engine (or indeed to any other form of computer program) that monitors what you type in and gives assistance in making your request effective before it is submitted to the main part of the program. For instance, it could check that the syntax of your commands is correct and if there is a problem either try to correct it or inform you of its nature and where it occurs.

The system analyzes a keyword search typed in by a reader and checks that it correctly obeys the syntax required by the search engine. Although not extensively developed in the following example, it would be possible to build into the system the capability to tell the reader, if he or she has made a mistake, exactly where the problem lies—for example, that he or she has omitted a closing parenthesis or has failed to enclose a phrase within quotation marks.

In this simple example, the reader's keyword request is checked and, if it does not match the required syntax, he or she is simply told that it is not acceptable. In a limited number of cases, the reader may be shown those parts of the request that *are* correct and after which the problem occurs. An example is shown in Figures 7.9 and 7.10. However, the system cannot work out the nature of the error, and in most cases will simply indicate that the syntax is not acceptable.

Figure 7.9 A search request with incorrect syntax.

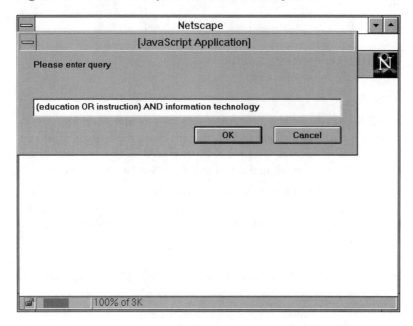

This system is essentially a rule-based system of the type introduced in Chapter 5. Recall from that chapter the techniques of negative explanation. These could be used to extend the system so that it would explain the exact nature of the problem when a reader enters a query that does not obey the search engine's required syntax. As in the example given in Chapter 5, the explanations could be derived from knowledge of exactly which rules have failed.

We will implement the following syntactical rules:

1. A *level 1 query* may consist of:
2.   *a level 2 query*; or
3.   *a level 2 query AND a level 1 query*

4. A *level 2 query* may consist of:
5.   *a phrase*; or
6.   *(a phrase)*; or
7.   *a phrase AND a level 1 query*; or
8.   *(a phrase AND a level 1 query)*; or

Figure 7.10 The system gives feedback on the request.

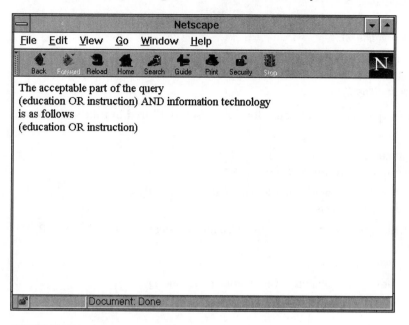

The acceptable part of the query
(education OR instruction) AND information technology
is as follows
(education OR instruction)

9.   *a phrase OR a level 1 query*; or
10.   *(a phrase OR a level 1 query)*

11. A *phrase* may consist of:
12.   a *word*; or
13.   *"one or more words"*

According to these rules, the following keyword requests do obey the syntax. Each example is followed by an indication in italics of which element of the rules it obeys.

learning
a phrase (line 12)

"learning strategies"
a phrase (line 13)

learning AND styles
a level 2 query (line 7)

(learning OR styles)
a level 2 query (line 10)

("learning styles" OR "learning strategies")
a level 2 query (line 10)

("learning styles" AND (computers OR "information technology"))
a level 2 query (line 8)

(computers OR workstations) AND (Internet OR "World Wide Web")
a level 1 query (line 3)

(learning AND (styles OR strategies)) AND ("computer assisted" AND (learning OR instruction))
a level 1 query (line 3)

The following queries are not valid, for the reason indicated in italics after each one:

"learning strategies
no closing quotation mark to indicate a phrase

("learning styles" AND (computers OR "information technology")
missing closing parenthesis

(learning AND (styles OR strategies)) AND ("computer assisted" AND (learning OR instruction)))
too many closing parentheses

("learning styles" AND (computers OR information technology))
no quotation marks surrounding two words (information technology) to indicate a phrase

Here is the code (Program 7-11 on the website). This version of the program is case and space sensitive. The operators AND and OR must be in uppercase, and any spaces in queries are interpreted as characters. Thus one or more spaces appearing before or after the query will result in the query's being rejected as invalid.

 Techniques introduced in the "Fuzzy Matching" section of this chapter would enable the system to be extended to handle lower-case operators and additional spaces.

```
<HTML>
<HEAD>
<SCRIPT>

var log = ""
var error = ""

function validQuery1 (input) {
if (validQuery2 (input)) {return true}
var i=0
```

```
while (i <= input.length) {
i++
var stringPrecedingOperator = input.substring (0,i)
var ANDoperator = input.substring (i+1,i+4)
var stringFollowingOperator = input.substring (i+5, input.length)
if (ANDoperator == "AND") {
if (validQuery2 (stringPrecedingOperator) && validQuery1 (stringFollowingOperator))
{return true} }
}
return false}

function validQuery2 (input) {
if (validPhrase (input)) {return true}
var i=0
while (i <= input.length) {
i++
var stringPrecedingOperator = input.substring (0,i)
var openingBracket = input.substring (0,1)
var stringBetweenBracketAndOperator = input.substring (1,i+1)
var ANDbetweenBrackets = input.substring (i+2,i+5)
var stringBetweenANDandBracket = input.substring (i+6,(input.length-1))
var ORbetweenBrackets = input.substring (i+2,i+4)
var stringBetweenORandBracket = input.substring (i+5,(input.length-1))
var ANDoperator = input.substring (i+1,i+4)
var stringFollowingAND = input.substring (i+5, input.length)
var ANDoperator = input.substring (i+1,i+3)
var stringFollowingAND = input.substring (i+4, input.length)
var stringBetweenBrackets = input.substring (1, (input.length-1))
var closingBracket = input.substring ((input.length-1), input.length)

if ((bracketValidPhrase (openingBracket,stringBetweenBrackets,closingBracket)
&& report (input))
|| (andPhrase (stringPrecedingOperator,ANDoperator,stringFollowingAND)
&& report (stringPrecedingOperator + " AND " + stringFollowingAND))
|| (andBracketPhrase
(openingBracket,stringBetweenBracketAndOperator,ANDbetweenBrackets,
stringBetweenANDandBracket,closingBracket)
&& report ("(" + stringBetweenBracketAndOperator + " AND " +
stringBetweenANDandBracket + ")"))
|| (orBracketPhrase
(openingBracket,stringBetweenBracketAndOperator,ORbetweenBrackets,
stringBetweenORandBracket,closingBracket)
&& report ("(" + stringBetweenBracketAndOperator + " OR "
+ stringBetweenORandBracket + ")"))
```

```
|| (orPhrase (stringPrecedingOperator,ANDoperator,stringFollowingAND))
&& report (stringPrecedingOperator + " OR " + stringFollowingAND))
{return true} }
return false}

function orBracketPhrase (A,B,C,D,E) {
if (
A == "(" && C == "OR" && validPhrase (B)
&& validQuery1 (D) && E == ")" )
{return true}
else {
return false}}

function andPhrase (A,B,C) {
if (B == "AND" && validPhrase (A) && validQuery1 (C))
{return true}
else {
return false}}

function andBracketPhrase (A,B,C,D,E) {
if (
A == "(" && C == "AND" && validPhrase (B)
&& validQuery1 (D) && E == ")" )
{return true}
else {
return false}}

function bracketValidPhrase (A,B,C) {
if (
A == "(" && C == ")" && validPhrase (B))
{return true}
else {
return false}}

function orPhrase (A,B,C) {
if (B == "OR" &&
validPhrase (A)
&& validQuery2 (C) )
{return true}
else {
return false}}

function validWord2 (input) {
var illegalCharacters = ' ()"'
```

```
for (i=0;i<input.length;i++) {
for (j=0;j<illegalCharacters.length;j++) {
if (input.substring (i,i+1) == illegalCharacters.substring (j,j+1))
{return false}}}
return true}

function validWord3 (input) {
var illegalCharacters = '"'
for (i=0;i<input.length;i++) {
for (j=0;j<illegalCharacters.length;j++) {
if (input.substring (i,i+1) == illegalCharacters.substring (j,j+1))
{return false}}}
return true}

function validPhrase (input) {
var A = input.substring (0,1)
var xyz = input.length
var B = input.substring (1,(xyz-1))
var C = input.substring (xyz -1,xyz)
if (validWord2 (input)
|| (A == '"'  && validWord3 (B) && C == '"' ))
{return true}
return false}

function report (A) {
log = A + "<br>"
return true
}

var query = prompt ("Please enter query ", "")
if (validQuery1 (query)) {
document.write ("Your query is fine!<br>")}
else {
if (log == "") {document.write ("<br>I am afraid that none of the query parsed suc-
cessfully<br>")}
else {document.write ("The acceptable part of the query <br>" + query
+ "<br>is as follows<br>" + log + "<p>") }
}

</SCRIPT>
</HEAD>
</HTML>
```

PROBLEM SOLVING
and Game Playing

8

It is unlikely that the main purpose of your Web pages will be to solve problems or play games. However, problem solving and game playing are excellent vehicles for introducing information processing techniques useful in developing programs capable of intelligent behavior.

Games are introduced here insofar as they require problem-solving techniques to enable computers to play them—for example, implementing strategic reactions to moves made by an opponent. Problem solving is central to many intelligent applications because functions can often be thought of as essentially "problems" requiring solutions. This holds true even where the function of an application is not problem solving in any formal or explicit sense, but rather simply behaving intelligently, so as to add value to your Web pages.

Halfway between bald technical explanations and realistic real-world applications, the problems and games introduced in this chapter are designed to illustrate complex procedures (such as double recursion and means-ends analysis) clearly and simply while tackling tasks that are meaningful to the experience of all readers. In this way, these concepts can be easily grasped and included in a repertoire of potentially useful techniques for the development of Web pages capable of displaying intelligent behavior.

Route Finding

Finding a route from a starting point to some destination is a process that can be generalized to a wide range of problems. We can represent many problems in terms of getting from some initial state (the current situation) to some end state (the desired situation). In the case of finding a travel route, the initial state is where we are now, and the end state is our destination. In the case of, say, diagnosing plant problems, the initial state is a sick plant, and the desired end state is a healthy plant. In terms of problem solving more generally, the initial state is the current problem situation; the end state is the problem solved.

Figure 8.1 A network of rail links.

Sheffield – Barnsley – Leeds – Durham – Newcastle
Manchester – Carlisle – Durham – Edinburgh

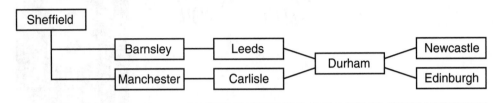

In order to introduce techniques clearly, we will stay with the *travel* problem: finding a route from one place to another. We will keep things simple at first and set up a series of rail links between a number of cities, as shown in Figure 8.1.

We can represent these links as a series of starting and ending points. Thus the first link starts at Sheffield and ends at Barnsley, the next starts at Barnsley and ends at Leeds, and so on.

```
Sheffield—Barnsley
Barnsley—Leeds
Leeds—Durham
Durham—Newcastle
Sheffield—Manchester
Manchester—Carlisle
Carlisle—Durham
Durham—Edinburgh
```

We want our system to be able to tell us how to get from one city to another. So, for example, if we ask for a route from Sheffield to Newcastle, we would expect the answer:

```
Sheffield—Barnsley—Leeds—Durham—Newcastle
```

However, if we removed the link between, say, Leeds and Durham, we would expect our system to reroute us as follows:

```
Sheffield—Manchester—Carlisle—Durham—Newcastle
```

This interaction is shown in Figures 8.2 and 8.3.

We will represent the links in JavaScript as members of an array. Each link will itself be an array, with two properties: a *start* and a *finish*. For clarity and simplicity, the names of cities have been replaced with letters in our code:

```
route[0][start] = "A"
route[0][finish] = "B"
```

Figure 8.2 The system finds a route.

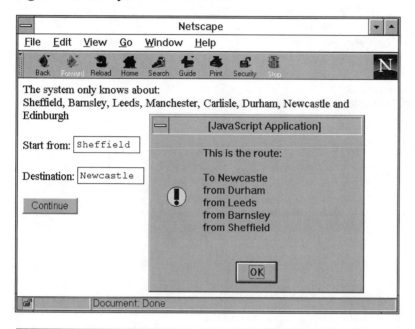

```
route[1][start] = "B"
route[1][finish] = "C"
route[2][start] = "C"
route[2][finish] = "D"
route[3][start] = "D"
route[3][finish] = "E"
```

and so on. We can create these arrays as follows:

```
route = new Array ()

function route_details (start, finish) {
this.start=start
this.finish=finish }

route[0] = new route_details ("A", "B")
route[1] = new route_details ("B", "C")
route[2] = new route_details ("C", "D")
route[3] = new route_details ("D", "E")
```

and so on.

Figure 8.3 The system finds an alternative route when a link is removed.

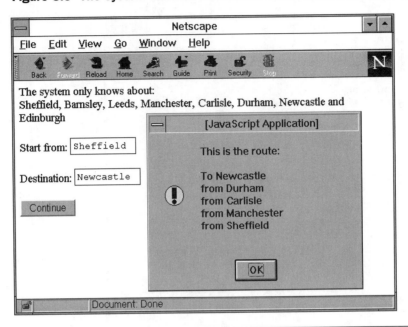

We've set up the links; here is the strategy we will build into the system so that it can successfully find routes between cities. The example is for a route from A to E.

1. Try to get from A to E
2.   I am at A—is this my destination?
3.   If yes, then stop.
4.   If no, then find where I can get to from A (try B)
5.   See if I can get from B to E (go to line 7)
6.   If I can, then add city A the route plan

7. Try to get from B to E
8.   I am at B—is this my destination?
9.   If yes, then stop.
10.   If no, then find where I can get to from B (try C)
11.   See if I can get from C to E (go to line 13)
12.   If I can, then add city B to the route plan

13. Try to get from C to E
14.   I am at C—is this my destination?
15.   If yes, then stop.
16.   If no, then find where I can get to from C (try D)

17.   See if I can get from D to E (go to line 19)
18.   If I can, then add city C to the route plan

19. Try to get from D to E
20.   I am at D—is this my destination?
21.   If yes, then stop.
22.   If no, then find where I can get to from D (try E)
23.   See if I can get from E to E (go to line 25)
24.   If I can, then add city D to the route plan

25. Try to get from E to E
26.   I am at E—is this my destination?
27.   If yes, then stop.

The program starts by trying to get from A to E (line 1). Because it is not yet at the destination, it goes to line 4. This line checks for links from A to anywhere else. If there is more than one link from A, it takes the first link it finds (in this case, the link from A to B). Note that in the JavaScript code there will be a loop here that—if the link from A to B fails to get us to the destination—will try all the other links from A to anywhere else. This is the means whereby the program can backtrack and try other solutions to the problem if one fails.

Line 6, in which the link just tried (A) is added to the route plan, will not be processed unless and until line 5 has successfully found a way of getting from B to the destination (E). If no way is found from B to E, A will not be added to the route plan. In this way, only links that prove to be successful will be added to the route plan. Thus line 6 will not be processed until lines 7 through 12 have been processed with a successful result. Similarly, line 12 will not be processed until line 11 has successfully found a way of getting from C to the destination, which entails processing lines 13 through 18.

Commands are "stacked up" and processed only when the destination is reached (line 27). At this point, the stacked-up commands (lines 24, 18, 12, and 6, in that order) are executed, and the successful route is compiled.

In pseudo-code, here is the rule that will implement this strategy.

```
function findRoute from CurrentPlace to Destination
IF CurrentPlace = Destination
THEN return true
    ELSE find a link from CurrentPlace to SomewhereElse AND
        IF findRoute from SomewhereElse to Destination returns true
        THEN add CurrentPlace to the route
```

Here is a worked example for finding a route from A to E:

1. function findRoute from A to E
2. IF A = E
3. THEN return true

4.　　ELSE find a link from A to B AND
5.　　　　IF **findRoute** from B to E returns true
　　　　　　[lines 7–12 will be processed before line 6]
6.　　　　THEN add A to the route

7.　function **findRoute** from B to E
8.　IF B = E
9.　THEN return true
10.　　ELSE find a link from B to C AND
11.　　　　IF **findRoute** from C to E returns true
　　　　　　[lines 13–18 will be processed before line 12]
12.　　　　THEN add B to the route

13. function **findRoute** from C to E
14. IF C = E
15. THEN return true
16.　　ELSE find a link from C to D AND
17.　　　　IF **findRoute** from D to E returns true
　　　　　　[lines 19–24 will be processed before line 18]
18.　　　　THEN add C to the route

19. function **findRoute** from D to E
20. IF D = E
21. THEN return true
22.　　ELSE find a link from D to E AND
23.　　　　IF **findRoute** from E to E returns true
　　　　　　[lines 25–27 will be processed before line 24]
24.　　　　THEN add D to the route

25. function **findRoute** from E to E
26. IF E = E
27. THEN return true

Here is the full code (Program 8-1 on the website):

```
<HTML>
<BODY>
<SCRIPT LANGUAGE="JavaScript">

var trace = ""
var routeFound = "no"

function route_details (start, finish) {
this.start=start
this.finish=finish }
```

```
route = new Array ()

route[0] = new route_details ("Sheffield", "Barnsley")
route[1] = new route_details ("Barnsley", "Leeds")
route[2] = new route_details ("Leeds", "Durham")
route[3] = new route_details ("Durham", "Newcastle")
route[4] = new route_details ("Sheffield", "Manchester")
route[5] = new route_details ("Manchester", "Carlisle")
route[6] = new route_details ("Carlisle", "Durham")
route[7] = new route_details ("Durham", "Edinburgh")

function find_route (from, to) {
if (from == to) {routeFound = "yes"; return true}
else {
for (i in route) {
if (route[i].start == from) {
if (find_route (route[i].finish, to))
{trace += "from " + from + "\n"
return true}}}
return false}
}

</SCRIPT>
The system only knows about:<BR>Sheffield, Barnsley, Leeds, Manchester, Carlisle,
Durham, Newcastle and Edinburgh
<FORM>
Start from:
<INPUT TYPE="text" NAME="param1" SIZE=10><P>
Destination:
<INPUT TYPE="text" NAME="param2" SIZE=10><P>
<INPUT TYPE="button" VALUE = "Continue" onClick="trace = ''; find_route
(this.form.param1.value, this.form.param2.value); if (routeFound == 'yes') {alert
('This is the route:\n\nTo ' + this.form.param2.value + '\n' + trace)} else {alert
('Sorry -- I have not been able to find a route')}">
</FORM>
</BODY>
</HTML>
```

It is important to note that when we set up a link between, say, Sheffield and Manchester, as far as JavaScript is concerned there is no link in the opposite direction between Manchester and Sheffield. Such bidirectional links, which we take for granted, must be explicitly programmed.

However, there is a danger in making a network of links that the traveler could get into a loop. The danger is that when it tries links from one place to another, JavaScript may end up with an infinite loop such as:

Sheffield—Manchester—Barnsley—Sheffield—Manchester—Barnsley—Sheffield and so on. To prevent this problem, it is necessary to set up a log in which previously tried routes are recorded. Each time a new move is being contemplated, the log is consulted, and the new move is not allowed if it repeats a move previously made.

This type of checking procedure, using a log to prevent looping, is explained and illustrated below.

The River-Crossing Problem

The river-crossing problem is one of those classic examples used for many years in courses on computing and psychology. It contains a number of elements that make it particularly useful in teaching problem solving: problem representation in terms of an initial state and a desired end state, a strategy, operators capable of changing the problem from one state to another in the search for a solution, and constraints on choice of operators.

The problem is as follows. On the left bank of a river are a woman, a goat, a wolf, and a cabbage. They need to get to the other side of the river. However, the woman can take only one item at a time with her across the river in the boat. The problem is that if at any stage she leaves the goat and cabbage alone on the riverbank, the goat will eat the cabbage. If she leaves the goat alone with the wolf, the wolf will eat the goat. So our problem-solving program needs to work out a series of moves to enable the woman to get the goat, wolf, and cabbage safely to the other side of the river.

This problem has a lot in common with the route-finding example introduced above. There is a starting point (an initial problem state, in this case the woman, goat, cabbage, and wolf on the left bank of the river) and a destination (the desired end state of the woman, goat, cabbage, and wolf being on the *right* bank of the river).

There are also a number of constraints. The wolf and the goat, as well as the goat and the cabbage, must not at any stage be left alone on either bank; otherwise, the goat or the cabbage will be in danger of being eaten. However, the woman can carry only one item from bank to bank at a time.

Let us examine the parallels with the route-finding example, in which we wanted to get from place A to place E. This program had the following structure:

1. To get from the initial state [A] to the desired end state [E]
2. Take the initial state [we are at place A]
3. Transform the initial state into a new state [by finding a rail link from A to B]
4. Try to get from this new state [B] to the desired end state [E]

Our new program has a similar structure in that we want to get from an initial state A (woman, goat, wolf, and cabbage on the left bank) to a desired end state E (woman, goat, wolf, and cabbage on the right bank). The structure is parallel:

1. To get from the initial state [woman, goat, wolf, and cabbage on left bank] to the desired end state [woman, goat, wolf, and cabbage on right bank]
2. Take the initial state
3. Find a way of transforming the initial state into a new state [find a "legal" boatload to move from one bank to the other—for instance, woman and goat to right bank]
4. Try to get from this new state [woman and goat on right bank; wolf and cabbage on left bank] to the desired end state [woman, wolf, goat, and cabbage on right bank]

In the route-finding example, the way of transforming the initial state into some new state was to find a rail link from place A to somewhere else. We then tried to get from that "somewhere else" to our destination.

In the river-crossing problem, the way of transforming one state into a new state is more complex. It entails identifying a "legal" boatload (for example, the woman and goat traveling from the left to the right bank) that will result in a changed state or a "somewhere else" (in this case, the woman and the goat on the right bank; the wolf and the cabbage on the left bank). We then need to identify another "legal" boatload that will transform this problem state into some new problem state from which we will be able to reach our desired end state. We also need to build in some check so that we do not get into a loop of identical moves.

Here is a solution that we want our program to be able to generate. It consists of the following series of moves:

1. The woman takes the goat from left to right bank.
2. The woman sails alone from right to left bank.
3. The woman takes the cabbage from left to right bank.
4. The woman takes the goat from right to left bank.
5. The woman takes the wolf from left to right bank.
6. The woman sails alone from right to left bank.
7. The woman takes the goat from left to right bank.

Let us start by representing the initial problem state and the desired end state. We can do this by creating four variables. The first two represent the initial problem state of the left and right riverbanks as they are now:

```
var left_now = " woman cabbage goat wolf "
var right_now = " "
```

The second two represent the goal state:

```
var left_goal = " "
var right_goal = " woman cabbage goat wolf "
```

We can represent the players as arrays:

```
player = new Array ()
player[0] = "cabbage"
player[1] = "goat"
player[2] = "wolf"
```

We can define the possible legal moves as follows:

1. The woman can go on her own from the left to right bank, if doing so does not result in an illegal combination of items (defined below).

2. The woman can go on her own from the right to left bank, if doing so does not result in an illegal combination of items.

3. The woman plus one item can go from left to right bank, if doing so does not result in an illegal combination of items.

4. The woman plus one item can go from right to left bank, if doing so does not result in an illegal combination of items.

An illegal combination of items consists of the goat and wolf being left together without the woman or the goat and cabbage being left together without the woman. We can create a function that will check a riverbank at any stage and say whether or not it is in a legal state:

```
function legal (bank) {
if (bank.indexOf ("woman", 0) < 0 &&
(( bank.indexOf ("wolf", 0) >= 0 && bank.indexOf ("goat", 0) >= 0)
|| (bank.indexOf ("goat", 0) >= 0 && bank.indexOf ("cabbage", 0) >= 0)))
{return false } else {return true } }
```

This function is passed details of the riverbank to be checked. This is passed to the function as its *bank* parameter. A typical *bank* might be "goat cabbage woman." The function first checks whether the woman is present on the bank. If she is, it returns *true*. If she's not, it goes on to check whether any illegal combination of players is present: the wolf and the goat or the goat and the cabbage. The function uses **indexOf**, which, if the text specified in its first argument is found in the *bank* string, returns its location in the string. If this value is greater than or equal to 0 this means the text has been found. If the *bank* contains an illegal state, the function returns *false*.

We can also set up a function that will check whether a particular state of the two banks has existed before. If it has, then we are in a loop. We will use this function to avoid this situation:

```
function previously_visited (side, bank) {
var holder=false
for (i in log) {
if (equivalent (side + " " + bank, log[i]) == true) {holder = true}
} return holder}
```

This function is passed the state of a bank as it would be if a projected move were made. If the function returns *true*, the move would only duplicate a move already made. Therefore, the main part of the program (explained below) would try a different move.

We are building strings to represent the state of the two banks each time a move is made. The order in which players appear in the string representing a bank depends on the order in which they are moved. Thus the string for a given bank may be "goat woman cabbage," "woman goat cabbage," or "cabbage woman goat." We therefore need to create a function **equivalent** that will return *true* if given two strings that contain the same players—even if they appear in a different order.

```
function equivalent (bank, log_item) {
if ( bothThere (bank, log_item, "woman")
&& bothThere (bank, log_item, "goat")
&& bothThere (bank, log_item, "cabbage")
&& bothThere (bank, log_item, "wolf")
&& bothThere (bank, log_item, "left")
&& bothThere (bank, log_item, "right") )
{return true}
return false}
```

This function is passed two arguments. The first is a string representing the state of a bank if a projected move were to be carried out. The second is an array containing strings representing all the previous moves made. This function checks whether each player is present or absent in both strings. If all players match, **equivalent** returns *true*. It uses another function, **bothThere**, to check in turn whether each player is present or absent in both the bank representation and the log of previous moves.

```
function bothThere (bank, log_item, thing) {
if ((bank.indexOf (thing, 0) >= 0 && log_item.indexOf (thing, 0) >= 0) ||
(bank.indexOf (thing, 0) < 0 && log_item.indexOf (thing, 0) < 0))
{return true}
return false}
```

The **bothThere** function is passed the string representing the state of the bank after the projected move, the name of the player to be checked, and the array representing all the moves previously made. Like the **legal** function, the **bothThere** function uses the **indexOf** method to check whether the player is present or absent in the bank and the log of previous moves.

Now let's examine the function **transform**, which handles the moves by transforming the current state of the two banks (represented by *bank1* and *bank2*) and the goal state (represented by *goal1* and *goal2*). The same function can be used whether we are moving from the left to right or the right to left banks. If the value of the variable *starting_side* is "left," *bank1* and *goal1* will represent the left bank and *bank2* and *goal2* the right bank. If *starting_side* is "right," the positions will be reversed.

The **transform** function uses exactly the same basic structure as the **findRoute** function we met in the route-finding section earlier in this chapter. It is more complex in that more actions are performed in each of the main sections.

```
1. function transform (starting_side, bank1, bank2, goal1, goal2)
2. {
3. if (starting_side=="right" && equivalent (bank2, " ") == true)
4. {document.write (bank2 + "---------------------" + bank1 + "<BR>")
5. return true}
6. else {for (i in player) {
7. var new_bank1 = move (i, bank1, bank2, "bank1", starting_side)
8. var new_bank2 = move (i, bank1, bank2, "bank2", starting_side)
9. if (starting_side == "left") {other_side = "right"}
10. else {other_side = "left"}
11. if (legal (new_bank1)== true
12. && legal (new_bank2)==true
13. && previously_visited (other_side, new_bank2)==false
14. && previously_visited (other_side, new_bank1)==false
15. && add_to_log (other_side + " " + new_bank2) == true
16. && transform (other_side, new_bank2, new_bank1, goal1, goal2) == true)
17. {
18. if (starting_side == "left") {document.write (bank1 + "---------------------" +
bank2 + "<BR>")}
19. else {document.write (bank2 + "---------------------" + bank1 + "<BR>")}
20. return true}}
21. return false }}

22. function move (player_number, bank1, bank2, return_element, side) {
// MOVE WOMAN
23. index = bank1.indexOf ("woman", 0)
24. bank1 = bank1.substring (0, (index) ) + bank1.substring (bank1.indexOf ("woman")
+ "woman".length, bank1.length)
25. bank2 = " " + bank2 + "woman" + " "
// MOVE A PLAYER
26. if ( (index = bank1.indexOf (player[player_number], 0)) >= 0 ) {
27. bank1 = bank1.substring (0, (index) ) + bank1.substring (bank1.indexOf
(player[player_number]) + player[player_number].length, bank1.length )
28. bank2 = " " + bank2 + player[player_number] + " "
29. }
30. if (return_element == "bank1") {return bank1}
31. if (return_element == "bank2") {return bank2}
32. }
```

Line 3 specifies a boundary condition telling JavaScript that the goal has been reached when the left bank is empty—in other words, when *starting_side* = "right" and *bank2* = " ". (Bear in mind that when *starting_side* = "left", *bank2* will represent the right bank.)

When the goal is reached, **transform** writes the final state of the two banks (line 4) and returns *true* (line 5). If the goal has not yet been reached (line 6), a move entailing each player in turn (line 6) is tried and checked to establish whether it is legal (lines 11 through 14).

If all of these checks are successful, the move is added to the log of moves made (line 15), and **transform** calls itself recursively (line 16) to try to get from the new state of the two banks brought about by the move (represented by *new_bank1* and *new_bank2*, line 16) to the goal state. Because the next move will start from the other bank, the starting side for the move is changed (lines 9 and 10) and passed in the recursive call (line 16).

Only if the entire cycle of recursive calls is ultimately successful—that is, only if the goal is finally reached—does JavaScript print the list of changes to the state of the two banks necessary to solve the problem (lines 18 and 19). Note that these changes are printed only *after* the solution has been found—that is, *after* **transform** has successfully called itself recursively (line 16).

In other words, all moves which were tried but did not eventually lead to the solution—even if they were entirely legal—are not printed out. This avoids the situation in which a series of legal moves fail somewhere down the line. JavaScript backtracks from this point to try alternative series of moves but does not print the failed ones.

The consequence is that the list of moves is printed in reverse order, as the recursion "unwinds" after having reached the goal. We will tackle this problem in a second version of the program.

Making a move entails processing the text strings representing the two banks. The word "woman" is removed from one bank (line 24) and added to the other (line 25), as is the name of the player the woman takes with her (lines 26 through 28). If the player to be moved is not present on the bank (in other words, if line 26 is not true), obviously it cannot be moved. In this case, the woman sails on her own from one bank to the other—that is, only the move relating to the woman (lines 23 through 25) is made.

 We do not actually need the *goal1* and *goal2* arguments in the **transform** function because we can specify that the goal has been reached simply if the left bank is empty (line 3). However, including them makes the comparison with the earlier route-finding problem easier.

Now here is the code (Program 8-2 on the website) in full:

```
<HTML>
<HEAD>
<SCRIPT LANGUAGE="JavaScript">
```

```
var left_now = " woman cabbage goat wolf "
var right_now = " "
var left_goal = " "
var right_goal = " woman cabbage goat wolf "
var log_counter = 0
player = new Array ()
player[0] = "cabbage"
player[1] = "goat"
player[2] = "wolf"
log = new Array ()

function legal (bank) {
if (bank.indexOf ("woman", 0) < 0 &&
(( bank.indexOf ("wolf", 0) >= 0 && bank.indexOf ("goat", 0) >= 0)
|| (bank.indexOf ("goat", 0) >= 0 && bank.indexOf ("cabbage", 0) >= 0)))
{return false } else {return true } }

function previously_visited (side, bank) {
var holder=false
for (i in log) {
if (equivalent (side + " " + bank, log[i]) == true) {holder = true}
} return holder}

function equivalent (bank, log_item) {
if ( bothThere (bank, log_item, "woman")
&& bothThere (bank, log_item, "goat")
&& bothThere (bank, log_item, "cabbage")
&& bothThere (bank, log_item, "wolf")
&& bothThere (bank, log_item, "left")
&& bothThere (bank, log_item, "right") )
{return true}
return false}

function bothThere (bank, log_item, thing) {
if ((bank.indexOf (thing, 0) >= 0 && log_item.indexOf (thing, 0) >= 0) ||
(bank.indexOf (thing, 0) < 0 && log_item.indexOf (thing, 0) < 0))
{return true}
return false}

function add_to_log (info) {
log[log_counter] = info
log_counter = log_counter + 1
return true}

function transform (starting_side, bank1, bank2, goal1, goal2) {
if (starting_side=="right" && equivalent (bank2, " ") == true)
{document.write (bank2 + "---------------------" + bank1 + "<BR>")
```

```
return true}
else {for (i in player) {
var new_bank1 = move (i, bank1, bank2, "bank1", starting_side)
var new_bank2 = move (i, bank1, bank2, "bank2", starting_side)
if (starting_side == "left") {other_side = "right"}
else {other_side = "left"}
if (legal (new_bank1)== true
&& legal (new_bank2)==true
&& previously_visited (other_side, new_bank2)==false
&& previously_visited (other_side, new_bank1)==false
&& add_to_log (other_side + " " + new_bank2) == true
&& transform (other_side, new_bank2, new_bank1, goal1, goal2) == true)
{
if (starting_side == "left") {document.write (bank1 + "---------------------" +
bank2 + "<BR>")}
else {document.write (bank2 + "---------------------" + bank1 + "<BR>")}
return true}}
return false }}

function move (player_number, bank1, bank2, return_element, side) {
// MOVE WOMAN
index = bank1.indexOf ("woman", 0)
bank1 = bank1.substring (0, (index) ) + bank1.substring (bank1.indexOf ("woman") +
"woman".length, bank1.length)
bank2 = " " + bank2 + "woman" + " "
// MOVE A PLAYER
if ( (index = bank1.indexOf (player[player_number], 0)) >= 0 ) {
bank1 = bank1.substring (0, (index) ) + bank1.substring (bank1.indexOf (player[play-
er_number]) + player[player_number].length, bank1.length )
bank2 = " " + bank2 + player[player_number] + " "
}
if (return_element == "bank1") {return bank1}
if (return_element == "bank2") {return bank2}
}

function changeSides (starting_side) {
if (starting_side == "left") {return "right"} else {return "left"}
}

</SCRIPT>
</HEAD>
<BODY>
<SCRIPT LANGUAGE="JavaScript">

document.write (" LEFT BANK-------------------RIGHT BANK<p>")
transform ("left", left_now, right_now, left_goal, right_goal)
```

```
</SCRIPT>
</BODY>
</HTML>
```

This version of the program solves the problem. However, it has been kept simple in order to illustrate the basic problem-solving technique. A consequence of this simplicity is that the way it presents its solution is far from ideal. As previously noted, it prints details of the left and right riverbanks after each move has been made in reverse order. The program's output is shown below:

```
LEFT BANK————————————————RIGHT BANK

——————————————— cabbage wolf woman goat
goat woman ——————————————— cabbage wolf
goat ——————————————— cabbage woman wolf
wolf woman goat ——————————————— cabbage
wolf ——————————————— goat woman cabbage
cabbage wolf woman ——————————————— goat
cabbage wolf ——————————————— woman goat
woman cabbage goat wolf ———————————————
```

Ideally, we would like it to print not simply the states of the left and right banks after each move has been made, but rather the moves themselves and in the correct order. The following version (Program 8-3 on the website) does precisely this. Changes from the previous code are shown in bold.

```
<HTML>
<HEAD>

<SCRIPT LANGUAGE="JavaScript">

var left_now = " woman cabbage goat wolf "
var right_now = " "
var left_goal = " "
var right_goal = " woman cabbage goat wolf "
var log_counter = 0
movement_log = new Array ()
player = new Array ()
player[0] = "cabbage"
player[1] = "goat"
player[2] = "wolf"
log = new Array ()

function legal (bank) {
if (bank.indexOf ("woman", 0) < 0 &&
(( bank.indexOf ("wolf", 0) >= 0 && bank.indexOf ("goat", 0) >= 0)
|| (bank.indexOf ("goat", 0) >= 0 && bank.indexOf ("cabbage", 0) >= 0)))
```

```
{return false } else {return true } }

function previously_visited (side, bank) {
var holder=false
for (i in log) {
if (equivalent (side + " " + bank, log[i]) == true) {holder = true}
} return holder}

function equivalent (bank, log_item) {
if ( bothThere (bank, log_item, "woman")
&& bothThere (bank, log_item, "goat")
&& bothThere (bank, log_item, "cabbage")
&& bothThere (bank, log_item, "wolf")
&& bothThere (bank, log_item, "left")
&& bothThere (bank, log_item, "right") )
{return true}
return false}

function bothThere (bank, log_item, thing) {
if ((bank.indexOf (thing, 0) >= 0 && log_item.indexOf (thing, 0) >= 0) ||
(bank.indexOf (thing, 0) < 0 && log_item.indexOf (thing, 0) < 0))
{return true}
return false}

function add_to_log (info) {
log[log_counter] = info
log_counter = log_counter + 1
return true}

function printLog (counter) {
var i = 0
while (i < counter) {
document.write (movement_log[i] + "<BR>")
i++}
}
function transform (starting_side, bank1, bank2, goal1, goal2, counter) {
if (starting_side=="right" && equivalent (bank2, " ") == true)
{printLog (counter)
return true}
else {for (i in player) {
var new_bank1 = move (i, bank1, bank2, "bank1", starting_side, counter)
var new_bank2 = move (i, bank1, bank2, "bank2", starting_side, counter)
if (starting_side == "left") {other_side = "right"}
else {other_side = "left"}
if (legal (new_bank1)== true
&& legal (new_bank2)==true
&& previously_visited (other_side, new_bank2)==false
```

```
&& previously_visited (other_side, new_bank1)==false
&& add_to_log (other_side + " " + new_bank2) == true
&& transform (other_side, new_bank2, new_bank1, goal1, goal2, counter + 1) == true)
{return true}}
return false }}

function move (player_number, bank1, bank2, return_element, side, counter) {
// MOVE WOMAN
index = bank1.indexOf ("woman", 0)
bank1 = bank1.substring (0, (index) ) + bank1.substring (bank1.indexOf ("woman") +
"woman".length, bank1.length)
bank2 = " " + bank2 + "woman" + " "
// MOVE A PLAYER
if ( (index = bank1.indexOf (player[player_number], 0)) >= 0 ) {
bank1 = bank1.substring (0, (index) ) + bank1.substring (bank1.indexOf (player[play-
er_number]) + player[player_number].length, bank1.length )
bank2 = " " + bank2 + player[player_number] + " "

movement_log[counter] = "Woman takes " + player[player_number] + " from " +
side
}
else {movement_log[counter] = "Woman on own from " + side }
if (return_element == "bank1") {return bank1}
if (return_element == "bank2") {return bank2}
}

function changeSides (starting_side) {
if (starting_side == "left") {return "right"} else {return "left"}
}

</SCRIPT>
</HEAD>
<BODY>
<SCRIPT LANGUAGE="JavaScript">

document.write ("SOLUTION <P>")
transform ("left", left_now, right_now, left_goal, right_goal, 0)

</SCRIPT>
</BODY>
</HTML>
```

This version stores each move as an element of an array **movement_log**, which is printed using the **printLog** function when the goal is reached. Each time a move is attempted, whether or not it turns out to be legal and whether or not it turns out to be one of the successful series of moves, the move is recorded in the **movement_log** array.

However, unsuccessful moves are overwritten by subsequent successful moves, so only those moves making up the correct solution to the problem are printed. This is achieved by adding a new argument *counter* to the **transform** function, which acts as an index for the storage of move details in the **movement_log** array.

The **move** function adds details of the current move to the array using the value of *counter*, which is passed to it from the **transform** function. So, for example, when *counter* = 0, the **move** function might store the following details of a move:

```
movement_log[0] = "woman takes wolf from left"
```

If *counter* = 1, then the details might be:

```
movement_log[1] = "woman on own from right"
```

The variable *counter* is incremented only in the recursive call of **transform** in the form of its last argument, *counter + 1*. What this means is that if a series of moves fails, JavaScript will backtrack to try an alternative series of moves. However, as it backtracks, the value of *count* also backtracks to previous values, in the sense that it remains the same in the same recursive cycle. In other words, if JavaScript backtracks to, say, the second recursive cycle of **transform**, it will find that *count* retains the value it originally had in that cycle.

So, the new attempt to find a successful series of moves from this point will share the same value of *counter* as the original unsuccessful one starting from the same point. Because the value of count is the same, details of the next new move will share the same index number (the value of count) and will thus overwrite the old ones. If, for example, JavaScript backtracks to the very beginning, its next attempted move might be:

```
movement_log[0] = "Woman takes goat from left"
```

thus overwriting the previous value of **movement_log[0]**.

When the solution is found, **printLog** displays the content of each element of the array **movement_log**. It is passed the latest value of *counter*—the value of *counter* when the goal is reached. In this way it knows how many of the elements of **movement_log** it should print. This is necessary because if a failed series of attempted moves was longer than the ultimate successful series of moves, **movement_log** would contain some redundant elements. These elements would, however, be indexed by numbers higher than the current value of *count*.

Figure 8.4 shows the improved output from version 2.

Towers of Hanoi

The towers of Hanoi puzzle is another classic problem-solving example. The purpose of including it here is to illustrate a powerful and elegant problem-solving technique entailing double recursion.

Figure 8.4 Solution to the river-crossing problem.

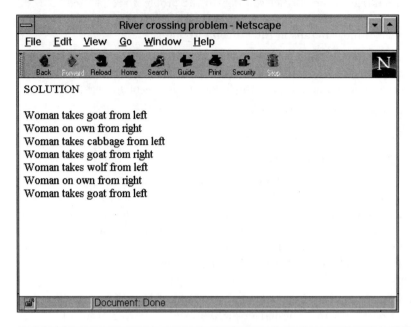

The puzzle consists of trying to move a number of disks from one pole to another. Figure 8.5 shows three disks, but in fact the program can find a solution for any number of disks (subject to computer memory).

The rules of the problem are as follows. Disks must be moved from the left pole to the middle pole. The right pole may be used in this process. However, only one disk may be moved at a time, and a disk may never be placed on top of a disk that is smaller than itself.

The solution, in the case of three disks, is as follows:

1. Move a disk from left to middle pole.
2. Move a disk from left to right pole.
3. Move a disk from middle to right pole.
4. Move a disk from left to middle pole.
5. Move a disk from right to left pole.
6. Move a disk from right to middle pole.
7. Move a disk from left to middle pole.

Here is the strategy. It entails using a function we will call **transfer**:

1. function **transfer**

2. To move a tower of 3 disks from left to middle, using the right as a spare
3.   first **transfer** a subtower of 2 disks from left to right
4.   then print "Move a disk from left to middle"
5.   then **transfer** the subtower of 2 disks from right to middle.

Bear in mind that only line 4 will move a disk (in fact, "moving" consists of simply printing what move should be made next). So only one disk at a time will be moved. The reference to transferring a subtower of more than one disk does not mean literally that a subtower will be moved. It refers to the fact that the **transfer** function will be called, line 4 of which moves only one tower each time the function is called.

The solution entails double recursion. This is illustrated in the pseudo-code below. The example uses only two disks in order to show the procedure more clearly. The line numbers show the order in which the lines are processed.

1. transfer 2 disks from left to middle (using right as spare)
2.   if 2 != 0
3.   transfer 1 disk from left to right (using middle as spare)
13.   move a disk from left to middle *[SECOND MOVE]*
14.   transfer 1 disk from right to middle (using left as spare)

4. transfer 1 disk from left to right (using middle as spare)
5.   if 1 != 0
6.   transfer 0 disks from left to middle (using right as spare)
9.   move a disk from left to right *[FIRST MOVE]*
10.   transfer 0 disks from middle to right (using left as spare)

7. transfer 0 disks from left to middle (using right as spare)
8.   if 0 != 0 *[This does not apply, so control is passed to line 9]*

Figure 8.5 The towers of Hanoi problem.

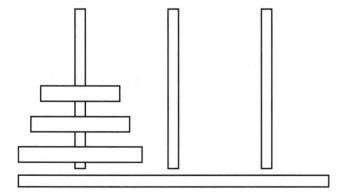

11. transfer 0 disks from middle to right (using left as spare)
12.   if 0 != 0 *[This does not apply, so control is passed to line 13]*

15. transfer 1 disk from right to middle (using left as spare)
16.   if 1 != 0
17.   transfer 0 disks from right to left (using middle as spare)
20.   move a disk from right to middle *[THIRD MOVE]*
21.   transfer 0 disk from left to middle (using right as spare)

18. transfer 0 discs from right to left (using middle as spare)
19.   if 0 != 0 *[This does not apply, so control is passed to line 20]*

22. transfer 0 disks from left to middle (using right as spare)
23.   if 0 != 0 *[This does not apply. No further lines to process.]*

Note the order in which the moves are made: lines 9, 13, and 20.

Now here is the full code. The first version (Program 8-4 on the website) solves the problem for three disks and displays each move in an alert message box.

```
<HTML>
<HEAD>
<SCRIPT LANGUAGE="JavaScript">

function hanoi (number, source, destination, spare) {
if (number != 0) {
hanoi (number - 1, source, spare, destination)
alert ("Move a disk from " + source + " to " + destination)
hanoi (number - 1, spare, destination, source) }
}

hanoi (3, "left", "middle", "right")

</SCRIPT>
</HEAD>
</HTML>
```

The second version below (Program 8-5 on the website) is somewhat more user-friendly. It asks the reader how many disks should be placed on the left pole and displays the results in the main window.

```
<HTML>
<HEAD>

<SCRIPT LANGUAGE="JavaScript">

solution = ""

function transfer (number, source, destination, spare) {
```

```
if (number != 0) {
transfer (number - 1, source, spare, destination)
solution += "Move a disk from " + source + " to " + destination + "<BR>"
transfer  (number - 1, spare, destination, source)}
}

</SCRIPT>
</HEAD>
<BODY>
Enter number of disks (no more than 5 recommended!)
<FORM>
<INPUT TYPE = "text" NAME = "input">
<INPUT TYPE = "button" VALUE = "Submit" onClick = "transfer
(this.form.input.value,'left', 'middle', 'right'); document.write (solution)">
</FORM>
</BODY>
</HTML>
```

Figure 8.6 shows the second version in action.

Implementing a Strategy:
Responding to an Opponent

Tic-tac-toe is a trivial game. However, it does provide an excellent simple example of how to implement a strategy capable of responding intelligently to an opponent's moves. In more general problem-solving terms, "an opponent's moves" can equate to changes in a problem situation, whether relatively neutral (changes in the market or economic conditions) or more specifically hostile (moves made by competing individuals or organizations).

Figure 8.7 shows the system in action. The reader clicks an empty box to make a move, then clicks the button. The **onBlur** event handler of the box triggers the system's response.

The strategy we will build into the program is very simple:

1. If any line (horizontal, vertical, or diagonal) has an empty cell that, if filled, would result in a win, then fill it.

2. If the center cell is free, then fill it.

3. Otherwise, fill any free cell.

These steps are tried in order so that a more valuable move is made before a less valuable one if possible.

```
<HTML>
<BODY>
```

Figure 8.6 Solution for 3 disks.

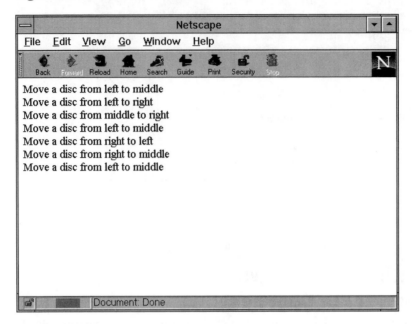

```
Click on a cell then click button
<FORM NAME="myForm">
<INPUT TYPE="text" NAME="text1" SIZE="6" VALUE="1" onBlur="check (1)">
<INPUT TYPE="text" NAME="text2" SIZE="6" VALUE="2" onBlur="check (2)">
<INPUT TYPE="text" NAME="text3" SIZE="6" VALUE="3" onBlur="check (3)">
<br>
<INPUT TYPE="text" NAME="text4" SIZE="6" VALUE="4" onBlur="check (4)">
<INPUT TYPE="text" NAME="text5" SIZE="6" VALUE="5" onBlur="check (5)">
<INPUT TYPE="text" NAME="text6" SIZE="6" VALUE="6" onBlur="check (6)">
<br>
<INPUT TYPE="text" NAME="text7" SIZE="6" VALUE="7" onBlur="check (7)">
<INPUT TYPE="text" NAME="text8" SIZE="6" VALUE="8" onBlur="check (8)">
<INPUT TYPE="text" NAME="text9" SIZE="6" VALUE="9" onBlur="check (9)">
<INPUT TYPE="button" VALUE="Move made">
</FORM>

<SCRIPT>

found = "no"

// set up objects
```

Figure 8.7 Implementing a simple strategy.

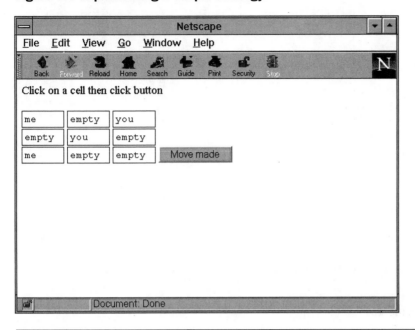

```
box = new Array ();
win = new Array ();
my_score = new Array ();
your_score = new Array ();
```

```
// set up each cell as empty
```

```
box[1]="empty"; box[2]="empty"; box[3]="empty"; box[4]="empty"; box[5]="empty";
box[6]="empty"; box[7]="empty"; box[8]="empty"; box[9]="empty";
```

```
// specify possible winning lines
```

```
win[1]="123"; win[2]="159"; win[3]="147"; win[4]="258"; win[5]="369"; win[6]="456";
win[7]="789"; win[8]="357";
```

```
// check that a selected cell is not already taken
// and make next move
```

```
function check (cellNumber) {
if (box[cellNumber] == 'empty') {box[cellNumber]='you'; update (); display ();
makeAmove (); update (); display ()} else {alert ('Sorry -- that square is taken')}
```

```
}
```

// update the position

```
function update () {
for (i in win) {
my_score[i] = 0;
your_score[i] = 0;
    for (j=0; j<3; j++) {
        if (box[win[i].charAt (j)]=="me")
            {my_score[i]+=1}
        if (box[win[i].charAt (j)]=="you")
            {your_score[i]+=1} }
}}
```

// display the new situation in the cells

```
function display () {
for (i=0; i<9; i++)
{document.forms[0].elements[i].value = box[i + 1]}
}
```

// strategy rules for my go

```
function makeAmove () {
```

// if any line has one cell left to win then fill it

```
for (i in win) {
    if (my_score[i] == 2 && your_score[i] == 0)
    {fill_in (i)}
  }
if (found == "yes") {found = "no"; return true}

for (i in win) {
    if (your_score[i] == 2 && my_score[i] == 0)
    {fill_in (i)}
  }
if (found == "yes") {found = "no"; return true}
```

// if the centre cell is free then fill it
```
if (box[5] == "empty") {box[5] = "me"; return true}
```

// otherwise fill any free cell
```
for (i in box) {
    if (box[i] == "empty") {box[i] = "me"; return true}}
alert ("I cannot make any move"); return false
```

```
}

function fill_in (i) {
for (j=0; j<3; j++)
         {if (box[win[i].charAt (j)] == "empty")
             {box[win[i].charAt (j)] = "me";
              found = "yes"; return true}}
return false}

display ()

</SCRIPT>
</BODY>
</HTML>
```

USING DYNAMIC
HTML with JavaScript

ynamic HTML allows us to enhance the look and behavior of our Web pages by using style sheets and layers controlled by JavaScript.

Style sheets allow us to specify how parts and the whole of our pages should appear. They enable us to control fonts, to position HTML content on the screen, to have layered blocks of content, overlapping if we want, and to apply borders and margins to blocks of content within each page. Layers of blocks can be positioned precisely on the screen. They can be moved, resized, created, made to appear and disappear, and have content written to them on the fly, making complex animation effects possible.

We can create style sheets using the widely accepted Cascading Style Sheets (CSS) syntax. However, Netscape Navigator 4 offers a JavaScript-based syntax for creating and manipulating styles. Navigator 4 also offers JavaScript control of layers. JavaScript-based style sheets and JavaScript control of layers are at present specific to the Navigator 4 (and upward) browser.

Defining a Style

The following code defines a JavaScript-based style specifying that any text appearing between the HTML <H1> </H1> tags should be red, and any block of text appearing within the <P> </P> tags should be in bold 17-point font with left and right margins taking up 15% of the block's total width.

```
1. <STYLE TYPE = "text/javascript">
2.      tags.H1.color = "red";
3.      tags.P.marginLeft = "15%"
4.      tags.P.marginRight = "15%"
5.      tags.P.fontSize = "17pt"
```

```
6.        tags.P.fontWeight = "bold"
7. </STYLE>
```

Line 1 specifies that this is a JavaScript-based style sheet, as opposed to one based on the CSS syntax, which would be specified by

```
<STYLE TYPE = "text/css">
```

The **tags** property is in fact a property of the document; **tags.H1.color** is shorthand for **document.tags.H1.color**. The element appearing after **tags** reflects the HTML tag to which the property value is to be applied. Thus line 2 specifies that any text appearing within the HTML <H1> tags should be colored red.

There is an alternative, shorter form of representation. The following code has the same effect as that above:

```
<STYLE TYPE = "text/javascript">
    with (tags.H1) {color = "red";}
    with (tags.P) {marginLeft = "15%"; marginRight = "15%";
    fontSize = "17pt"; fontWeight = "bold"; }
</STYLE>
```

Styles for Blocks of Content

So-called block-level elements—HTML elements like <H1>, <P>, and so on that start on a new line—can have their own style of margins, borders, padding, and background image or color. The following code specifies that blocks of HTML content appearing within the <P> tags should have a 25-point margin on all sides:

```
<STYLE TYPE = "text/javascript">
tags.P.margins ("25pt");
</STYLE>
```

The code below specifies the top ("5pt"), right ("10pt"), bottom ("8pt"), and left ("15pt") margins:

```
<STYLE TYPE = "text/javascript">
tags.P.margins ("5pt","10pt","8pt","15pt");
</STYLE>
```

Styles for Combinations of HTML Elements

Besides specifying styles for individual HTML elements, we can also specify styles for combinations of elements. The following code, for example, specifies that any text that *both* is bold *and* appears within an H2 tag should be red:

```
<STYLE TYPE = "text/javascript">
contextual (tags.H2, tags.B).color = "red";
</STYLE>
```

Applying Styles

Once a style is defined, the HTML code making up our Web page will use it automatically. So if we have defined styles for, say, the HTML attributes <BODY>, <H1>, and <B>, we need only write normal HTML code as shown below in order to apply the styles:

```
<BODY>
<H1> This will appear in H1 style </H1>
This will appear in BODY style, <B> this in B style </B> and this in BODY style.
</BODY>
```

Note that if a style is defined for an element (in this case, <B>) embedded within another element (in this case, <BODY>), the embedded style will override that of the parent style.

Styles in Files

Styles can be written and stored in separate files. Let us assume that the following code is stored in a file called styles1.html:

```
tags.P.color = "blue"
tags.P.fontSize = "17pt"
tags.P.fontWeight = "bold"
```

We can apply this style by using the LINK attribute, including the URL of the styles1.html document, in the HTML file for our page as follows:

```
<HTML>
<HEAD>
<LINK REL = STYLESHEET TYPE = "text/javascript"
HREF = "http://abc.com/styles1.html">
</HEAD>
<BODY>
Welcome to my page.
</BODY>
</HTML>
```

The words "Welcome to my page" will appear in blue 17-point bold text.

We can include different style sheets in the same document and can mix styles written in both JavaScript and CSS syntax, as in the example below:

```
<STYLE TYPE = "text/javascript"
SRC = "http://abc.com/styles1.html">
</STYLE>
<STYLE TYPE = "text/css"
SRC = "http://abc.com/styles2.html">
</STYLE>
```

```
<STYLE TYPE = "text/javascript"
SRC = "http://abc.com/styles3.html">
</STYLE>
```

Defining Styles on the Fly

The STYLE attribute can be used to define a style when it occurs in your Web page. CSS syntax can be used as in the following example:

```
<BODY>
This will be normal text
<P STYLE = "color:red; margin-left:30; margin-right:30;">
This will be red with left and right margins of 30 pixels </P>
<P> But this text will be normal again </P>
</BODY>
```

The style specified in the <P> tag above will apply only to the block of text to which that particular tag applies. Text in the next <P> tag will be unaffected. Full details of CSS and JavaScript syntax can be found in Netscape's "Dynamic HTML in Netscape Communicator" guide noted in Chapter 11.

Applying Styles Selectively

We can apply a particular style to an arbitrary selection of HTML content using the SPAN attribute. SPAN enables us to mark the beginning and end of where a particular style should be applied, as in the following example (also using CSS syntax):

```
<BODY>
This will be normal text
<SPAN STYLE = "color:blue; font-weight:bold;">
This will be blue and bold. The text will return to normal </SPAN> from here
</BODY>
```

We can also apply a style selectively by giving it a name, then calling that name whenever we want to apply the style. The following code defines a style, called **myStyle1**, consisting of red italic text:

```
<STYLE TYPE = "text/javascript">
classes.myStyle1.all.color = "red";
classes.myStyle1.all.fontWeight = "italic";
</STYLE>
```

We can apply this style as follows:

```
<BODY>
<P CLASS = myStyle1> This text will be red italic </P>
<P> but this will be normal </P>
</BODY>
```

Positioning the Content of Your Web Pages with Layers

Layers are blocks of content on your Web page that can be manipulated in a variety of ways. They can be positioned, moved, resized, and made to overlap, appear, and disappear. They can be transparent or opaque. Their content can also be changed on the fly. Layers can be created using either CSS or JavaScript syntax. In keeping with the focus of this book, we will concentrate here on JavaScript.

The following code creates two layers:

```
<LAYER>
Text for first layer
</LAYER>
<LAYER>
Text for second layer
</LAYER>
```

Layers have a number of properties and attributes that can be specified in order to control their position, size, and appearance. The following can be specified when creating a layer:

above: The layer above the current layer.

background: The image to be used as the background to the layer.

bgColor: The background color of the layer.

below: The layer below the current layer.

clip.bottom: Specifies the bottom of the clipping area, the visible part of the layer.

clip.height: Specifies the height of the clipping area, the visible part of the layer.

clip.left: Specifies the left of the clipping area, the visible part of the layer.

clip.right: Specifies the right of the clipping area, the visible part of the layer.

clip.top: Specifies the top of the clipping area, the visible part of the layer.

clip.width: Specifies the width of the clipping area, the visible part of the layer.

left: The horizontal position of the left side of the layer.

ID: Name given to the layer, prefer to NAME.

name: Name given to the layer in the NAME or ID attribute.

pageX: The horizontal position of the layer relative to the page.

pageY: The vertical position of the layer relative to the page.

src: URL of the file containing the contents of the layer.

top: The vertical position of the top of the layer.

visibility: Specifies whether the layer should be visible.

zIndex: Index of depth of layers; higher-value layers are stacked above lower-value layers.

Positioning Layers

We can position a layer specifying an absolute position or a relative position. The following code creates a layer, named **layer1**, 250 pixels wide and 200 high, with a yellow background. It positions the layer 10 pixels from the left of the screen and 5 pixels from the top:

```
<LAYER ID = layer1 TOP = 5 LEFT = 10 BGCOLOR = "yellow"
WIDTH = 250 HEIGHT = 200>
Text for layer1
</LAYER>
```

We can also position a layer wherever it happens to occur in the flow of text or other content. The following layer is signified by the tag ILAYER meaning "inline layer." It is "inline" in the sense that it is displayed where it naturally falls following other content on the page.

```
This text will be followed immediately by layer2
<ILAYER ID = layer2 WIDTH = 250 HEIGHT = 200>
This is layer 2
</LAYER>
and this text follows layer2
```

We can position an inline layer relative to where it would naturally occur as follows. The values in TOP and LEFT are relative, not absolute, so this layer will be positioned 4 pixels from the left and 10 pixels down from where it would otherwise occur:

```
This text will be followed immediately by layer3
<ILAYER ID = layer3 TOP = 10 LEFT = 4
WIDTH = 250 HEIGHT = 200>
This is layer3
</LAYER>
and this text follows layer3
```

Animating Your Web Pages

JavaScript can be used to produce animated effects on your Web pages. Layers of content can be modified—moved, resized, hidden, and revealed—on the fly. Content can be dynamically written to layers, and images within them can be rapidly changed to produce the illusion of movement.

Accessing Layer Features

In order to modify layers, we need to be able to refer to them and access their features, such as size and position. This is possible because a JavaScript object is created for each layer. The properties and methods associated with it can be accessed using its full address. For example, assuming that we have created a layer called **myLayer1**, we can retrieve information about its properties as follows:

```
document.myLayer1.visibility
```

A value of "show" for this property means that the layer is visible. A value of "hide"" indicates that it is not visible, and "inherit" signifies that it inherits its level of visibility from its parent layer.

Properties can also be accessed using different forms of address. The same information can be retrieved using either of the following. The second example assumes that the layer is the first layer:

```
document.layers["myLayer1"].visibility
document.layers[0].visibility
```

Modifying Layer Features

Layers also have a number of methods associated with them that can be called upon to change and animate the layers and their contents. The following command, for example, moves **myLayer1** 10 pixels to the right and 5 pixels down:

```
document.myLayer1.moveBy (10, 5)
```

The following resizes the layer by 5 pixels horizontally and vertically:

```
document.myLayer1.resizeBy (5, 5)
```

Here are some of the other methods that can be used to change layers. (See Appendix A for a list of all the methods and properties associated with layers.)

load (*fileName, layerWidth*): This will replace the source of the layer with what is in the file specified in fileName. It will also change the width of the layer to the number of pixels specified as the second argument.

moveAbove (*layerName*): This will move the current layer above the layer specified in layerName.

moveBelow (*layerName*): This will move the layer below layerName.

moveBy (*pixelsLeft, pixelsDown*): Moves the layer to the left by the number of pixels specified in pixelsLeft and down by the pixels specified in pixelsDown.

moveTo (*horizontalPixels, verticalPixels*): Moves the layer to a new place in the layer as specified by the horizontal and vertical pixel coordinates.

moveToAbsolute (*horizontalPixels, verticalPixels*): Moves the layer to the specified pixel coordinates relative to the page, not the layer.

resizeBy (*pixelsWidth, pixelsHeight*): Resizes the layer by the specified number of pixels.

resizeTo (*horizontalPixels, verticalPixels*): Resizes the layer to the specified horizontal and vertical pixels coordinates.

Writing Content to Layers

So far we have included the text we want to appear in a layer between the LAYER tags when we created the layer. However, we can also use the **document.write** command. This command can write to a layer from within the layer:

```
<LAYER ID="myLayer1">
<H1> Welcome </H1>
<SCRIPT>
document.write ("This page is new! <P>")
</SCRIPT>
<HR> Enjoy...
</LAYER>
```

The **document.write** command can also write content to a layer after it has been created. The new content will replace the original content. The document must be closed after it is written to. The following code would write to **myLayer1**:

```
document.myLayer1.document.write ("Here is new content <P>")
document.myLayer1.document.close ()
```

Animation

Animated effects can be achieved by resizing layers, moving them horizontally or vertically, hiding them behind other layers, or bringing them to the top.

However, producing attractive animation entails coordinating a series of movements rather than making a single move. JavaScript offers useful features enabling us to do this easily. The following example uses the **setTimeout** command gradually to resize a layer, 3 pixels at a time, until it reaches 500 pixels in width:

```
function resizeLayer (layerName) {
if (layerName.clip.width < 500) {
```

```
layerName.resizeBy (3, 3)
setTimeout (resizeLayer, 5, layerName) }
return false
}
```

The name of the layer to be resized is passed to the function when it is called. The function checks the width of the visible area of the layer and, assuming that it is narrower than 500 pixels, resizes it by 3 pixels horizontally and vertically. The **setTimeout** command (described more fully below) calls the function recursively after 5 milliseconds.

Here are details of commands enabling actions to be performed after some delay, including repeating loops of actions:

setTimeout (*"expression", milliseconds*): Evaluates a JavaScript expression after the specified number of milliseconds. The JavaScript expression must appear in quotes; otherwise, it is executed immediately, before the specified delay.

setTimeout (*"function", milliseconds, argument1, argument2, etc.*): Calls a function after the specified number of milliseconds. The function must appear in quotes. Arguments are passed to the function.

clearTimeout (*timeoutName*): If called before the **setTimeout** delay has passed, this cancels the activity of **setTimeout**. For example:

timeoutName = setTimeout (myFunction, 500)

clearTimeout (timeoutName)

The second line cancels the activity set up in the previous line to take place in 5 seconds.

setInterval (*"expression", milliseconds*): Evaluates a JavaScript expression repeatedly after the specified number of milliseconds. The expression must be enclosed in quotes.

setInterval (*"function", milliseconds, argument1, argument2, etc.*): Calls a function repeatedly after the specified number of milliseconds. The function name must appear in quotes. Arguments are passed to the function.

clearInterval (*intervalName*): If called before the **setInterval** delay has passed, this cancels the activity of **setInterval**. For example:

intervalName = setInterval (myFunction, 500)

clearInterval (intervalName)

As with **clearTimeout**, the second line cancels the activity set up in the previous line to take place in 5 seconds.

Images can be inserted into moving layers. They can also be changed on the fly to increase the complexity of the animation by specifying new values in the IMG SRC attribute. The following example will change the source of the first image in myLayer1:

```
document.myLayer1.document.images[0].src = "image2.gif"
```

In order to avoid delay in the loading of images, we can fetch the images we want to use ahead of time so that they are stored in the browser's cache and will appear rapidly. We can do this by creating a hidden layer containing the images. When the layer is loaded, the images will be fetched into the cache. We can then use them in other layers by referring to their address in the hidden layer.

It is also possible to suppress the appearance of icons and empty frames that appear as placeholders before images are fully loaded. We can do this by means of the SUPPRESS attribute in the IMG tag. If SUPPRESS is set to *true*, the icons and frames will not appear.

SERVER-SIDE
JavaScript

10

The JavaScript introduced so far in this book is downloaded from a server, along with the HTML making up your Web pages, and interpreted by the reader's browser, also called the *client*. For development and testing purposes, the Web pages can be written and run on a standalone computer, unconnected to any server or to the Internet, running a browser capable of interpreting JavaScript.

However, JavaScript commands in your Web pages can also be executed on the server as opposed to the client machine. Server-side JavaScript can take information from the client, process it to add value, then generate and send HTML, incorporating the results of this processing, to the client browser. The fact that this processing has taken place on the server rather than the client is irrelevant to the reader; the display of information is the same.

Server-side JavaScript requires a server running Netscape's server software.

Although it is by no means always the case, servers are often more powerful machines than clients. Running JavaScript on the server can therefore be appropriate for applications requiring more speed, power, and memory. Client-side JavaScript must be downloaded to, then interpreted by, the client browser.

However, the advantages of using server-side JavaScript are not limited to questions of power, size, and speed. Server-side JavaScript also offers facilities not available to client-side JavaScript. It enables read and write access to files stored on the server as well as to databases. Client-side JavaScript, for security reasons, has no such access (except to the cookies text file). It also allows calls to C libraries on the server.

We have seen how it is possible to create cookies on the client machine; cookies enable small amounts of information to be stored and remain after the current session has finished. Server-side JavaScript offers a much more flexible and powerful way of doing this. However, it also allows access to information that relates to clients other than the current one. Applications can access and share global information about visitors to a particular page, or indeed to the server.

Client-side and server-side JavaScript can be mixed within the same Web page, and it is useful to allocate various tasks appropriately to one or the other. For example, client-side JavaScript is particularly suitable for smaller tasks, especially concerned with the user interface. It is ideal for validating and preprocessing reader input to HTML forms. Doing so can often reduce bandwidth when sending the results to the server. Processing and storing information about large numbers of visitors using client-side JavaScript can reduce load on the server.

Server-side JavaScript is written in the same way as client-side JavaScript: as text embedded in HTML. As shown in Figure 10.1, the text file is then sent to the JavaScript compiler, where the file is compiled into bytecode and stored on the server.

When a client requests the Web page, the HTML and client-side JavaScript are sent to the client and interpreted on the client browser. The server-side JavaScript, however, is executed on the server. Commands in the server-side JavaScript to write information to the client browser generate HTML and send it to the client browser for

Figure 10.1 Client- and server-side JavaScript.

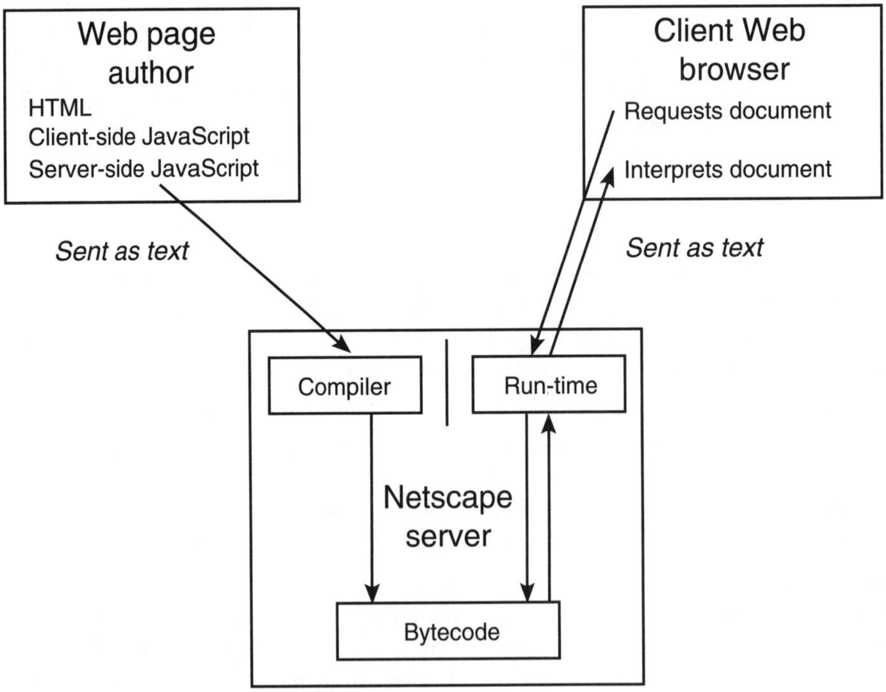

display as normal. This HTML can, of course, incorporate information that represents the results of processing other server-side commands in the Web page.

Writing Server-Side JavaScript

Server-side JavaScript is basically the same JavaScript that we have been exploring in earlier sections of the book, but with additional features.

It can be included in your Web pages using the <SERVER> </SERVER> tags as follows:

```
<HTML>
<HEAD>
<TITLE> Server-side JavaScript </TITLE>
</HEAD>
<BODY>
Normal HTML
<SCRIPT>
Client-side JavaScript
</SCRIPT>
<SERVER>
Server-side JavaScript
</SERVER>
</BODY>
</HTML>
```

In the code below, **request.ip** is a server-side JavaScript object containing the IP address of the current visitor (explained in the next section of this chapter). This server-based information can be displayed to the client as follows:

```
<HTML>
<HEAD>
<TITLE> Server-side JavaScript </TITLE>
</HEAD>
<BODY>

Hello there -- your IP address is <SERVER> request.ip </SERVER>

</BODY>
</HTML>
```

Server-side statements may not be included in event handlers.

Obtaining Information

In order to add value to information provided by the readers of our Web pages, we need to obtain and store this information. However, with server-side JavaScript, we can also obtain information to inject into the process of adding value from files and databases accessed by the server. This section explores these various ways of obtaining information.

Server-Side Objects

Server-side JavaScript automatically creates a number of objects that are useful in enabling effective interaction between client and server.

The request Object

When a reader requests a Web page from the server, the server creates a **request** object relating to that interaction. This object is the shortest-lasting server-side JavaScript object. It remains on the server only until the request has been responded to.

The **request** object stores information as follows:

request.ip: The IP address of the client.

request.agent: The name and version of the client browser.

request.imageX: The horizontal position of the mouse when the client clicked an image map.

request.imageY: The vertical position of the mouse when the client clicked an image map.

request.method: The HTTP method associated with the request (POST, GET or HEAD).

request.protocol: The HTTP protocol level supported by the client software.

request.auth_type: The authorization type.

request.auth_user: The name of the local HTTP user of the browser, if HTTP access authorization is active for the URL.

request.query: Information from the request; material that appears after the question mark.

request.url: URL of the request, minus the protocol, host name, and optional port number.

Your Web pages can also store information on the server in the **request** object. When an HTML form is submitted, the names of its elements (text boxes, radio buttons, checkboxes, and the like) become properties of the **request** object. For example:

```
1. <HTML>
2. <BODY>
3. <FORM METHOD = "post" ACTION = "mypage.html">
4. <INPUT = "text" NAME = "readerName">
5. <INPUT TYPE="submit" VALUE = "Submit">
```

```
6. </FORM>
7. </BODY>
8. </HTML>
```

When this form is submitted (line 5), a request is made to the server for the document mypage.html (line 3). This causes the **request** object to be created on the server and for this object to receive the property *readerName*: The value stored in

```
request.readerName
```

will be whatever the reader typed into the text box "readerName."

Properties for the **request** object can also be created by including their names and values within a URL as follows:

```
<A HREF = "myPage.html?itemAorder=4&itemBorder=3"> Send your order </A>
```

The variable names and values are separated from the URL using a question mark and variables and their values are separated from one another by an ampersand as shown above. This code will result in the following properties and corresponding values being added to the **request** object:

```
request.itemAorder = 4
request.itemBorder = 3
```

The client Object

When your application is accessed, the server also sets up a **client** object. This object can be used to share information between visits by the same client. By default, it will expire after 10 minutes of reader inactivity. We can, however, specify that it remain longer using the command:

```
client.expiration (expiryTime)
```

where *expiryTime* is the number of seconds the object should remain. It can also be destroyed at any time using:

```
client.detroy ()
```

We cannot use the **client** object on an application's initial page (run when the application is started on the server). The properties of the **client** object are created by you. So, for example, you could create properties such as:

```
client.dateOfLastVisit
client.numberOfVisits
```

to keep track of a reader's visits to your page.

However, the property values of the **client** object are converted to strings. This means that numbers and Boolean *true* or *false* values must be handled differently than in client-side JavaScript. It also means that objects cannot be stored as values of properties of the **client** object. Ways around these limitations are explained in the section "Adding Value" later in this chapter.

 In fact, a new **client** object is created each time a request is made to the server. Values of existing **client** object properties can be maintained across requests using a variety of methods. These include storing information as cookies on the client, in URLs sent to the client, or on the server. This is explained in more detail in the section "Storing Client Information More Permanently" later in this chapter.

The project Object

The **project** object stores information relating globally to the Web application, such as information about all the readers who have accessed it. This object remains on the server for as long as the application is present.

Using the **project** object, for example, each person accessing your application could be given a unique identification number:

    project.readerNumber

which could be incremented by 1 for each visitor. To avoid two or more readers visiting your pages at the same time being given the same number, it is possible to lock and unlock the **project** object:

```
project.lock ()
project.readerNumber ++
client.readerID = project.readerNumber
project.unlock ()
```

This code will temporarily lock the **project** object to ensure temporary sequential access, then check the count of readers who have accessed the application and allocate the next number to this particular client, then unlock the **project** object to allow normal access.

The server Object

The **server** object remains on the server for as long as the server is running. If it stops, the server object is destroyed. This object stores information that can be shared between all the applications running on the server.

A number of properties are created automatically:

server.hostname: Full hostname including port number, such as "www.abc.com:80."

server.host: Server, domain, and subdomain, such as "www.abc.com."

server.port: Server port.

server.protocol: Communication protocol supported by the server (such as HTTP).

server.jsVersion: Server version and platform.

The **server** object can be locked and unlocked in the same way as the **project** object:

```
server.lock ()
server.unlock ()
```

 We can also create our own instances of **lock** that we can use to lock any shared object.

Storing Client Information More Permanently

We can store client object property values more permanently using a variety of techniques. The technique to be used can be selected and changed from the Application Manager. Basically, information can be stored on the client or the server, or a mixture of the two.

Storing information on the server places extra load on server memory. However, space is not limited as it is on the client. Storing information on the client increases network traffic because the information must be communicated to it from the server. Information stored on the client will not be lost when the server stops running.

Client-Side Techniques

Client-side techniques include storing information in cookies on the client, and client URL encoding.

Cookies are stored on the client in the following form:

```
NETSCAPE_LIVEWIRE.propertyName=propertyValue
```

Property values for storage as cookies are passed from the server to the client in the header of the document sent in response to a request. When this technique is used, no extra memory is used on the server. Information is sent only once per page, although a separate cookie is created for each property value. Client-side cookies are also limited in space.

In client URL encoding, object property values are added to the URLs on your Web page that refer to other parts of the application when the document is sent from the server to the client. When the reader requests the URL by, for example, clicking a hyperlink, this information is returned to the server with the request.

<blockquote>
NOTE The space allocated to cookies stored on the client is limited. Each cookie can be no bigger than 4K (including name and value). Any cookie larger than this will be truncated to 4K. No more than 20 cookies are allowed for each application. If more are created, the oldest will be deleted to make room for the new ones. The cookie file can contain a maximum of 300 cookies. If more are created, the oldest will be deleted.
</blockquote>

However, if any URLs appear within the <SERVER> tags, property values will not be appended to them. For example, in the following code:

```
<BODY>
<A HREF = "details.html" > Further details </A>
</BODY>
```

property values will be added to the URL when it is downloaded to the client. This will not happen, however, in the following example:

```
<BODY>
<SERVER>
write ("<A HREF = 'details.html' > Further details </A>")
</SERVER>
</BODY>
```

If you want property values to be appended to URLs generated by the server (that is, appearing within the <SERVER> tags), use the **addClient** command:

```
<BODY>
<SERVER>
write (addClient ("<A HREF = 'details.html' > Further details </A>"))
</SERVER>
</BODY>
```

This is also necessary if we use the **redirect** command to redirect the client to another URL. The command:

```
redirect ("http://www.abc.newdoc.html")
```

will not add property values to URLs in the new document. We can ensure that they are added by using instead:

```
redirect (addClient ("http://www.abc.newdoc.html"))
```

If we want to prevent property values being appended to URLs that do not appear within the <SERVER> tags, we can enclose them within backquotes (also known as *ticks*) as follows:

```
<BODY>
<A HREF = `'details.html'` > Further details </A>
</BODY>
```

Client-side URL encoding increases network traffic because information is appended to each URL on a Web page and is transferred from server to client, then from client to server.

Server-Side Techniques

Server-side techniques store property values in server memory, and retrieve this information using server-side cookies, URL encoding, or IP addresses. Server-side techniques are not subject to the space limitations of client-side cookies. Because less information must be passed between server and client, network traffic is low compared to client-side techniques. However, storing information relating to large numbers of clients will take up extra memory.

The cookie technique creates a cookie on the client, as in the client-side technique. However, in the client-side approach, a separate cookie is created for each property value. In the server-side approach, a cookie is created containing index information allowing property values relevant to the client to be retrieved from the server.

Server-side URL encoding, rather than adding property value details to URLs sent to the client, simply encodes index information that will enable relevant information to be retrieved from the server. IP addresses can be used similarly to index information stored on the server. Using knowledge of the client's IP address does not require the passing of information from server to client. This is the fastest technique. However, it does rely on the client's using the same IP, which may not be the case if the client is using an Internet provider that dynamically allocates IP addresses or is using a proxy server, which will return the same IP address for different clients.

Creating Other Objects and Variables

We can create our own objects and variables as in client-side JavaScript; for example:

```
var total = 0
```

or

```
orders = new Array ()
```

We can store in these objects and variables information from server-side objects; for example:

```
var thisReaderNumber = 1 + project.numberOfReaders
```

They have the same lifetime as the **request** object—in other words, they are destroyed as soon as the current request has been responded to.

However, information can be retained for longer periods by storing it as values of properties of appropriately durable server-side objects.

The following code stores the date of a reader's visit in an array stored in the **project** object, indexed by the reader's number:

```
project.clientVisits = new Array ()
project.clientVisits[thisReaderNumber] = new Date ()
```

Server-side JavaScript provides an easy way to obtain the value(s) of options chosen by readers in response to HTML select objects. If, for example, we have the following list of options contained within a form in the HTML making up our Web page:

```
<SELECT NAME = "mySelectList">
<OPTION SELECTED> First item
<OPTION> Second item
<OPTION> Third item
<OPTION> Fourth item
<OPTION> Fifth item
</SELECT>
```

we can retrieve the value of the selected option in server-side JavaScript as follows:

```
<SERVER>
var readerChoice = getOptionValue ("mySelectList")
</SERVER>
```

If the reader were to make multiple selections where this is permitted by the select object—for example:

```
<SELECT NAME = "mySelectList" MULTIPLE SIZE = 4>
<OPTION SELECTED> First item
<OPTION> Second choice
<OPTION> Third choice
<OPTION> Fourth choice
<OPTION> Fifth choice
</SELECT>
```

we can retrieve the multiple selections using a simple loop as follows:

```
<SERVER>
var numberOfChoices = getOptionValueCount ("mySelectList")
var i = 0
while (i < numberOfChoices) {
    var choice = getOptionValue ("mySelectList", i)
    write ("Item number: " + choice + "<BR>")
    i++
}
</SERVER>
```

getOptionValueCount returns the number of options that the reader has selected. **getOptionValue** returns the value of a single choice. Where multiple choices have been made, as in the second example, a second argument will return the value of the specified choice. Choice 1 can be retrieved using:

```
getOptionValue ("mySelectList", 0)
```

Choice 2 can be retrieved with:

```
getOptionValue ("mySelectList", 1)
```

and so on.

Accessing Files

Server-side JavaScript can read and write to files stored on the server. This ability can be contrasted with client-side JavaScript, which allows no access to files stored on the reader's computer, except for the cookies.txt file.

A new file can be created on the server using the command:

```
visitorNames = new File ("c:\project\visitors.txt")
```

If we assume that the server has a directory called **project** on the C: drive, this command sets up a file named visitors.txt in that directory. We want to use the name **visitorNames** when referring to the file in JavaScript.

We can open this file as follows:

```
result = visitorNames.open ("r")
```

The parameter "r" is one of several that can be used to open a file. These parameters are as follows:

"r" opens the file for reading. Returns *true* if the file exists, *false* if not.

"w" opens the file for writing. Creates a new empty file even if the file already exists.

"a" appends new information at the end of the file. Creates a new file if it does not exist.

"r+" opens the file for reading and writing (from the beginning of the file). Returns *true* if the file exists, *false* if not.

"w+" creates a new empty file for reading and writing.

"a+" opens the file for reading and appending. Creates a new file if it does not exist.

"b" can be appended to any of the others to indicate binary, as opposed to ASCII data (Windows only).

Files are closed using the **close** command:

```
visitorNames.close ()
```

Reading Information from Files

Information can be read from a file using the commands **read** and **readln**. For instance:

```
var content = visitorNames.readln ()
```

will read a line from the file and store it (without the line break) as the value of the variable *content*.

```
var content = visitorNames.read (40)
```

will read 40 bytes (starting at 0) from the file and store them as the value of *content*.

```
var content = visitorNames.readByte ()
```

will read the next byte and return the byte number or *–1* in case of an error.

We can set the position of the pointer so that, for example, we can retrieve 40 bytes starting at byte number 100 relative to the beginning of the file (which begins at 0):

```
visitorNames.setPosition (100)
```

setPosition allows an optional second argument:

setPosition (100, 0): 100 bytes from the beginning of the file (the default).

setPosition (100, 1): 100 bytes from the current pointer position.

setPosition (100, 2): 100 bytes from the end of the file.

The following will store the current position in the variable *position*. The command **getPosition** returns the position (starting at 0) or *–1* if there is an error:

```
var position = visitorNames.getPosition ()
```

When reading from a file, we will often need to know when the pointer has reached the end of the file. The following code opens a file myfile.txt, then reads a line at a time, adding it (along with an HTML line break) to the variable *information*:

```
var information
var result
result = visitorNames.open ("r")
while (!visitorNames.eof ()) {
    information + = visitorNames.readln () + "<BR>" }
result = visitorNames.close ()
```

visitorNames.eof () returns *true* if the pointer is at the end of the file, *false* if not.

To generate an appropriate message, we can check to see whether a file exists using **exists**. This command returns *true* if the file does exist, *false* if not. The following code displays the message "Cannot find this file!" if it does not exist. If the file does exist, its contents are written line by line to the reader's browser. (The command **write** is introduced in the section "Communicating the Results to Your Readers" later in this chapter.)

```
var result
myFile = new File ("c:\project\myfile.txt")
if (!myFile.exists ()) {
    write ("Cannot find this file! <BR>") }
else {
result = myFile.open ("r")
while (!myFile.eof ()) {
    write (myFile.readln () + "<BR>") }
result = myFile.close ()
```

Writing Information to Files

We can also write to files. The following **write** commands all return *true* if successful, *false* if not:

```
myFile = new File ("c:\project\myfile.txt")
result = myFile.open ("a")
myFile.write ("Text for the file")
result = myFile.close ()
```

Alternatively:

```
myFile.writeln ("Text for the file")
myFile.writeByte (number)
```

will write a line of text and a byte, specified by *number*, to the file.

The **write** commands actually write to a buffer rather than directly to the file. To cause the contents of the buffer to be written to the file, use the **flush** command:

```
myFile.flush ()
```

This command also returns *true* if successful, *false* if not.

Other File Commands

Other commands that can be used with files include:

fileName.byteToString (*number*): Converts a number into a one-character string.

fileName.StringToByte (*string*): Converts the first character of a string to a number.

fileName.getLength (): Returns the number of characters in a text file, the number of bytes in other files, and *–1* in case of an error.

fileName.error (): Returns *–1* if the file is not open or cannot be opened. Otherwise, it returns the error code (specific to the platform).

fileName.clearError (): Clears the value of both **error** and **eof**.

 Server-side JavaScript can also call external libraries. These are functions written in other programming languages such as C or C++ and stored in compiled form as files on the server. In Windows, these are called Dynamic Link Libraries (DLLs). This advanced aspect of JavaScript programming is not covered in this book.

Accessing Databases

LiveWire allows Structured Query Language (SQL) access to a range of databases, including DB2, Informix, Oracle, Sybase, and databases compliant with the Open Database Connectivity standard (ODBC).

Retrieving and Displaying Data

The simplest way of accessing a database is to use the **database.connect** command. The following code assumes the existence of an Oracle database called *Products*, which contains a *Suppliers* table. The contents of *Suppliers* are shown in Table 10.1.

The second and third arguments in the first command refer to the name of the server on which the database is mounted and a password (left as an empty string if a password is not required).

```
<SERVER>
database.connect ("ORACLE", "databaseSeverName", "myPassword", "Products")
database.SQLTable ("select * from Products")
database.disconnect ()
</SERVER>
```

Table 10.1. Suppliers Table in Products Database

SupplierName	Item	Code	Type
Jones Inc.	bolts	C22	component
Jones Inc.	grinder	T22	tool
Jones Inc.	polisher	T32	tool
Matlock Plc.	paper	O45	officeSupplies
Matlock Plc.	photocopier	O34	officeSupplies
Smith Inc.	screws	C43	component

This code will retrieve details of all customers in the database and display them in a table on the reader's browser using the **database.SQLTable** command. It is possible to check whether a database is connected by using **database.connected**, which returns *true* if there is a connection, *false* if not, as in the example below:

```
if (!database.connected ()) {write ("The database is not open.")}
```

Cursors also allow us to retrieve data and manipulate them more flexibly. The following command also retrieves customer details from the database:

```
<SERVER>
database.connect ("ORACLE", "databaseSeverName", "myPassword", "Products")
myCursor = database.cursor ("select * from Suppliers where Type = tool")
database.disconnect ()
</SERVER>
```

The following code will write the name of the first supplier of tools:

```
Suppliers of tools: <BR>
<SERVER>
myCursor.next ()
write (myCursor.SupplierName + "<BR>")
</SERVER>
```

The **next** command is necessary because the pointer is located on the row before the first record. The **next** command returns *false* if the current record is the last in the cursor; otherwise, it returns *true*.

The following **while** loop will retrieve the names of all suppliers:

```
<SERVER>
while (myCursor.next ()) {
write (myCursor.supplierName + "<BR>")
```

```
}
myCursor.close ()
</SERVER>
```

Other features of cursors include these:

colName: Returns the name of the current column.

Columns: Returns the number of columns in the cursor.

columnNames: Returns the names of the columns in the cursor.

updateRow: Updates the records in the current row of the table specified in the cursor.

insertRow: Inserts a new row in the table specified in the cursor.

deleteRow: Deletes the current row in the table specified in the cursor.

Adding, Deleting, and Updating Data

The final three features listed in the previous section allow us to change the contents of a database. However, in order to do this, we must first specify that a cursor should be updatable. We do this by adding *true* as a second argument to the command creating the cursor:

```
myCursor = database.cursor ("select * from Suppliers where Item = component", true)
```

To delete a row in the specified table, **next** must be used to move the pointer to the desired row; then

```
myCursor.deleteRow ()
```

will delete the record. To replace a record, we must specify what we want to replace it with. Each column name in a database table specified in a cursor has a corresponding property in the cursor. We can use this to specify the new data. So, **myCursor.supplierName** refers to the corresponding column in the database, as does **myCursor.item**. The following commands, for example, specify a new record:

```
myCursor.SupplierName = "Twinings Plc."
myCursor.Item = "envelopes"
myCursor.Code = "O58"
myCursor.Type = "officeSupplies"
```

We can insert this record using the command:

```
myCursor.insertRow ()
```

Alternatively, we can replace a record by moving to it using **next**, then using the command:

```
myCursor.upDateRow ()
```

Other commands supported by the database server that do not return a cursor can be executed using the **execute** command. These commands include DELETE, UPDATE, ADD, and other Data Definition Language (DDL) statements.

Transactions (groups of database commands that are performed—and that succeed or fail—together) can be executed using these commands:

database.beginTransaction (): This is followed by the database commands to be performed.

database.commitTransaction (): Commits the transaction.

database.rollbackTransaction (): Undoes any updates performed since the last **beginTransaction**.

Adding Value

Chapter 3 introduced techniques for adding value to information provided by the readers of your Web pages. These techniques were extended in Chapters 5 through 8 of this book.

Server-side JavaScript can use all these techniques. However, it can also inject into the process of adding value information retrieved from files and databases accessed by the server.

Server-side JavaScript also displays a number of differences from client-side JavaScript, including other additional commands.

The remainder of this chapter concentrates on these differences, and on those facilities and commands not previously covered that are available in server-side but not client-side JavaScript.

Variables

Variables created in server-side JavaScript last as long as the **request** object. In other words, they are destroyed as soon as the current request has been responded to. It is possible, however, to store variable values more permanently, before they are destroyed, by transforming them into property values in the server-side objects introduced in the section "Server-Side Objects" earlier in this chapter.

It is also important to note that in the **client** object, property values are stored as *strings*. This means that if we store a number, a Boolean value, or an object, they will not be retrievable as such; they will be converted into strings.

In client-side JavaScript, if we have a function:

```
function answer (readerAnswer, correctAnswer) {
if (readerAnswer == correctAnswer)
```

```
{return true}
else {return false}
}
```

we can use the value returned by this function as follows:

```
if (answer () == true)
{alert ("You are correct!")}
else {alert ("You are wrong.")}
```

In server-side JavaScript, however, we would have to surround "true" with quotes because it is a string (not a Boolean value):

```
if (answer () == "true")
{alert ("You are correct!")}
else {alert ("You are wrong.")}
```

The same problem applies to numbers. If a **client** object property contains a number:

```
client.totalPreTax = 150
```

the value will be stored as a string "150." A function will experience similar problems if it is required to perform calculations using numbers—for example:

```
addTax (client.totalPreTax)

function addTax (preTax) {
var total = preTax + (preTax * 10/100)
return total
}
```

We can overcome this problem by using the commands **parseInt** and **parseFloat** as follows:

```
function addTax (preTax) {
var total = parseFloat (preTax) + (parseFloat (preTax) * 10/100)
return total
}
```

The command **parseInt** translates a string into an integer; **parseFloat** translates a string into a floating point number.

Communicating the Results to Your Readers

Chapter 4 explored client-side techniques for communicating information, including the results of processing reader input, to the reader. This section introduces ways of communicating information to the reader from the server. Server-side JavaScript offers a number of commands enabling e-mails to be automatically sent, the reader's browser to be redirected automatically to load a different Web page, and HTML—incorporating the results of server-side processing—to be written to the client.

Writing HTML

The **write** command works like the client-side **document.write** command, except that it writes HTML from the server to the reader's browser. The command:

```
write ("<H1> Home Page </H1> <HR> Welcome ")
```

will generate the HTML and to send it to the reader's browser, which interprets and displays it as normal.

In fact, the **write** command will write the information to an internal buffer on the server, prior to sending it to the reader's browser. We can control when it is actually sent by using the command:

```
flush ()
```

The code below reads lines from a file, writing each line to the buffer. The text is sent to the reader's browser, using the **flush** command, only when the end of the file is reached and the file has been closed:

```
var result
result = myFile.open ("r")
while (!myFile.eof ()) {
   write (myFile.readln () + "<BR>") }
result = myFile.close ()
flush ()
```

Writing JavaScript and Variable Values

Server-side object property values and other variable values can be integrated within HTML sent to the reader's browser. For example:

```
write ("<HR> Hello there " + project.readerName)
```

will send to the client the HTML and text concatenated with the value of the **project** object's *readerName* property. The following code will write to the client JavaScript code, which creates a variable *totalOrders* and sets its value to the content of the **client** object's *orders* property:

```
write ("<SCRIPT> var totalOrders = " + client.orders + "</SCRIPT>")
```

Values can be integrated within HTML tags written to the client. The following example writes an HTML form element and sets its VALUE to the contents of the **client** object's *orders* property. This is done by surrounding the name of the server-side object with backquotes (ticks):

```
<INPUT TYPE = "text" NAME = "orders" SIZE = 8 VALUE = `client.orders`>
```

The values of server-side object properties can also be integrated into other HTML tags—for example:

```
<A HREF = `project.relatedLinks`> Related links </A>
```

Redirecting the Reader

The **redirect** command allows you to load a different page into the reader's browser. This may be useful if, for example, you want to redirect the reader to a more up-to-date version of your Web page if he or she has clicked on an old hyperlink with the address of an older version:

```
redirect ("http://www.abc.com/newdoc.html")
```

Recall from the section "Storing Client Information More Permanently" that if you redirect the reader to another Web page, **client** object property values will not be appended to the URLs on that page when it is downloaded to the reader's browser. This means that values stored in the **client** object will be lost and therefore cannot be shared across pages in your application. You can ensure that these values are appended to the URLs by using the **addClient** command as follows:

```
redirect (addClient ("http://www.abc.com/newdoc.html"))
```

Sending E-Mail

Server-side JavaScript can send e-mail messages containing simple text or complex MIME-compliant messages and attachments. The following code illustrates some of the properties of the **SendMail** object:

```
<SERVER>
myMessage = new SendMail ()
myMessage.To = "f.smith@poppleton.ac.uk"
myMessage.From = "j.myers@abc.com"
myMessage.Subject = "Contract"
myMessage.Body = "Here are details of the contract we discussed..."
myMessage.send ()
</SERVER>
```

Other properties are as follows:

myMessage.Cc: Other recipients of the message, in a list separated by commas.

myMessage.Bcc: Other recipients — but not shown in the message, in a list separated by commas.

myMessage.Smtpserver: The name of the mail server.

We can also add other properties (see the RFC 822 standard for the format of Internet text messages). These are sent in the message header fields. For example:

```
myMessage["Reply-to"] =
```

MIME-compliant messages can be sent by adding a "Content-type" property and specifying the MIME value. The following example sends a GIF image file:

```
<SERVER>
myMessage = new SendMail ()
myMessage.To = "f.smith@poppleton.ac.uk"
myMessage.From = "j.myers@abc.com"
myMessage.Subject = "Picture"
myMessage["Content-type"] = "image/gif"
myMessage["Content-Transfer-Encoding"] = "base64"
myFile = new File ("c:\images\picture1.gif")
fileOpen = myFile.open ("r")
if (fileOpen) {
lengthOfFile = myFile.getLength ()
myMessage.Body = myFile.read (lengthOfFile)
myMessage.send ()
}
</SERVER>
```

WHERE TO GO
from Here

There are some excellent sources of information to support you in learning more about JavaScript. A great deal of information is available on the Web, the most notable being Netscape's online documentation, details of which are given in the "Tutorials and Reference Resources" section of this chapter.

Sources of free JavaScript code are listed in the "JavaScript Code" section. Inspecting code written by others can be an extremely valuable and rapid way of learning new techniques.

Establishing contact with fellow JavaScripters can also be an invaluable source of help and support. Details are given in the section "Contacting Other JavaScripters." One thing JavaScripters are good at is creating lists of JavaScript resources. A selection is included in the section "Resource Lists." There is also an increasing number of good books, listed in the "Print Resources" section.

The following lists are highly selective and represent a useful starting point only. New resources are appearing all the time, and it is a good idea periodically to update the lists with an online search. Tips on how to do this effectively are given in the "Keeping Up to Date" section.

Resources

The following are some good resources for information on JavaScript.

Tutorials and Reference Resources

Netscape's JavaScript Guide

http://developer.netscape.com/library/documentation/communicator/jsguide4/ index.htm

Netscape's JavaScript Reference
http://developer.netscape.com/library/documentation/communicator/jsref/index.htm

Netscape's Guide to Server-Side JavaScript
http://developer.netscape.com/library/documentation/enterprise/wrijsap/index.htm

Netscape's Guide to Dynamic HTML
http://developer.netscape.com/library/documentation/communicator/dynhtml/index.htm

Dynamic HTML
http://home.earthlink.net/~/illyming/Dynamic.html

A Beginner's Guide to JavaScript
http://www.webconn.com/java/javascript/intro/tutorial/htm

The JavaScript Forum: Basic Tutorial
http://www.geocities.com/ResearchTriangle/1828/basic.html

The JavaScript Forum: Advanced Tutorial
http://www.geocities.com/ResearchTriangle/1828/advanced.html

Javascript Articles
http://developer.netscape.com/news/viewsource/index.html
http://www.netscapeworld.com/netscapeworld/common/nw.backissues.column.html

JavaScript Code

Cut-N-Paste JavaScript
http://www.infohiway.com/javascript/

Developer.com
http://www.developer.com/directories/pages/dir.javascript.html

JavaScript Archive
http://planetx.bloomu.edu/~mpscho/jsarchive/

JavaScript 411 Library
http://www.freqgrafx.com/411/library.html

JS Resources
http://www.tradepub.com/javascript/

Contacting Other JavaScripters

Newsgroups
news:comp.lang.javascript

Mailing Lists
snews://secnews.netscape.com/netscape.devs-javascript
http://www.netspace.org/cgi-bin/lwgate/JAVASCPT/

Frequently Asked Questions
http://developer.netscape.com/support/faqs/champions/javascript.html

Resource Lists

Netscape's List of JavaScript Resources
http://developer.netscape.com/library/documentation/jsresource.html

JavaScript Index
http://www.cob.ohio-state.edu/~lindeman/javascript/andrew.html

JavaScript WebRing
http://145.72.65.138/ageytenb/jswr/

Yahoo!'s JavaScript List
http://www.yahoo.com/Computers_and_Internet/Programming_Languages/JavaScript/

Print Resources

The ABCs of JavaScript. Lee Purcell and Mary Jane Mara, Sybex, 1997. ISBN: 0782119379

The Complete Idiot's Guide to JavaScript. Aaron Weiss et al. Que, 1997. ISBN: 0789711362

Danny Goodman's JavaScript Handbook. Danny Goodman, IDG, 1996. ISBN: 0764530038

Designing With JavaScript : Creating Dynamic Web Pages. Nick Heinle, O'Reilly & Associates, 1997. ISBN: 1565923006

JavaScript Bible. Danny Goodman, IDG, 1998. ISBN: 0764531883

JavaScript Cookbook. Yosef Cohen, Wiley, 1997. ISBN: 0471181455

JavaScript for Dummies. Emily A. Vanderveer, IDG, 1997. ISBN: 0764502239

JavaScript Interactive Course. Arman Danesh, Waite Group, 1997. ISBN: 1571690840

JavaScript One Step at a Time. David A. Wall, IDG, 1997. ISBN: 076453100X

JavaScript Sourcebook. Gordon McComb, Wiley, 1996. ISBN: 0471161853

JavaScript Unleashed. Richard Wagner, Sams, 1997. ISBN: 1575213060

Learn Advanced JavaScript Programming. Yehuda Shiran et al. Wordware, 1997. ISBN: 1556225520

Netscape Developer's Guide to JavaScript. Bill Anderson, Prentice-Hall, 1998. ISBN: 0137192797

Netscape Visual JavaScript for Dummies. Emily Vanderveer, IDG, 1998. ISBN: 0764502867

Practical JavaScript Programming. Reaz Hoque, M & T books, 1997. ISBN: 1558515135

Server Scripts With Visual JavaScript. Dan Rahmel, McGraw-Hill, 1997. ISBN: 007913694X1997

Teach Yourself JavaScript 1.2 in a Week. Arman Danesh, Sams, 1997. ISBN: 1575213044

Keeping Up to Date

Web Sources

To keep up to date, search the Web periodically. Here are some tips for retrieving relevant information. To search for Web-based documents, I recommend Alta Vista's Advanced Search option at:

http://altavista.digital.com/cgi-bin/query?pg=aq

If you use both the main Search box and the Ranking box, you will get the best of both worlds: a Boolean search enabling close control over keywords as well as best-match searching that will rank the search results in order of relevance.

Keep the keywords all in lowercase (any uppercase letter will force an exact-case match, which could result in some useful documents not being retrieved). *NEAR* means "within 10 words of." Enter the following keywords into the main search box:

javascript NEAR (tutorial OR guide OR introduction)

and enter the following keyword into the Ranking box:

javascript beginner

or:

javascript advanced

To search for phrases, enclose them within double quotes—for example:

"server side javascript"

You can enter a starting date, enabling you to restrict the search to items appearing since your last search. Why not write a JavaScript program that will automatically run such an updated search?

Finding Books

An excellent source of information on recent books is Amazon.com's online bookstore at:

http://www.amazon.com/

You can search Amazon's catalog, which contains millions of titles. Simply enter JavaScript as a keyword search.

CONCISE JAVASCRIPT
Reference

This book has introduced JavaScript concepts in terms of things we may want to achieve using them—in other words, the concepts have been grouped according to types of use, this use being reflected in the chapter and section headings of the book.

However, it may also be useful now to group these concepts in terms of how they are defined and how they fit into the JavaScript language in a technical sense. This appendix presents a systematic overview of JavaScript concepts arranged according to this technical specification.

Its main purpose is to provide the following:

- A full listing of JavaScript concepts, including those not already introduced in detail earlier in the book

- A concise description of each concept, enabling you to assess how useful it would be in developing a given application

- A means of checking the compatibility of each concept with different versions of browser and server software

This appendix is designed as a quick reference to be used as a means of identifying the facilities that may be useful for a particular application. It should be used in conjunction with Netscape's excellent online documentation, which provides full details of each concept, along with examples showing precisely how to use it.

Netscape's JavaScript Reference can be found at:

http://developer.netscape.com/library/documentation/communicator/jsref/ index.htm

Basic JavaScript Concepts

Although an open standard, supported by a range of browsers, JavaScript is closely associated with Netscape's Navigator browser. Different versions of the browser support different versions of JavaScript; the current version is JavaScript 1.2, supported by Navigator 4 used in Netscape Communicator.

Navigator Objects

As a document is read into the browser, a hierarchy of objects is automatically created, some reflecting the content of the particular HTML page, as follows:

```
window
          document
                    area
                    Anchor
                    applet
                    form
                              object
                              checkbox
                              fileUpload
                              hidden
                              option
                              password
                              radio
                              reset
                              select
                              submit
                              text
                              textarea
                    layer
                    link
                    plugin
          frames
          history
          location
navigator
          mimeType
          plugin
screen
```

When referring to objects, you must include the elements of the hierarchy in the address. The top level element **window** can be omitted. The following example assumes a form named **myForm** that contains a text box named **myTextBox**. The value of the text box can be retrieved using the address:

```
document.myForm.myTextBox.value
```

It is also important to note that the objects are loaded into the browser sequentially as it reads an HTML document from the top downward. So, if an object is referred to before it is created, JavaScript will generate an error message. This will happen if, for example, we include the command:

```
alert (document.myForm.myTextBox.value)
```

before the HTML that creates the object referred to:

```
<FORM NAME = "myForm">
<INPUT TYPE = "text" NAME = "myTextBox" VALUE = "Your name">
</FORM>
```

Object Properties and Methods

Objects have properties and methods. *Properties* are declarative; they have descriptive values. For example, the *bgColor* property of the **document** object reflects the color specified in the document:

```
<BODY BGCOLOR="red">
```

and the value of the *location* property of the **window** object is the URL of the document currently loaded in the window.

Methods are procedural as opposed to declarative; they perform actions. So, for example, the *toUpperCase* method of the **String** object performs a transformation on that object. If we have an object as follows:

```
var myString = "hello"
```

then the value of

```
myString.toUpperCase ()
```

is "HELLO".

Things are not always quite so clear cut. Some properties can do things in the sense that they have an immediately visible effect if they are changed; so, for example, the command:

```
document.myForm.myTextBox.value = "Hello"
```

will instantly change what appears in a text box. Similarly, the command:

```
document.bgColor = "red"
```

will change the background color of the document currently being displayed.

Objects and Their Methods, Properties, and Event Handlers

The following section lists JavaScript objects in alphabetical order. Each is associated with a set of characteristics, which may include properties, methods, and event handlers. Information is given indicating the version of JavaScript, and therefore the Netscape Navigator version, in which each is implemented. In the case of objects applying to server-side JavaScript, the relevant version of Netscape's server software is given. Where a characteristic (a property, method, or event handler) of an object is added or changed in a subsequent version of JavaScript, the version number is indicated in the description of the characteristic appearing in the entry for the object.

Anchor

Client-side. An object representing a place in a document that acts as a target for a hyperlink, defined using the HTML A tag or the string.anchor method (see **String** object).

JavaScript 1.0. Navigator 2 and above. The anchors in a document are indexed in an array as follows:

document.anchors[0] refers to the first anchor
document.anchors[1] refers to the second anchor

The anchors array has the following property:

length [the number of items in the array]
document.anchors.length returns the number of anchors in the document

Applet

Client-side. An object representing a Java applet in a document, included using the HTML tag APPLET.

JavaScript 1.1. Navigator 3 and above. The applets in a document are indexed in an array as follows:

document.applets[0] refers to the first applet
document.applets[1] refers to the second applet

The applets array has the following property:

length [the number of items in the array]
document.applets.length returns the number of applets in the document

Area

Client-side. An object representing an area of an image map, created using the HTML AREA tag.

JavaScript 1.1. Navigator 3 and above.

See the **Link** object for details of area characteristics.

Array

Client-side and Server-side. An object representing an array. Also enables the creation of new arrays. For example:

myObject = new Array ()

creates a new array object. (See JavaScript Reference for details of optional arguments.)
JavaScript 1.1. Navigator 3 and above.
LiveWire 1 and Netscape 3 servers.

Methods

concat	[Joins two arrays] JavaScript 1.2. Navigator 4. Netscape 3 servers
join	[Joins the elements of an array into a string]
pop	[Returns the last element of an array and removes it from the array] JavaScript 1.2. Navigator 4. Netscape 3 servers
push	[Adds one or more elements to an array and returns the last one added] JavaScript 1.2. Navigator 4. Netscape 3 servers
reverse	[Reverses the elements of an array]
shift	[Returns the first element of an array and removes it from the array] JavaScript 1.2. Navigator 4. Netscape 3 servers
slice	[Returns an array having taken out a section] JavaScript 1.2. Navigator 4. Netscape 3 servers
splice	[Adds elements and/or removes them from an array] JavaScript 1.2. Navigator 4. Netscape 3 servers
sort	[Sorts the elements of an array; different sort criteria can be specified] Behavior modified in JavaScript 1.2. Navigator 4
toString	[Converts the array to a string]
unshift	[Adds elements to the beginning of an array and returns the new length] JavaScript 1.2. Navigator 4. Netscape 3 servers

Properties

index	[A number representing each element in the array, the first being 0]
input	[The original expression, which, when matched to a regular expression, resulted in an array]
length	[The number of items in the array]
prototype	[Allows new properties to be added to an array]

Blob

Server-side. An object that enables BLOb (Binary Large Objects, used for multimedia content) data to be displayed and linked to.
LiveWire 1 and Netscape 3 servers.

Properties

blobImage	[Enables BLOb data to be retrieved from a database]
blobLink	[Creates a hyperlink to a BLOb]

Boolean

Client-side and Server-side. Enables you to create objects with a Boolean (*true* or *false*) value—e.g.

    newBooleanObject = new Boolean (true)

JavaScript 1.1. Navigator 3 and above.

LiveWire 1 and Netscape 3 servers.

Methods

toString	[Returns a string representation of the object]

Properties

prototype	[Allows new properties to be added to the object]

Button

Client-side. An object representing a button created with the HTML tag INPUT TYPE="button".

JavaScript 1.0. Navigator 2 and above.

Methods

blur	[Causes the checkbox to lose the focus] JavaScript 1.1. Navigator 3 and above
click	[Has the same effect as the user clicking the checkbox]
focus	[Causes the checkbox to receive the focus] JavaScript 1.1. Navigator 3 and above
handleEvent	[Calls the event handler for the specified type of event, as though the event had occurred] JavaScript 1.2. Navigator 4

Properties

form	[The FORM containing the checkbox]
name	[The value of the HTML NAME attribute]
type	[The value of the HTML TYPE attribute] JavaScript 1.1. Navigator 3 and above
value	[The value of the HTML VALUE attribute]

Event handlers

onBlur	[Activated when the object loses the focus] JavaScript 1.1. Navigator 3 and above

onClick	[Activated when the object is clicked]
onFocus	[Activated when the object receives the focus] JavaScript 1.1. Navigator 3 and above
onMouseDown	[Activated when the mouse button is pressed when over the object] JavaScript 1.2. Navigator 4
onMouseUp	[Activated when the mouse button is released when over the object] JavaScript 1.2. Navigator 4

Checkbox

Client-side. An object representing a checkbox created with the HTML tag INPUT TYPE="checkbox".
JavaScript 1.0. Navigator 2 and above.

Methods

blur	[Causes the checkbox to lose the focus] JavaScript 1.1. Navigator 3 and above
click	[Has the same effect as the user clicking the checkbox]
focus	[Causes the checkbox to receive the focus] JavaScript 1.1. Navigator 3 and above
handleEvent	[Calls the event handler for the specified type of event, as though the event had occurred] JavaScript 1.2. Navigator 4

Properties

checked	[*True* if the checkbox is checked, *false* otherwise]
defaultChecked	[*True* if the HTML CHECKED attribute is present, otherwise *false*]
form	[The FORM containing the checkbox]
name	[The value of the HTML NAME attribute]
type	[The value of the HTML TYPE attribute— in this case, "checkbox"] JavaScript 1.1. Navigator 3 and above
value	[The value of the HTML VALUE attribute]

Event handlers

onBlur	[Activated when the object loses the focus] JavaScript 1.1. Navigator 3 and above
onClick	[Activated when the object is clicked]
onFocus	[Activated when the object receives the focus] JavaScript 1.1. Navigator 3 and above

Client

Server-side. An object containing information relating to the client.
LiveWire 1 and Netscape 3 servers.

Methods

destroy	[Destroys the client object]
expiration	[Specifies when the client object should be destroyed]

Connection

Server-side. An object representing a connection to a database.
Netscape 3 servers.

Methods

beginTransaction	[Begins a database transaction; statements to be performed follow this command]
commitTransaction	[Commits the database operations specified after beginTransaction]
connected	[Checks whether there is a connection to a database]
cursor	[Returns a cursor containing the results of an SQL select database query]
execute	[Executes specified database operations that do not return a cursor]
majorErrorCode	[Major database error code]
majorErrorMessage	[Major database error message]
minorErrorCode	[Minor database error code]
minorErrorMessage	[Minor database error message]
release	[Releases the connection back to the database pool]
rollbackTransaction	[Undoes all updates performed since the last *beginTransaction*]
SQLTable	[Displays as an HTML table the results of an SQL database search]
storedProc	[Creates and runs a stored procedure object]
toString	[Returns a string representation of the object]

Properties

prototype	[Enables new properties to be added to the object]

Cursor

Server-side. An object containing the results of an SQL select database search.
LiveWire 1 and Netscape 3 servers.

Methods

close	[Closes a query]
columnName	[The name of the cursor column specified by a number, the first column being 0]

---

columns	[The number of columns in a cursor]
deleteRow	[Deletes the current row in the cursor]
insertRow	[Inserts the row specified in the cursor]
next	[Moves the pointer to the next row in the cursor]
updateRow	[Updates the row with data specified in the cursor]

Properties

| cursorColumn | [Contains the name of a column in a cursor] |
| prototype | [Enables new properties to be added to the object] |

Database

Server-side. An object representing a connection to a database.
LiveWire 1 and Netscape 3 servers.

Methods

beginTransaction	[Begins a database transaction; statements to be performed follow this command]
commitTransaction	[Commits the database operations specified after *beginTransaction*]
connect	[Creates a connection to a database]
connected	[Checks whether there is a connection to a database]
cursor	[Creates a cursor containing the results of an SQL select database query]
disconnect	[Disconnects the database]
execute	[Executes database commands that do not return a cursor]
majorErrorCode	[Major database error code]
majorErrorMessage	[Major database error message]
minorErrorCode	[Minor database error code]
minorErrorMessage	[Major database error message]
rollbackTransaction	[Undoes all updates performed since the last *beginTransaction*]
SQLTable	[Displays as an HTML table the results of an SQL database search]
storedProc	[Creates and runs a stored procedure object] Netscape 3 servers
storedProcArgs	[Relates to a Sybase stored procedure] Netscape 3 servers
toString	[Returns a string representation of the object]

Properties

| prototype | [Enables new properties to be added to the object] |

Date

Client-side and Server-side. An object representing a date.
JavaScript 1.0. Navigator 2 and above.
LiveWire 1 and Netscape 3 servers.

Methods

getDate	[Returns the day of the month for the Date object as a number from 1 to 31]
getDay	[Returns the day of the week for the Date object as a number: 0 = Sunday, 1 = Monday, etc.]
getHours	[Returns the hour of day of the Date object as a number from 0 to 23]
getMinutes	[Returns the minutes of the Date object as a number from 0 to 59]
getMonth	[Returns the month of the Date object as a number: 0 = January, 1 = February, etc.]
getSeconds	[Returns the seconds of the Date object as a number from 0 to 59]
getTime	[Returns the time of the Date object as milliseconds since 1 Jan 1970 at 00:00:00]
getTimezoneOffset	[Returns the difference in minutes between local time and GMT]
getYear	[Returns the last two digits of the year of the Date object]
parse	[Returns the difference in milliseconds between 1 Jan 1970 at 00:00:00 and the data specified; the date is specified as a string formatted in the prescribed way]
setDate	[Sets the day of the Date object]
setHours	[Sets the hour of the Date object]
setMinutes	[Sets the minutes of the Date object]
setMonth	[Sets the month of the Date object]
setSeconds	[Sets the seconds of the Date object]
setTime	[Sets the number of milliseconds that have elapsed since 1 January 1970 00:00:00]
setYear	[Sets the year of the Date object]
toGMTString	[Converts a Date object into a string in GMT format]
toLocaleString	[Converts a Date object to a string using the conventions of the current locale]
UTC	[Converts a string of comma-separated date parameters into a normal string date representation]

Properties

prototype	[Enables new properties to be added to the object] JavaScript 1.1. Navigator 3 and above

DbPool

Server-side. Represents a pool of connections to a database.
Netscape 3 servers.

Methods

DbPool	[Creates a pool of database connection]
connect	[Connects the pool to a database]
connected	[Checks whether the pool is connected]
connection	[Retrieves an available connection]
disconnect	[Disconnects the pool from the database]
majorErrorCode	[Code representing a major error]
majorErrorMessage	[Message representing a major error]
minorErrorCode	[Code representing a minor error]
minorErrorMessage	[Message representing a minor error]
storedProcArgs	[Creates a prototype for a Sybase stored procedure]
toString	[Returns a string representation of the object]

Document

Client-side. An object representing the document loaded in the browser window or frame.
JavaScript 1.0. Navigator 2 and above.

Methods

captureEvents	[Specifies which events should be captured by the object] JavaScript 1.2. Navigator 4
close	[Closes the document]
getSelection	[Returns text currently selected by the user] JavaScript 1.2. Navigator 4
handleEvent	[Calls the event handler for the specified type of event, as though the event had occurred] JavaScript 1.2. Navigator 4
open	[Opens a document that can be written to using *write* and *writeln*]
releaseEvents	[Releases the specified captured event to be handled further down the event hierarchy] JavaScript 1.2. Navigator 4
routeEvent	[Passes the specified captured event down the event hierarchy] JavaScript 1.2. Navigator 4
write	[Writes HTML and text to the document]
writeln	[Writes HTML and text to the document, followed by a newline character]

Properties

alinkColor	[The color of the active link]

anchors	[An array of anchors in order of appearance in the document; *document.anchors[0]* refers to the first, and so on]. The anchors array has its own property: length [The number of anchors in the document]
applets	[An array of applets in order of appearance in the document. *document.applets[0]* refers to the first, and so on]. JavaScript 1.1. Navigator 3 and above. The applets array has its own property: length [The number of applets in the document]
bgColor	[The background color of the document]
cookie	[Cookie information stored as a name=value string]
domain	[Domain name of the server that supplied the document] JavaScript 1.1. Navigator 3 and above
embeds	[An array of all the plugins in the document] JavaScript 1.1. Navigator 3 and above
fgColor	[The foreground color of the document]
formName	[This represents a separate property for each named form in the document] JavaScript 1.1. Navigator 3 and above
forms	[An array of forms in order of appearance in the document; *document.forms[0]* refers to the first, and so on] JavaScript 1.1. Navigator 3 and above. The forms array has its own property: length [The number of forms in the document]
images	[An array of the images contained in the document] JavaScript 1.1. Navigator 3 and above
lastModified	[Date on which the document was last modified]
layers	[An array of all the layers contained in the document] JavaScript 1.2. Navigator 4
linkColor	[The color of links in the document]
links	[An array of links in order of appearance in the document; *document.links[0]* refers to the first, and so on]. The links array has the property: length [The number of links in the document]
plugins	[An array of plugins in order of appearance in the document; document.plugins[0] refers to the first, and so on]. JavaScript 1.1. Navigator 3 and above. The plugins array has the property: length [The number of plugins in the document]
referrer	[The URL of the calling document]
title	[The value of the HTML TITLE attribute]
URL	[The address, or URL, of the document]
vlinkColor	[The color of links that have been clicked]

Event handlers

onBlur	[Activated when the object loses the focus] Specified in the BODY tag of a document but in fact this one of the **Window** object's event handlers
onClick	[Activated when the mouse is clicked when over the object]
onDblClick	[Activated when the mouse is double-clicked when over the object]
onFocus	[Activated when the object receives the focus] Specified in the BODY tag of a document but in fact this one of the **Window** object's event handlers
onKeyDown	[Activated when a key is pressed] JavaScript 1.2. Navigator 4
onKeyPress	[Activated when a key is held down] JavaScript 1.2. Navigator 4
onKeyUp	[Activated when a key is released] JavaScript 1.2. Navigator 4
onMouseDown	[Activated when the mouse button is pressed when over the object] JavaScript 1.2. Navigator 4
onMouseUp	[Activated when the mouse button is released when over the object] JavaScript 1.2. Navigator 4

Event

Client-side. Object containing information passed to an event handler when an event occurs.
JavaScript 1.2. Navigator 4.

Properties

data	[An array containing the URLs of objects that have been dragged and dropped]
height	[Height of the window or frame]
layerX	[For a resize event, the object width, or the cursor's horizontal position relative to the layer]
layerY	[For a resize event, the object height, or the cursor's vertical position relative to the layer]
modifiers	[Any modifier keys pressed with the mouse or a key: CONTROL, SHIFT, etc.]
pageX	[The cursor's horizontal position on the page in pixels]
pageY	[The cursor's vertical position on the page in pixels]
screenX	[The cursor's horizontal position relative to the screen in pixels]
screenY	[The cursor's vertical position relative to the screen in pixels]
target	[The object to which the event was sent]
type	[The type of event]
which	[Which mouse button or which key (ASCII value) was pressed]
width	[Width of the window or frame]

File

Server-side. An object enabling access to files stored on the server.
LiveWire 1 and Netscape 3 servers.

Methods

byteToString	[Converts a number representing a byte to its string character]
clearError	[Clears the error status]
close	[Closes the file]
eof	[Represents the end of the file]
error	[The current error status]
exists	[Checks whether the file exists]
flush	[Writes the contents of the internal buffer to the file]
getLength	[Length of the file]
getPosition	[Position of the pointer in the file]
open	[Opens the file]
read	[Reads from the file]
readByte	[Reads a byte from the file]
readln	[Reads a line from the file]
setPosition	[Sets the position of the pointer in the file]
stringToByte	[Converts the first character of a string into its numerical byte representation]
write	[Writes to the file]
writeByte	[Writes a byte to the file]
writeln	[Writes a line to the file]

Properties

prototype	[Enables new properties to be added to the file]

FileUpload

Client-side. An object representing a file reference created with the HTML tag
INPUT TYPE="file".
JavaScript 1.0. Navigator 2 and above.

Methods

blur	[Causes the object to lose the focus]
focus	[Causes the object to receive the focus]
handleEvent	[Calls the event handler for the specified type of event, as though the event had occurred] JavaScript 1.2. Navigator 4
select	[Causes the object to be selected]

Properties

form	[The FORM containing the checkbox]

name	[Reflects the value of the HTML NAME attribute]
type	[Reflects the value of the HTML TYPE attribute] JavaScript 1.1. Navigator 3 and above
value	[Reflects the value of the HTML VALUE attribute]

Event handlers

onBlur	[Activated when the object loses the focus]
onChange	[Activated when the value of the object is changed]
onFocus	[Activated when the object receives the focus]

Form

Client-side. An object representing a form created with the HTML tag FORM. JavaScript 1.0. Navigator 2 and above.

Methods

handleEvent	[Calls the event handler for the specified type of event, as though the event had occurred] JavaScript 1.2. Navigator 4
reset	[Resets the form] JavaScript 1.1. Navigator 3 and above
submit	[Submits the form]

Properties

action	[A string specifying the URL to which the form should be submitted]
elements	[An array of objects on the form in order of appearance in the document; *document.myForm.elements[0]* refers to the first, and so on]
encoding	[The MIME encoding specified in the HTML ENCTYPE attribute]
length	[The number of elements in the form]
method	[The value of the HTML METHOD attribute]
name	[The name of the form as specified in the HTML NAME attribute]
target	[Reflects the HTML TARGET attribute]

Event handlers

| onReset | [Activated when the form is reset] |
| onSubmit | [Activated when the form is submitted] |

Frame

Client-side. An object representing a frame created with the HTML FRAME tag. JavaScript 1.0. Navigator 2 and above. JavaScript represents a frame as a window. The **Frame** object therefore share methods and properties with the **Window** object.

Function

Client-side and Server-side. An object representing a function. Enables the creation of new functions; e.g.

myFunction = new Function ("alert ('Hello there') ")

JavaScript 1.1. Navigator 3 and above.
LiveWire 1 and Netscape 3 servers.

Methods

toString   [Returns the string representation of the object]

Properties

arguments   [An array containing the arguments of a function, starting at
                        0] Modified in JavaScript 1.2. Navigator 4
arity   [The number of arguments that the function allows] JavaScript
                        1.2. Navigator 4
caller   [Specifies which function called the present function]
length   [The number of arguments actually passed to the function]
prototype   [Enables new properties to be added to the function]

Hidden

Client-side. An object representing a hidden input element created with the HTML tag INPUT TYPE="hidden".
JavaScript 1.0. Navigator 2 and above.

Properties

form   [The FORM containing the checkbox]
name   [The name of the hidden element as specified in the HTML
                        NAME attribute]
type   [The value of the HTML TYPE attribute] JavaScript 1.1.
                        Navigator 3 and above
value   [The value of the HTML VALUE attribute]

History

Client-side. An array containing the URLs of the documents previously loaded during the session.
JavaScript 1.0. Navigator 2 and above.

Methods

back   [Loads the previous document in the list of documents visited
                        during the session]

| forward | [Loads the next document in the list of documents visited during the session] |
| go | [Specifies the document to be loaded from the list of documents visited during the session; for example, *history.go (-3)* will load the document three back in the list; *history.go ("My Page")* will load the nearest document containing the string in its URL] |

Properties

current	[The URL of the currently loaded document] JavaScript 1.1. Navigator 3 and above
length	[The number of entries in the history list]
next	[The URL of the document next in the history list relative to the currently loaded document] JavaScript 1.1. Navigator 3 and above
previous	[The URL of the previous document in the history list relative to the current document] JavaScript 1.1. Navigator 3 and above

Image

Client-side. An object representing an image created with the HTML IMG tag. Enables the creation of new images; e.g.

myImage = new Image ()

JavaScript 1.1. Navigator 3 and above.

Methods

| handleEvent | [Calls the event handler for the specified type of event, as though the event had occurred] JavaScript 1.2. Navigator 4 |

Properties

border	[Reflects the HTML BORDER attribute]
complete	[Returns true if the loading of the image has been completed]
height	[The height in pixels of the image]
hspace	[Reflects the HTML HSPACE attribute]
lowsrc	[Reflects the HTML LOWSRC attribute]
name	[Reflects the HTML NAME attribute]
prototype	[Enables new properties to be added to the object]
src	[URL of the image file to be displayed]
vspace	[Reflects the HTML VSPACE attribute]
width	[The width in pixels of the image]

Event handlers

onAbort	[Activated when loading of the image is stopped]
onError	[Activated when an error occurs]
onKeyDown	[Activated when a key is pressed when over the object] JavaScript 1.2. Navigator 4
onKeyPress	[Activated when a key is held down] JavaScript 1.2. Navigator 4
onKeyUp	[Activated when a key is released when over the object] JavaScript 1.2. Navigator 4
onLoad	[Activated when the image has loaded]

Layer

Client-side. An object representing a layer created with the HTML tags LAYER or ILAYER. JavaScript 1.2. Navigator 4.

Methods

captureEvents	[Specifies which events should be captured by the object]
handleEvent	[Calls the event handler for the specified type of event, as though the event had occurred]
load	[Changes the source and width of the layer]
moveAbove	[Moves the layer above the specified layer]
moveBelow	[Moves the layer below the specified layer]
moveBy	[Moves the layer by the specified number of pixels]
moveTo	[Moves the layer to a new place in the layer as specified by pixel coordinates]
moveToAbsolute	[Moves the layer to the specified pixel coordinates relative to the page, not the layer]
releaseEvents	[Releases the specified captured event to be handled further down the event hierarchy]
resizeBy	[Resizes the layer by the specified number of pixels]
resizeTo	[Resizes the layer to the specified pixels coordinates]
routeEvent	[Passes the specified captured event down the event hierarchy]

Properties

above	[The layer above the current layer]
background	[The image to be used as the background to the layer]
bgColor	[The background color of the layer]
below	[The layer below the current layer]
clip.bottom	[Specifies the bottom of the clipping area, the visible part of the layer]
clip.height	[Specifies the height of the clipping area, the visible part of the layer]
clip.left	[Specifies the left of the clipping area, the visible part of the layer]

clip.right	[Specifies the right of the clipping area, the visible part of the layer]
clip.top	[Specifies the top of the clipping area, the visible part of the layer]
clip.width	[Specifies the width of the clipping area, the visible part of the layer]
document	[Each layer contains a document, via which the contents of the layer can be accessed; for example: document.layer1.visibility]
ID	[Name given to the layer; prefer to NAME]
left	[The horizontal position of the left side of the layer]
name	[Name given to the layer in the NAME or ID attribute]
pageX	[The horizontal position of the layer relative to the page]
pageY	[The vertical position of the layer relative to the page]
parentLayer	[The layer containing the current layer or the window if there is no parent layer]
siblingAbove	[The layer with the same parent above the current layer in the z-index]
siblingBelow	[The layer with the same parent below the current layer in the z-index]
src	[URL of the file containing the contents of the layer]
top	[The vertical position of the top of the layer]
visibility	[Specifies whether the layer should be visible]
zIndex	[Index of depth of layers; higher-value layers are stacked above lower-value layers]

Event handlers

onBlur	[Activated when the object loses the focus]
onFocus	[Activated when the object receives the focus]
onLoad	[Activated when the object has been loaded]
onMouseOut	[Activated when the mouse is moved away from the object, having been over it]
onMouseOver	[Activated when the mouse is moved over the object]

Link

Client-side. A **Link** object of represents a link created with the HTML tag A HREF, or with the link method of the **String** object (JavaScript 1.0—Navigator 2 and above), or with the HTML tag AREA HREF (JavaScript 1.1—Navigator 3 and above).

Methods

| handleEvent | [Calls the event handler for the specified type of event, as though the event had occurred] JavaScript 1.2. Navigator 4 |

Properties

hash	[Indicates (is followed by) the anchor name in a URL]
host	[The host and domain name of the URL in the link]
hostname	[The host and port part of the URL in the link]
href	[The URL of the link]
pathname	[The path part of the URL of the link]
port	[The port of the link's URL]
protocol	[The protocol of the link's URL]
search	[Information appearing after the "?" in the URL appended a GET request]
target	[The name of the window or frame specified in the HTML TARGET attribute]
text	[The content of the HTML A tag]

Event handlers

Area objects
(JavaScript 1.1—Navigator 3 and above)

onDblClick	[Activated when the mouse button is double-clicked when over the link] JavaScript 1.2. Navigator 4
onMouseOut	[Activated when the mouse moves away from being over the link]
onMouseOver	[Activated when the mouse moves over the link]

Other links ˙

onClick	[Activated when the link is clicked]
onDblClick	[Activated when the mouse button is double-clicked when over the link] JavaScript 1.2. Navigator 4
onKeyDown	[Activated when the mouse button is pressed when over the link] JavaScript 1.2. Navigator 4
onKeyPress	[Activated when a key is pressed when over the link] JavaScript 1.2. Navigator 4
onKeyUp	[Activated when a key is released when over the link] JavaScript 1.2. Navigator 4
onMouseDown	[Activated when the mouse button is pressed when over the link] JavaScript 1.2. Navigator 4
onMouseOut	[Activated when the mouse moves away from being over the link] JavaScript 1.1. Navigator 3 or above
onMouseUp	[Activated when the mouse button is released when over the link] JavaScript 1.2. Navigator 4
onMouseOver	[Activated when the mouse moves over the link]

Location

Client-side. The current URL.
JavaScript 1.0. Navigator 2 and above.

Methods

reload   [Reloads the current document] JavaScript 1.1. Navigator 3 or above

replace   [Loads the specified document] JavaScript 1.1. Navigator 3 or above

Properties

hash   [The name of the anchor name in the currently loaded document's URL]

host   [The host and domain name or IP address of the currently loaded document's URL]

hostname   [The host and port par of the currently loaded document's URL]

href   [The currently loaded document's full URL]

pathname   [The path name of the currently loaded document's URL]

port   [The port number of the currently loaded document's URL]

protocol   [The protocol of the currently loaded document's URL]

search   [Information appearing after the "?" in a URL passed as a GET request]

Lock

Server-side. An object enabling sections of code to be "locked" to prevent simultaneous access by other client requests.
Netscape 3 servers.

Methods

isValid   [Checks whether the object was correctly constructed]

lock   [Locks the object]

unlock   [Unlocks the object]

Math

Client-side and Server-side. An object enabling various mathematical calculations to be performed.
JavaScript 1.0. Navigator 2 and above.
LiveWire 1 and Netscape 3 servers.

Methods

abs   [Returns the absolute value of the specified number]

acos   [Returns the arc cosine of the specified number as radians]

asin   [Returns the arc sine of the specified number as radians]

atan   [Returns the arc tangent of the specified number as radians]

atan2   [Returns the angle from the X axis to a point, in radians]

ceil	[Returns the next integer bigger than the specified number]
cos	[Returns the cosine of the specified angle, expressed as radians]
exp	[Returns E to the power of the specified number]
floor	[Returns the next integer smaller than the specified number]
log	[Returns the log of the specified number]
max	[Returns the bigger of the two numbers making up its arguments]
min	[Returns the smaller of the two numbers making up its arguments]
pow	[Returns the first of its two arguments to the power of the second]
random	[Returns a random number between 0 and 1]
round	[Rounds a number up or down to the nearest integer]
sin	[Returns the sine of the specified number as radians]
sqrt	[Returns the square root of the specified number]
tan	[Returns the tangent of the specified number as radians]

Properties

E	[Euler's constant—approx. 2.718]
LN10	[Natural logarithm of 10]
LN2	[Natural logarithm of 2]
LOG10E	[Base 10 logarithm of E]
LOG2E	[Base 2 logarithm of E]
PI	[pi—approx. 3.14159]
SQRT1_2	[Square root of 1/2—1 over the square root of 2]
SQRT2	[Square root of 2]

MimeType

Client-side. A Multipart Internet Mail Extension type supported by the client. JavaScript 1.1. Navigator 3 and above.

Each MIME type is a member of the **Navigator** object's mimeTypes array. Each MIME type in the array has its own array of properties, such as *navigator.mimeTypes["images/jpeg"].description*

Properties

description	[Description of the MIME type]
enabledPlugin	[Refers to the plugin object configured for the particular MIME type]
suffixes	[A list of file name extensions relevant to the MIME type]

navigator

Client-side. An object representing the version of Netscape Navigator.
JavaScript 1.0. Navigator 2 and above.

Methods

javaEnabled	[Checks whether Java is enabled in the browser] JavaScript 1.1. Navigator 3 or above
plugins.refresh	[Makes available newly installed plugins]
preference	[Allows certain Navigator preferences to be set; requires a signed script] JavaScript 1.2. Navigator 4
taintEnabled	[Specifies whether data tainting is enabled] JavaScript 1.1. Navigator 3 or above

Properties

appCodeName	[Code name of the browser]
appName	[Name of the browser]
appVersion	[Navigator version]
language	[Two-letter code indicating the language of the client Navigator browser] JavaScript 1.2. Navigator 4
mimeTypes	[Array of MIME types supported] JavaScript 1.1. Navigator 3 or above
platform	[The type of machine for which the Navigator version was compiled, such as Win32, Mac68k] JavaScript 1.2. Navigator 4
plugins	[Array of plugins installed] JavaScript 1.1. Navigator 3 or above
userAgent	[User agent header]

Number

Client-side and Server-side. An object containing various numerical information.
Enables the creation of new number objects; e.g.

myNumber = new Number (10)

JavaScript 1.1. Navigator 3 and above.
LiveWire 1 and Netscape 3 servers.
JavaScript 1.2. Navigator 4 modified the operation of the Number constructor.
See also **Global Functions**.

Properties

MAX_VALUE	[The biggest number that can be represented]
MIN_VALUE	[The smallest number that can be represented]
NaN	[Value that is "Not a Number"]
NEGATIVE_INFINITY	[Negative infinity value]
POSITIVE_INFINITY	[Infinity value]
prototype	[Enables new properties to be added to the object]

Object

Client-side and Server-side. Represents an object, and enables the creation of new objects:

myObject = new Object ()

JavaScript 1.0. Navigator 2 and above.

Methods

eval	[Evaluates a JavaScript expression] JavaScript 1.1 Navigator 3 and Livewire 1 only. See Global functions
toString	[A string representing the object]
unwatch	[Removes a watchpoint from a property belonging to the object] JavaScript 1.2. Navigator 4 and Netscape 3 servers
valueOf	[Returns the object's primitive value] JavaScript 1.1. Navigator 3 and above. LiveWire 1 and Netscape 3 servers
watch	[Adds a watchpoint to a property belonging to the object] JavaScript 1.2. Navigator 4 and Netscape 3 servers

Properties

constructor	[Specifies the function that created the object's prototype] JavaScript 1.1. Navigator 3 and above. LiveWire 1 and Netscape 3 servers
prototype	[Allows the addition of new properties to the object] JavaScript 1.1. Navigator 3 and above

Option

Client-side. An object representing an option created with the HTML OPTION tag, or with the option constructor.

JavaScript 1.0. Navigator 2 and above.

Properties

defaultSelected	[The initial selected state of the option - *true* or *false*] JavaScript 1.1. Navigator 3 or above
selected	[The current selected state of the option - *true* or *false*]
text	[The text of the option] JavaScript 1.1 (Navigator 3 or above) allows the text property to change an option's text
value	[Relects the HTML VALUE attribute]

Password

Client-side. An object representing a password input element created with the HTML tag INPUT TYPE="password".

JavaScript 1.0. Navigator 2 and above.

Methods

blur	[Causes the object to lose the focus]
focus	[Causes the object to receive the focus]
handleEvent	[Calls the event handler for the specified type of event, as though the event had occurred] JavaScript 1.2. Navigator 4
select	[Causes the object to be selected]

Properties

defaultValue	[The default value when the document is loaded]
form	[The FORM containing the checkbox]
name	[Reflects the value of the HTML NAME attribute]
type	[Value of the HTML TYPE attribute] JavaScript 1.1. Navigator 3 or above
value	[Value of the HTML VALUE attribute]

Event handlers

onBlur	[Activated when the object loses the focus] JavaScript 1.1. Navigator 3 or above
onFocus	[Activated when the object receives the focus] JavaScript 1.1. Navigator 3 or above

Plugin

Client-side. An object representing a plug-in module installed in the browser. JavaScript 1.1. Navigator 3 and above.

Each plugin is a member of the **Navigator** object's plugins array. Each plugin in the array has its own array of properties, such as *navigator.plugins[0].name*

Properties

description	[Description provided by the plugin]
filename	[Reflects the file enabling the plugin to be viewed]
length	[The number of plugins available in the browser]
name	[The name of the selected plugin]

Project

Server-side. An object containing information relating to a particular application. LiveWire 1 and Netscape 3 servers.

Methods

lock	[Locks the project object]
unlock	[Unlocks the project object]

Radio

Client-side. An object representing a radio button created with the HTML tag INPUT TYPE="radio".
JavaScript 1.0. Navigator 2 and above.

Methods

blur	[Causes the object to lose the focus] JavaScript 1.1. Navigator 3 or above
click	[Has the same effect as the user clicking the object]
focus	[Causes the object to receive the focus] JavaScript 1.1. Navigator 3 or above
handleEvent	[Calls the event handler for the specified type of event, as though the event had occurred] JavaScript 1.2. Navigator 4

Properties

checked	[The value reflects whether the radio button has been clicked]
defaultChecked	[Reflects whether the radio button is marked CHECKED as the default]
form	[The FORM containing the checkbox]
name	[Reflects the value of the HTML NAME attribute]
type	[Reflects the value of the HTML TYPE attribute] JavaScript 1.1. Navigator 3 or above
value	[Reflects the HTML VALUE attribute]

Event handlers

onBlur	[Activated when the object loses the focus]
onClick	[Activated when the object is clicked]
onFocus	[Activated when the object receives the focus]

RegExp

Client-side and Server-side. Allows patterns of characters to be matched against text—for example, to find occurrences of particular strings. See Netscape's JavaScript Reference for full details.
JavaScript 1.2. Navigator 4.
Netscape 3 servers.

Request

Server-side. An object containing information relating to the current client request.
LiveWire 1 and Netscape 3 servers.

Properties

agent	[Name and version of the client software]
imageX	[The horizontal position of the mouse over an image map when the request was made]
imageY	[The vertical position of the mouse over an image map when the request was made]
ip	[The IP address of the client making the request]
method	[The method, such as POST, GET, used by the request]
protocol	[The protocol of the request]

Reset

Client-side. An object representing a reset button created with the HTML tag INPUT TYPE="reset".
JavaScript 1.0. Navigator 2 and above.

Methods

blur	[Causes the object to lose the focus] JavaScript 1.1. Navigator 3 or above
click	[Has the same effect as the user clicking the object]
focus	[Causes the object to receive the focus] JavaScript 1.1. Navigator 3 or above
handleEvent	[Calls the event handler for the specified type of event, as though the event had occurred] JavaScript 1.2. Navigator 4

Properties

form	[The FORM containing the checkbox]
name	[The name given to the reset button, reflecting the HTML NAME element]
type	[Reflects the HTML TYPE attribute] JavaScript 1.1. Navigator 3 or above
value	[The text to appear on the reset button]

Event handlers

onBlur	[Activated when the object loses the focus] JavaScript 1.1. Navigator 3 or above
onClick	[Activated when the object is clicked]
onFocus	[Activated when the object receives the focus] JavaScript 1.1. Navigator 3 or above

Resultset

Server-side. Represents a virtual table resulting from a stored procedure.
Netscape 3 servers.

Methods

close	[Closes the resultset object]
columnName	[Returns the a column name in the resultset]
columns	[Returns the number of columns in the resultset]
next	[Moves to the next row]

Properties

prototype	[Allows new properties to be added to the object]

Screen

Client-side. Object containing details of the screen display.
JavaScript 1.2. Navigator 4.

Properties

availHeight	[Available height in pixels, excluding space taken up by interface features, such as toolbars]
availWidth	[Available width in pixels, excluding space taken up by interface features, such as toolbars]
colorDepth	[The number of colors available for display]
height	[The height of the screen in pixels]
pixelDepth	[The number of bits per pixel]
width	[The width of the screen in pixels]

Select

Client-side. An object representing a set of options created with the HTML tag
SELECT.
JavaScript 1.0. Navigator 2 and above.

Methods

blur	[Causes the object to lose the focus]
focus	[Causes the object to receive the focus]
handleEvent	[Calls the event handler for the specified type of event, as though the event had occurred] JavaScript 1.2. Navigator 4

Properties

form	[The FORM containing the checkbox]
length	[Reflects the number of options in the Select object]

name	[Name given to the object in the HTML NAME attribute]
options	[An array reflecting all of the options]
selectedIndex	[An integer representing the array number of the option selected]
type	[Reflects the HTML TYPE attribute which enables multiple selections] JavaScript 1.1. Navigator 3 or above

Event handlers

onBlur	[Activated when the object loses the focus]
onChange	[Activated when the selection is changed]
onFocus	[Activated when the object receives the focus]

SendMail

Server-side. An object enabling e-mails to be sent.
Netscape 3 servers.

Methods

errorCode	[Returns the error code]
errorMessage	[Returns the error message]
send	[Sends the e-mail]

Properties

Bcc	[List of recipients of the message not visible in the message]
Body	[The text of the message]
Cc	[List of people to whom the message should copied]
Errorsto	[Person to whom error messages should be sent]
From	[Person from whom the message is being sent]
Organization	[Organization of the person sending the message]
Replyto	[Person to whom replies should be sent]
Smtpserver	[The mail server name]
Subject	[The subject of the message]
To	[List of main recipients of the message]

Server

Server-side. An object containing information relating to server.
LiveWire 1 and Netscape 3 servers.

Methods

| lock | [Locks the server object] |
| unlock | [Unlocks the server object] |

Properties

host	[The host and domain name or IP address]
hostname	[The host and port number]
port	[The port number]
protocol	[The protocol]

Stproc

Server-side. Represents a call to a database stored procedure.
Netscape 3 servers.

Methods

close	[Closes the object]
outParamCount	[Returns the number of output parameters]
outParameters	[Returns the values of the output parameters]
resultSet	[Retrieves a new resultset]
returnValue	[Returns the return value for the stored procedure]

Properties

prototype	[Enables new properties to be added to the object]

String

Client-side and Server-side. An object representing a string.
JavaScript 1.0. Navigator 2 and above.
LiveWire 1 and Netscape 3 servers.
JavaScript 1.1 (Navigator 3 and LiveWire 1) added the String constructor enabling
new strings to be constructed as follows: myString = *new String ("Hello there")*
See also **Global Functions**.

Methods

anchor	[Converts the string to an HTML anchor with the string as the value of the NAME attribute]
big	[Converts to a string surrounded by the HTML BIG tags]
blink	[Converts a string to a blinking string]
bold	[Converts a string to a bold string]
charAt	[Returns the character at a specified location in the string]
charCodeAt	[Returns the ISO Latin 1 codeset value for the character at the specified location]
concat	[Combines two strings into a new one] JavaScript 1.2. Navigator 4 and Netscape 3 servers
fixed	[Applies a fixed-pitch font]
fontcolor	[Changes the color of the text]

fontsize	[Changes the font size of the text]
fromCharCode	[Returns a string for the specified ISO Latin 1 codeset values]
indexOf	[Returns the location of the first occurrence of specified text in a string]
italics	[Converts a string to an italic string]
lastIndexOf	[Returns the last occurrence of specified text in a string]
link	[Converts the string to an HTML hyperlink with the string as the value of the HREF attribute]
	See the entry for Link for details.
match	[Matches a regular expression against a string] JavaScript 1.2. Navigator 4 and Netscape 3 servers
replace	[Replaces a substring matched against a regular expression] JavaScript 1.2. Navigator 4 and Netscape 3 servers
search	[Searches for a match between a regular expression and a string] JavaScript 1.2. Navigator 4 and Netscape 3 servers
slice	[Returns a new string having extracted a specified part of it] JavaScript 1.2. Navigator 4 and Netscape 3 servers
small	[Converts the string to small text using the HTML SMALL tags]
split	[Splits a string into an array of strings] JavaScript 1.1. Navigator 3 and above. LiveWire 1 and Netscape 3 servers
strike	[Converts a string to a string in strikethrough font]
sub	[Converts the string to subscript]
substr	[Returns the specified number of characters in a string from the specified place in the string] JavaScript 1.2. Navigator 4 and Netscape 3 servers
substring	[Returns a substring between two specified locations in the string]
sup	[Converts the string to superscript]
toLowerCase	[Converts a string to a lower case string]
toUpperCase	[Converts a string to an upper case string]

Properties

length	[The length of the string in characters including blanks]
prototype	[Enables new properties to be added to the object] JavaScript 1.1. Navigator 3 and above. LiveWire 1 and Netscape 3 servers

Submit

Client-side. An object representing a submit button created with the HTML tag INPUT TYPE="submit".
JavaScript 1.0. Navigator 2 and above.

Methods

blur	[Causes the object to lose the focus] JavaScript 1.1. Navigator 3 and above
click	[Has the same effect as the user clicking the object]
focus	[Causes the object to receive the focus] JavaScript 1.1. Navigator 3 and above
handleEvent	[Calls the event handler for the specified type of event, as though the event had occurred] JavaScript 1.2. Navigator 4

Properties

form	[The FORM containing the checkbox]
name	[Reflects the value of the HTML NAME attribute]
type	[Reflects the value of the HTML TYPE attribute] JavaScript 1.1. Navigator 3 and above
value	[Reflects the value of the HTML VALUE attribute]

Event handlers

onBlur	[Activated when the object loses the focus] JavaScript 1.1. Navigator 3 and above
onClick	[Activated when the object is clicked]
onFocus	[Activated when the object receives the focus] JavaScript 1.1. Navigator 3 and above

Text

Client-side. An object representing a text box created with the HTML tag INPUT TYPE="text".
JavaScript 1.0. Navigator 2 and above.

Methods

blur	[Causes the object to lose the focus]
focus	[Causes the object to receive the focus]
handleEvent	[Calls the event handler for the specified type of event, as though the event had occurred] JavaScript 1.2. Navigator 4
select	[Causes the object to be selected]

Properties

defaultValue	[Reflects the value of the HTML VALUE attribute]
form	[The FORM containing the checkbox]
name	[Reflects the value of the HTML NAME attribute]
type	[Reflects the value of the HTML TYPE attribute, as in "text"] JavaScript 1.1. Navigator 3 and above

| value | [The current value of the text box, the default value if nothing has been typed into the text box] |

Event handlers

onBlur	[Activated when the object loses the focus]
onChange	[Activated when the value of the object is changed, such as. when the text box is typed into]
onFocus	[Activated when the object receives the focus]
onSelect	[Activated when the object is selected]

Textarea

Client-side. An object representing a text area created with the HTML tag TEXTAREA.
JavaScript 1.0. Navigator 2 and above.

Methods

blur	[Causes the object to lose the focus]
focus	[Causes the object to receive the focus]
handleEvent	[Calls the event handler for the specified type of event, as though the event had occurred] JavaScript 1.2. Navigator 4
select	[Causes the object to be selected]

Properties

defaultValue	[Reflects the value of the HTML VALUE attribute]
form	[The FORM containing the checkbox]
name	[Reflects the value of the HTML NAME attribute]
type	[Reflects the HTML TYPE attribute] JavaScript 1.1. Navigator 3 and above
value	[Reflects the HTML VALUE attribute]

Event handlers

onBlur	[Activated when the object loses the focus]
onChange	[Activated when the value of the object is changed]
onFocus	[Activated when the object receives the focus]
onKeyDown	[Activated when a key is pressed] JavaScript 1.2. Navigator 4
onKeyPress	[Activated when a key is held done] JavaScript 1.2. Navigator 4
onKeyUp	[Activated when a key is released] JavaScript 1.2. Navigator 4
onSelect	[Activated when the object is selected]

Window

Client-side. An object representing a browser window or frame.
JavaScript 1.0. Navigator 2 and above.

Methods

alert	[Displays an *alert* message box]
back	[Loads the previous document in the history list] JavaScript 1.2. Navigator 4
blur	[Causes the object to lose the focus] JavaScript 1.1. Navigator 3 and above
captureEvents	[Specifies which events should be captured by the object] JavaScript 1.2. Navigator 4
clearInterval	[Cancels the repetition of actions initiated by *setInterval*] JavaScript 1.2. Navigator 4
clearTimeout	[Cancels the action set by *setTimeout* if within the time delay]
close	[Closes the window]
confirm	[Displays a *confirm* message box]
disableExternalCapture	[Disables *enableExternalCapture* described below] JavaScript 1.2. Navigator 4
enableExternalCapture	[Allows windows with frames to capture events in documents loaded from different locations; used in signed scripts.] JavaScript 1.2. Navigator 4
find	[Finds the specified string in the currently loaded document] JavaScript 1.2. Navigator 4
focus	[Causes the window to receive the focus] JavaScript 1.1. Navigator 3 and above
forward	[Loads the next document in the history list] JavaScript 1.2. Navigator 4
handleEvent	[Calls the event handler for the specified type of event, as though the event had occurred] JavaScript 1.2. Navigator 4
home	[Has the effect of clicking the browser's Home button] JavaScript 1.2. Navigator 4
moveBy	[Move the window by the specified number of pixels on the x and y axes] JavaScript 1.2. Navigator 4
moveTo	[Move the window to the specified location, x and y coordinates of the top left of the screen] JavaScript 1.2. Navigator 4
open	[Opens a new window; this includes a variety of properties that control the appearance and behavior of the window]
print	[Emulates the browser's Print button]
prompt	[Displays a *prompt* message box]
releaseEvents	[Releases the specified captured event to be handled further down the event hierarchy] JavaScript 1.2. Navigator 4

resizeBy	[Resizes the window by the specified pixels relating to the x and y axes] JavaScript 1.2. Navigator 4
resizeTo	[Resizes the window to the x and y dimensions specified in pixels] JavaScript 1.2. Navigator 4
routeEvent	[Passes the specified captured event down the event hierarchy] JavaScript 1.2. Navigator 4
scroll	[Scrolls] JavaScript 1.1 (Navigator 3) only
scrollBy	[Scrolls the window by the specified number of pixels] JavaScript 1.2. Navigator 4
scrollTo	[Scrolls the window to the specified location in pixels] JavaScript 1.2. Navigator 4
setInterval	[Specifies that a function should be called or an expression evaluated repeatedly after a specified time, expressed as milliseconds, has elapsed] JavaScript 1.2. Navigator 4
setTimeout	[Calls a function or evaluates an expression after a specified time, expressed as milliseconds, has elapsed]
stop	[Stops a document or image loading] JavaScript 1.2. Navigator 4

Properties

closed	[Specifies whether the window has been closed] JavaScript 1.1. Navigator 3 and above
defaultStatus	[The message that appears in the status bar when the document is loaded]
document	[The document currently loaded in the window]
frames	[An array indexing the windows frames]
history	[List of previously visited URLs] JavaScript 1.1. Navigator 3 and above
innerHeight	[Height of the window's content area, in pixels] JavaScript 1.2. Navigator 4
innerWidth	[Width of the window's content area, in pixels] JavaScript 1.2. Navigator 4
length	[The number of frames in the window]
location	[The current URL]
locationbar	[Allows control of the window's location bar] JavaScript 1.2. Navigator 4. locationbar has the following property:
	visible [*myWindow.locationbar.visible*= *true* (or *1*) makes the location bar visible; making the value of the visible property *false* (or *0*) hides the location bar; can be set only using a signed script]
menubar	[Allows control of the window's menu bar] JavaScript 1.2. Navigator 4. menubar has the following property:

	visible	[*myWindow.menubar.visible*= *true* (or *1*) makes the menu bar visible; making the value of the visible property *false* (or *0*) hides the menu bar; can be set only using a signed script]
name		[Name given to the window]
opener		[The name of the window of the document that opened the window] JavaScript 1.1. Navigator 3 and above
outerHeight		[Height of the window's outer boundary] JavaScript 1.2. Navigator 4
outerWidth		[Width of the window's outer boundary]
pageXOffset		[The x position of the page relative to the x y position of the window's upper-left corner] JavaScript 1.2. Navigator 4
pageYOffset		[The y position of the page relative to the x y position of the window's upper-left corner] JavaScript 1.2. Navigator 4
parent		[Window containing the frame]
personalbar		[Allows control of the Navigator 4 personal bar] JavaScript 1.2. Navigator 4. personalbar has the following property:
	visible	[*myWindow.personalbar.visible*= *true* (or *1*) makes the personal bar visible; making the value of the visible property *false* (or *0*) hides the personal bar; can be set only using a signed script]
scrollbars		[Allows control of the window's scroll bars] JavaScript 1.2. Navigator 4. scrollbars has the following property:
	visible	[*myWindow.scrollBars.visible*= *true* (or *1*) makes the scrollbars visible; making the value of the visible property *false* (or *0*) hides the scrollbars; can be set only using a signed script]
self		[Refers to the current window]
status		[Information displayed in the window's status bar]
statusbar		[Allows control of the window's status bar] JavaScript 1.2. Navigator 4. statusbar has the following property:
	visible	[*myWindow.statusbar.visible*= *true* (or *1*) makes the status bar visible; making the value of the visible property *false* (or *0*) hides the status bar; can be set only using a signed script]
toolbar		[Allows control of the window's tool bar] JavaScript 1.2. Navigator 4. toolbar has the following property:
	visible	[*myWindow.scrollBars.visible*= *true* (or *1*) makes the tool bar visible; making the value of the visible property *false* (or *0*) hides the tool bar; can be only set using a signed script]
top		[Refers to the top window]
window		[Refers to the current window]

Event handlers

onBlur	[Activated when the object loses the focus] JavaScript 1.1. Navigator 3 and above
onDragDrop	[Activated when objects are dragged and dropped] JavaScript 1.2. Navigator 4
onError	[Activated when an error occurs] JavaScript 1.1. Navigator 3 and above
onFocus	[Activated when the object receives the focus] JavaScript 1.1. Navigator 3 and above
onLoad	[Activated when the window is loaded]
onMove	[Activated when the window is moved] JavaScript 1.2. Navigator 4
onResize	[Activated when the window is resized] JavaScript 1.2. Navigator 4
onUnload	[Activated when the window is unloaded]

Reserved Words

The words in Table A.1 cannot be used as JavaScript variables, functions, methods, or object names.

Table A.1 JavaScript Reserved Words

abstract	boolean	break
byte	case	catch
char	class	const
continue	default	delete
do	double	else
extends	false	final
finally	float	for
function	goto	if
implements	import	in
instanceof	int	interface
long	native	new
null	package	private
protected	public	return
short	static	super
switch	synchronized	this
throw	throws	transient
true	try	typeof
var	void	while
with		

Operators

Except where otherwise specified, these are implemented in JavaScript 1.0 (Navigator 2 and above, LiveWire 1 and Netscape 3 servers).

Arithmetic Operators

+	Adds numbers.
++	Increments by one.
–	Subtracts.
– –	Decreases by one.
*	Multiplies.
/	Divides.
%	Modulus.

String Operators

+	Concatenates strings.
+=	Adds a new string to an existing string.

Logical Operators

&&	AND
||	OR
!	NOT

Bitwise Operators

&	AND
^	XOR
|	OR
~	NOT
<<	Left shift.
>>	Sign propagating right shift.
>>>	Zero fill right shift.

Assignment Operators

=	Assigns a value such as a = b
+=	a += b is the same as a = a + b

−=	a −= b is the same as a = a − b
*=	a * b is the same as a = a * b
/=	a /= b is the same as a = a / b
%=	a %= b is the same as a = a % b
&=	a &= y is the same as a = a & b
^=	a ^= y is the same as a = a ^ b
|=	a |= y is the same as a = a | b
<<=	a <<= y is the same as a = a << b
>>=	a >>= y is the same as a = a >> b
>>>=	a >>>= y is the same as a = a >>> b

Comparison Operators

==	Returns *true* if the operands are equal.
!=	Returns *true* if the operands are not equal.
>	Returns *true* if the first operand is greater than the second.
>=	Returns *true* if the first operand is greater than or equal to the second.
<	Returns *true* if the first operand is smaller than the second.
<=	Returns *true* if the first operand is smaller than or equal to the second.

Special Operators

?:	Shorthand way of implementing IF... THEN... ELSE... rules.
,	Evaluates two expressions, returning the result of the second expression.
delete	Deletes an element in an array, or a property of an object.
new	Enables the creation of a new instance of a type of object.
this	Shorthand way of referring to the current object (in which this is used).
typeof	Returns the type of object; for example, if we create a variable

var myMessage="Hello there"; var myNumber=5

then the value of *typeof myMessage* is *string*, and the value of *typeof myNumber* is *number*.

(JavaScript 1.1. Navigator 3 and above)

void	Evaluates a JavaScript expression without returning any value. (JavaScript 1.1. Navigator 3 and above)

Statements

break

Causes a loop to be terminated and control to pass to the command following the loop.
JavaScript 1.0. Navigator 2 and above.
LiveWire 1 and Netscape 3 servers.

comment

Enables comments to be written in a program that will not be interpreted as JavaScript commands.
JavaScript 1.0. Navigator 2 and above.
LiveWire 1 and Netscape 3 servers.

continue

Causes the current iteration of a loop to be terminated and the next iteration of the loop to be started.
JavaScript 1.0. Navigator 2 and above.
LiveWire 1 and Netscape 3 servers.

delete

Deletes an element in an array, or an object's property.
JavaScript 1.2. Navigator 4.
Netscape 3 servers.

do...while

A loop in which statements following *do* are processed until a condition specified after *while* is evaluated as false.
JavaScript 1.2. Navigator 4.
Netscape 3 servers.

export

Allows other scripts to access properties, functions, and objects of a signed script.
JavaScript 1.2. Navigator 4.
Netscape 3 servers.

for

Component of a *for* loop—e.g.

```
        for (var i = 0; i < 4; i++) {
        document.write (i + " ") }
    will write "0 1 2 3"
```
JavaScript 1.0. Navigator 2 and above.
LiveWire 1 and Netscape 3 servers.

for...in

A type of loop - e.g.
```
        myArray = new Array ("a","b","c")
        for (var i in myArray) {
        document.write (myArray[i] + " ") }
    will write "a b c"
```
JavaScript 1.0. Navigator 2 and above.
LiveWire 1 and Netscape 3 servers.

function

Declares a JavaScript function.
JavaScript 1.0. Navigator 2 and above.
LiveWire 1 and Netscape 3 servers.

if...else

Enables rules to be written of the form
    IF some condition(s)
    THEN some conclusion(s) or action(s)
    ELSE some alternative conclusion(s) or action(s)
JavaScript 1.0. Navigator 2 and above.
LiveWire 1 and Netscape 3 servers.

import

Enables a script to access properties, functions, and objects from a signed script.
JavaScript 1.2. Navigator 4.
Netscape 3 servers.

labeled

A section of a loop can be labeled so that a *break* or *continue* command can be limited to that particular section.
JavaScript 1.2. Navigator 4.
Netscape 3 servers.

return

Indicates the value to be returned by a function.
JavaScript 1.0. Navigator 2 and above.
LiveWire 1 and Netscape 3 servers.

switch

Enables you to specify a series of alternative condition-action pairs, so that if *switch*'s argument matches the condition of a particular pair, then the corresponding action is executed. The condition must be a valid JavaScript expression. The action can be one or a series of JavaScript statements. An optional *break* command can be included for any match, as can a default action in case no match is found.
JavaScript 1.2. Navigator 4.
Netscape 3 servers.

var

A statement declaring a new variable.
JavaScript 1.0. Navigator 2 and above.
LiveWire 1 and Netscape 3 servers.

while

A type of loop - e.g.
```
var i = 0
while(i < 4) {
document.write (i + " ")
i++ }
```
will write *"0 1 2 3"*
JavaScript 1.0. Navigator 2 and above.
LiveWire 1 and Netscape 3 servers.

with

Specifies a default object that applies to a set of following statements. If any of the statements refer to properties or methods without specifying an object, they are assumed to belong to the default object.
JavaScript 1.0. Navigator 2 and above.
LiveWire 1 and Netscape 3 servers.

Global Functions (i.e. not associated with any object)

addClient

Adds property values of the client object to a URL that is generated by the server, or to a URL to which the client is redirected by the server.
LiveWire 1 and Netscape 3 servers.

addResponseHeader

Adds information to the header of the response sent to the client from the server.
Netscape 3 servers.

blob

Links a BLOb (Binary Large Objects, used for multimedia content) to a database cursor.
LiveWire 1 and Netscape 3 servers.

callC

Enables an external function to be called.
LiveWire 1 and Netscape 3 servers.

debug

Allows the value of a JavaScript expression to be displayed for debugging purposes.
LiveWire 1 and Netscape 3 servers.

deleteResponseHeader

Deletes information from the header of the response sent to the client from the server.
Netscape 3 servers.

escape

Converts strings containing characters not permitted in a URL (e.g. spaces) to an acceptable form.
JavaScript 1.0. Navigator 2 and above.
LiveWire 1 and Netscape 3 servers.

eval

Causes a JavaScript string to be evaluated—e.g.
>   *document.write (eval ("3 * 2 + 4"))*
>   will write "10".

In JavaScript 1.1 (Navigator 3 and LiveWire 1) *eval* was a method of every object.
In JavaScript 1.2. (Navigator 4 and Netscape 3 servers) it is a global function only.

flush

Sends the contents of the server's internal buffer, in which a server-generated HTML page is stored prior to sending, to the client. The contents are sent automatically when they reach 64K.
LiveWire 1 and Netscape 3 servers.

getOptionValue

Returns the text associated with an option in a SELECT element in an HTML form.
LiveWire 1 and Netscape 3 servers.

getOptionValueCount

Returns the number of options selected in a multiple-choice SELECT element in an HTML form.
LiveWire 1 and Netscape 3 servers.

isNaN

Checks whether its argument is *Not a Number*.
JavaScript 1.0. Navigator 2. Unix only.
JavaScript 1.1. Navigator 3 and above.
LiveWire 1 and Netscape 3 servers.

Number

Converts an object to a number. If *myDate* is a **Date** object
>   *document.write (Number (myDate))*
>   will write the number of milliseconds between the date stored in myDate and 1 January 1970.

JavaScript 1.2. Navigator 4.
Netscape 3 servers.

parseFloat

Converts a string to a floating point number.
JavaScript 1.0. Navigator 2 and above.

LiveWire 1 and Netscape 3 servers.

parseInt

Converts a string to an integer.
JavaScript 1.0. Navigator 2 and above.
LiveWire 1 and Netscape 3 servers.

redirect

Redirects the client to a different URL.
LiveWire 1 and Netscape 3 servers.

registerCFunction

Registers an external function for use by server-side JavaScript.
LiveWire 1 and Netscape 3 servers.

ssjs_generateClientID

Generates a unique client object identification.
Netscape 3 servers.

ssjs_getCGIVariable

Enables environmental variables to be accessed.
Netscape 3 servers.

ssjs_getClientID

Returns a unique client object identification.
Netscape 3 servers.

String

Converts an object to a string. If the object is a **Date** object, it will be converted to
a string representation of the date.
JavaScript 1.2. Navigator 4.
Netscape 3 servers.

taint

Tainting prevents private specified information from being communicated without
the user's permission.
JavaScript 1.1 only (Netscape 3 only).
LiveWire 1 and Netscape 3 servers.

unescape

Converts strings transformed using *escape* to their original form.
JavaScript 1.0. Navigator 2 and above.
LiveWire 1 and Netscape 3 servers.

untaint

Removes tainting from specified information.
JavaScript 1.1 only (Netscape 3 only).
LiveWire 1 and Netscape 3 servers.

write

Writes to the HTML page being generated by server-side JavaScript for sending to the client.
LiveWire 1 and Netscape 3 servers.

List of Event Handlers

onAbort

JavaScript 1.1. Navigator 3 and above.
Applies to: Image.
Triggered when an image stops loading prematurely.

onBlur

JavaScript 1.0. Navigator 2 and above.
Applies to: Button (JavaScript 1.1—Navigator 3 and above), Checkbox (JavaScript 1.1—Navigator 3 and above), FileUpload (JavaScript 1.1—Navigator 3 and above), Frame (JavaScript 1.1—Navigator 3 and above), Layer (JavaScript 1.2—Navigator 4), Password (JavaScript 1.1—Navigator 3 and above), Radio (JavaScript 1.1—Navigator 3 and above), Reset (JavaScript 1.1—Navigator 3 and above), Select, Submit (JavaScript 1.1—Navigator 3 and above), Text, Textarea, Window (JavaScript 1.1—Navigator 3 and above).
Triggered when the object loses the focus.

onChange

JavaScript 1.0. Navigator 2 and above.
Applies to: FileUpload (JavaScript 1.1—Navigator 3 and above), Select, Text, Textarea.
Triggered when the value of the object is changed.

onClick

JavaScript 1.0. Navigator 2 and above. JavaScript 1.1. Navigator 3 and above.
allows you to return *false* to cancel the onClick event.
Applies to: Button, Checkbox, document, Link, Radio, Reset, Submit.
Activated when the object is clicked with the mouse.

onDblClick

JavaScript 1.2. Navigator 4.
Applies to: document, Link.
Activated when the object is double clicked by the mouse.

onDragDrop

JavaScript 1.2. Navigator 4.
Applies to: Window.
Triggered when an object is dragged and dropped with the mouse.

onError

JavaScript 1.1. Navigator 3 and above.
Applies to: Image, Window.
Applies when an error occurs.

onFocus

JavaScript 1.0. Navigator 2 and above.
Applies to: Button (JavaScript 1.1—Navigator 3 and above), Checkbox (JavaScript
1.1—Navigator 3 and above), FileUpload (JavaScript 1.1—Navigator 3 and above),
Frame (JavaScript 1.1—Navigator 3 and above), Layer (JavaScript 1.2—Navigator
4), Password (JavaScript 1.1—Navigator 3 and above), Radio (JavaScript 1.1—
Navigator 3 and above), Reset (JavaScript 1.1—Navigator 3 and above), Select,
Submit (JavaScript 1.1—Navigator 3 and above), Text, Textarea, Window
(JavaScript 1.1—Navigator 3 and above).
Triggered when the object receives the focus.

onKeyDown

JavaScript 1.2. Navigator 4.
Applies to: document, Image, Link, Textarea.
Applies when a key is pressed.

onKeyPress

JavaScript 1.2. Navigator 4.

Applies to: document, Image, Link, Textarea.
Triggered when a key is held down.

onKeyUp

JavaScript 1.2. Navigator 4.
Applies to: document, Image, Link, Textarea.
Activated when a key is released.

onLoad

JavaScript 1.0. Navigator 2 and above.
Applies to: Image (JavaScript 1.1—Navigator 3 and above), Layer, Window.
Activated when the object is loaded.

onMouseDown

JavaScript 1.2. Navigator 4.
Applies to: Button, document, Link.
Activated when the mouse button is pressed.

onMouseMove

JavaScript 1.2. Navigator 4.
Applies when the mouse is moved.

onMouseOut

JavaScript 1.1. Navigator 3 and above.
Applies to: Layer (JavaScript 1.2—Navigator 4), Link.
Activated when the mouse moves away from the object, having been over it.

onMouseOver

JavaScript 1.0. Navigator 2 and above.
Applies to: Layer (JavaScript 1.2—Navigator 4), Link (JavaScript 1.1—Navigator 3 and above—added this event handler to links created with the HTML AREA HREF tag).
Triggered when the mouse moves over the object.

onMouseUp

JavaScript 1.2. Navigator 4.
Applies to: Button, document, Link.
Triggered when the mouse button is released.

onMove

JavaScript 1.2. Navigator 4.
Applies to: Window.
Applies when the window is moved.

onReset

JavaScript 1.1. Navigator 3 and above.
Applies to: Form.
Triggered when the form is reset.

onResize

JavaScript 1.2. Navigator 4.
Applies to: Window.
Activated when the window is resized.

onSelect

JavaScript 1.0. Navigator 2 and above.
Applies to: Text, Textarea.
Activated when the object is selected.

onSubmit

JavaScript 1.0. Navigator 2 and above.
Applies to: Form.
Activated when the form is submitted.

onUnload

JavaScript 1.0. Navigator 2 and above.
Applies to: Window.
Activated when a document is unloaded from the window.

THE COMPANION
WEBSITE

B

Y<span></span>ou will find the companion website containing the programs introduced in the book at: **www.wiley.com/compbooks/ford**. The website will save you from typing a lot of code in order to try out the various techniques introduced in the book. However, it will also enable you to download the code to modify or utilize the techniques in your own applications.

Hardware/Software Requirements

To run the programs on the website you will need a connection to the Internet and a Web browser enabled to run JavaScript version 1.1 or above, such as Netscape Navigator version 3 or above.

Using the Website

This website enables you to run the programs introduced in the book. They are listed on the website according to the chapter of the book in which they are introduced. Where appropriate, tips for suitable input to a program are given where this is not immediately apparent.

To copy all or parts of the code for a program, simply click the appropriate link to run the program, then select the appropriate SAVE AS option in your browser's menu. Alternatively, select the VIEW SOURCE or equivalent command from your browser. The code is then displayed, and can be copied and pasted into your own word processor file. In this way, you can use and modify the code for your own applications.

User Information

The software accompanying this book is being provided as is without warranty or support of any kind. Should you require basic installation assistance, or if your media is defective, please call our product support number at (212) 850-6194 weekdays between 9 A.M. and 4 P.M. Eastern Standard Time. Or, we can be reached via e-mail at: **wprtusw@wiley.com**.

To place additional orders or to request information about other Wiley products, please call (800) 879-4539.

INDEX

METHOD attribute, 293
NAME attribute, 284, 285, 293, 304, 307, 310
NAME element, 305
pages, 1, 6, 9
select objects, 262
syntax, 202
table, 287
tags, 68, 243, 244, 271, 272, 293, 296, 297, 302, 306, 308–311, 326
TARGET attribute, 293
text, 35, 37
TYPE attribute, 285, 303–305, 307, 310
usage. *See* JavaScript
VALUE attribute, 285, 302, 303, 304
writing, 271

I

Identification/classification, 86
IF, 23, 24, 52–54
if...else, 319
IF...THEN rules, 23, 29, 86–89, 125, 166
<ILAYER> tag, 296
Image object, 295–296
  event handlers, 296
  methods, 295
  properties, 295
Images, 80, 82–83
<IMG> tag, 19, 252, 295
import statement, 319
Index address, 82
indexOf function, 224
Indicator phrase technique, 193
Inferences, making, 86–103
Information. *See also* Client information
  writing. *See* Files; Frames; Text; Text
  confirmation, 22–24
  management, 87, 88, 91, 92, 96, 104
  obtaining, 255–269. *See also* Reader
  processing, 35–63
  reading, 264. *See also* Files
  retrieval, 38–51
  storage, 14–15, 38–51
  writing, 265
information_window(), 118
Informix, 266
Inheritance, 151–166
  economical approach, 160–166
  mechanism, 158

usage, 152–160
inherits function, 165
Initial state, 223
Inline layer, 248
Input. *See* Reader
  sentence, 204
Intellectual processing, 1
Intelligent front end, 207
Intelligent knowledge based systems, 86
Intelligent systems, 6, 85, 86, 103
Intelligent Web pages, 1, 2
Interactive product information, 1
Interactive sales assistant, 2
Interactive service, 1
Interactive training, 2, 6–8
  program, 14
Interactive tutorial. *See* Web-based
  interactive tutorial
Internet, 6, 194
  provider, 261
  search engines, 118, 127, 207
  text messages, 273
Intranets, 194
IP address, 255, 260
isNaN function, 322
isNumber function, 178, 179

J

Java, 9
JavaBean, 9
JavaScript, 1, 8–9, 11, 14, 15, 22, 26, 28, 35–38, 40, 47, 60, 61, 67, 74, 88, 92, 94, 96, 97, 99, 106, 115–117, 156, 176, 179, 201, 216, 221, 226, 227, 233, 243, 250, 253, 263, 266, 271–272 275, 278, 315. *See also* Client-side JavaScript; Server-side JavaScript
  Application Manager, 258, 259
  code, 6, 35, 66, 129, 158, 219, 271, 275, 276
  commands, 17, 18, 32, 35–37, 66, 76, 80, 279–327
  defined, 8
  dynamic HTML, usage, 243–252
  error message, 16, 56, 103
  format, 52
  Javascript 1.1, 102, 103
  Javascript 1.2, 48, 70, 80, 198, 280
  objects, 128, 248, 255. *See also* Built-in
    JavaScript object

Javascript, *(Continued)*
  operators, 316
  reference, 279–327
  reserved words, 315
  syntax, 243, 245, 247
  techniques, 13
JavaScripters, 275
  contact, 276–277

K

Keyword, 118, 126, 127, 134, 141, 207,
  209, 278
Knowledge base, usage, 145–151
Knowledge based systems, 86. *See also*
  Intelligent knowledge based systems
Knowledge-based techniques. *See* Expert
  system knowledge-based techniques

L

labeled statement, 319
Layer object, 243,247–252, 296–297. *See also*
  Inline layer
  animation and, 250
  content writing, 250
  event handlers, 297
  features, 249–250
  methods, 249, 296
  positioning, 248
  properties, 247, 296–297
  usage. *See* Web
<LAYER> tag, 250, 296
Leading blanks, 188, 189
Legal operators, 203
Librarianship, 87, 96
Library management, 88, 91, 92, 96, 104
Line break, 264. *See also* HyperText Markup
  Language
Lines of reasoning, 4
  explanation, pages programming, 103–123
Linguistic pattern matching, 191
Link object, 297–298
  event handlers, 298
  methods, 297–298
  properties, 298
LINK attribute, 245
List boxes, 30–32, 181
list variable, 133
LiveConnect, 9
LN. *See* Logical necessity

load method, 249
Local variables, 46, 47, 57
Location object, 298–299
  methods, 299
  properties, 281, 299
lock, 259
Lock object, 299
  methods, 299
Logical necessity (LN)
  factor, 167
  properties, 172
Logical operators, 316
Logical sufficiency (LS)
  factor, 167, 168
  properties, 172
Looping, 222
Loops, 29, 43, 55–59, 224, 263. *See also* For
  loops; For...in; While loops
LS. *See* Logical sufficiency

M

Master array, 148
Matches. *See* Pattern
Matching. *See* Fuzzy matching; Linguistic
  pattern matching; Pattern; Template-
  based pattern matching
  arrays, 146, 165
Math object, 299–300
  methods, 299–300
  properties, 300
Means-end analysis, 215
Message box, 66, 72. *See also* alert
  header fields, 273
Methods. *See* Objects
MIME. *See* Multipart Internet Mail Extension
MIME-compliant messages, 272, 273
MimeType object, 300
  properties, 300
MimeTypes array, 300
moveAbove method, 249
moveBelow method, 249
moveBy method, 250
movement_log array, 232, 233
moveTo method, 250
moveToAbsolute method, 250
Multipart Internet Mail Extension
  (MIME), 300
  value, 273

N

NAME attribute, 25
Narrower terms, 128, 129, 147–149
   array, 165
narrowerTerms array, 148, 149
Natural-language constructions, 203
Natural-language processing techniques, 191
Navigator object, 301
   methods, 301
   properties, 301
Negative explanation, 107–110, 114, 115, 208
Netscape, 3, 4, 48, 102, 103, 198, 243, 280
Netscape Dynamic HTML, 9
Netscape Navigator, 8, 36, 81, 280–281
   Communicator, 280
   directory, 49
Network. *See* Semantic networks
   traffic, 259, 261
Network-based knowledge, 145
next command, 267, 268
nextPage, 18
new Image() command, 83
Nodes, 125
Nonbold code, 183
Noncommercial context, 4
Notes, 12, 13, 16–18, 26, 40, 41, 65, 76, 87,
   93, 118, 127, 172, 197, 207, 227,
   258–260, 262, 266
Noun phrase, 202, 205
noun_phrase rule, 204
Number object, 301, 322
   properties, 301
NULL, 262
Numerical operators, 176

O

ODBC. *See* Open Database Connectivity
Object object, 302
   methods, 302
   properties, 302
object, variable, 42
Objects, 128
   creation 261–263
   naming, 25
   server-side, 256–259
Open Database Connectivity (ODBC), 266
Operators, 54, 61, 176, 316–317
Opponent response, strategy
   implementation, 237–241

Option object, 302
   properties, 302
OR operator, 135, 210
Oracle database, 266
Orders property, 271
Output template, 197

P

<P> tags, 67, 243, 244, 246
Pages. *See* HyperText Markup Language;
   Intelligent Web pages; Web
   programming. *See* Lines of reasoning
Parameters, 70, 71, 263–264. *See also*
   Cookies
   cookies and, 51
Parent
   concepts, 151, 152
   document, 79
   frame, 74
parseFloat function, 322–323
parseFloat command, 270
parseInt funcion, 323
parseInt command, 270
Password object, 302–303
   event handlers, 303
   methods, 303
   properties, 303
path, 51. *See also* URL
Pattern matching, 191–202. *See also*
   Linguistic pattern matching; Template-
   based pattern matching
Plugin object, 303
   properties, 303
Plug-in applications, 9
Popup window, 17
Pragmatics, 194
Pre-analysis, 6
Print resources, 277–278
printLog function, 232, 233
Proactivity, 35–38
Probabilities, 166–173
probabilityOf function, 172
Problem solving, 89–93, 215–241
processKeywords function, 139
Product advice, 2
Project object, 258, 263, 303
   methods, 303
prompt command, 20, 21, 22, 23, 24, 38, 49,
   55, 99, 116

Server-based information, 255
Server-side commands, 255
Server-side cookies, 261
Server-side JavaScript, 8–9, 39, 84, 145,
    253–273, 323
  object, 255, 256
  writing, 255–273
Server-side objects, 256–259, 262, 269,
    271, 272
Server-side processing, 271
Server-side programming, 160
Server-side techniques, 261
setInterval command, 251
setPosition command, 264
setTime command, 50
setTimeout command, 250, 251
Shared object, 259
Shopping cart, 68
showMessage function, 44, 45, 47
Simple variables, 40–42
<SMALL> tag, 309
SPAN attribute, 246
Special operators, 317
Specialist activities, 6
speciesArray, 160
splice command, 201
split command, 201
SQL. *See* Structured Query Language
ssjs_generateClientID function, 323
ssjs_getCGIvariable function, 323
ssjs_getClientID function, 323
Stacked-up commands, 219
Start button, 101
Starting point, 222
Statements, 318–320
Status bar, 17
Stproc object, 308
  methods. 308
String, 129, 224, 225, 257, 269, 304,
    308–309, 323. *See also* Comma-
    separated strings; Text
  constructor, 308
  function, 323
  operators, 316
String object, 281, 297, 308–309
  methods, 308–309
  properties, 309
stripBlanks function, 189

Structured Query Language (SQL), 266
  select databases, 286
STYLE attribute, 246
Style, 243–244, 245–246. *See also* Files;
    HyperText Markup Language,
    Cascading Style Sheets; JavaScript-
    based style
Style sheets, 243
Submit, 74, 135, 139
Submit operator, 309–310
  event handlers, 310
  methods, 310
  properties, 310
Subordinate component concepts, 128
Subordinate topics, 127, 151
Subtower, 235
Sun Microsystems, 8
SUPPRESS attribute, 252
Sybase, 266
Syntactical analysis, 202–213
Syntax, 194, 207, 210. *See also* Cascading
    Style Sheets; HyperText Markup
    Language; JavaScript; JavaScript
    syntax

T

taint function, 323
TARGET attribute, 74
Targeted frame, 76
Technical documentation, 87
Template-based pattern matching, 194
Templates, 191, 192, 193–195. *See also*
    Catchall template; Output template
Text, 60–61, 93, 227. *See also* Free text
Text areas, 20, 27–28, 31, 72–74, 83, 142
Text boxes, 11, 20, 24–27, 31, 41, 45, 46,
    72–74, 83, 175, 181, 256, 281, 310
Text object, 310–311
  event handlers, 311
  methods, 310
  properties, 310–311
Textarea object, 311
  event handlers, 311
  methods, 310–311
  properties, 311
Text-handling facilities, 60
THEN, 23, 24, 52
Ticks, 261